John Keble, Edward Bouverie Pusey

Sermons for Lent to Passiontide

John Keble, Edward Bouverie Pusey
Sermons for Lent to Passiontide
ISBN/EAN: 9783743349452
Manufactured in Europe, USA, Canada, Australia, Japa
Cover: Foto ©Lupo / pixelio.de

Manufactured and distributed by brebook publishing software (www.brebook.com)

John Keble, Edward Bouverie Pusey

Sermons for Lent to Passiontide

SERMONS

FOR

THE CHRISTIAN YEAR

BY THE LATE

REV. JOHN KEBLE,

AUTHOR OF "THE CHRISTIAN YEAR."

SOLD BY

JAMES PARKER AND CO. OXFORD,
AND 377, STRAND, LONDON.

1881.

SERMONS

FOR

LENT TO PASSIONTIDE

BY THE LATE

REV. JOHN KEBLE,

AUTHOR OF "THE CHRISTIAN YEAR."

FIFTH THOUSAND.

SOLD BY

JAMES PARKER AND CO. OXFORD,
AND 377, STRAND, LONDON.
1881.

ADVERTISEMENT.

The following Sermons, with one exception[a], were preached by the revered Author to his village flock at Hursley, and that mostly between the years 1840 and 1855, when he began to preach extempore. "After that time, or at least 1856, there are," I am informed, "very few finished sermons. Up to that time, they are as a rule perfectly finished."

Being preached then between the time when he had nearly finished his forty-ninth year and his sixty-fourth, they represent the teaching, which, with the experience of years spent among his people, and of his own advancing age, he thought most adapted to their needs. They are specimens, mere fragments of his teaching. They were poured forth from the pastor's heart; for (as usual in his early days) the days upon which they were preached are marked upon them, and one third only were preached a second time, one only, thrice. Of the rest, some he gave away; of one remarkable series, on the penitential Psalms, (preached upon the Wednesdays and Fridays in Lent) all but one are lost. The one which remained has a notice that it was to be finished on the following Friday, and referred to other sermons, on Ashwednesday, and the intervening Friday. The rest of the series has been carefully sought for, in vain.

[a] Serm. xli.

The characteristics of these sermons (if one may venture so to speak) seem to me their intense reality, their awe of God, their sense of the exceeding sinfulness of sin, of the malice and wiles of our unseen enemy, of the deep repentance with which God ought to be sought again, yet of the certainty of His being found, by all who really seek Him; and with regard to his own people, the anxiety for each soul of the Pastor's little flock, which was burned into him. Bright and cheerful outwardly, he himself, in that beautiful sermon, "Suffering the measure of love," describes the sufferings of one who loves our Lord, at the apparent waste of souls, or the jarring against God's holy Will. "[b] How can it" (his inmost soul bursts out) "have one moment's perfect quiet, in such a world as this?" Yet the writer's truthfulness shews itself in the addition, "*perfect* quiet:" quiet, relative to our state, the soul might have; only not "perfect quiet."

Being Lenten Sermons, these Sermons are consequently strict. One object was apparently to unveil his hearers' hearts to themselves, to impress on them the misery and sinfulness of sin, and to draw off for them that covering of self-deceit, which self-love gathers around it. He appears to have avoided, purposely, all oratory; nay (which, until he had entirely trained himself to it, must have involved considerable self-denial to his poetic mind) even illustration from God's works in nature which he so loved. It is only in some two or three places, that imagery, as it were, involuntarily escapes him. Almost all his illustrations are from the types of the Old Testament; and these too are full of awe, how he tells his people that tempers to

[b] p. 71.

which we now too are by nature, one or other, inclined,
are the beginnings of the sins of Achan, or Cain, or Balaam, or the men of Sodom; or nearest to our Lord, of
Judas, or that Esau's profaneness was "but a shadow of
a Christian's wilful sin[c]." It is the pastor, not preaching,
but speaking to, almost talking to, expostulating with
his flock; in the Prophet's words, "[d] Why will ye die,
O house of Israel? For I have no pleasure in the death
of him that dieth, saith the Lord God; wherefore also
turn and live ye."

It belongs to his simple earnest style that he mostly
closes his Sermons, not with an empassioned appeal to his
people, but with a brief sentence (of which there are many
in the course of the sermons) calculated to abide with
them, and such as the poor often carry off, and live upon.
And any one who would profit by these Sermons, would
do well to weigh single words, as, e. g. where, speaking of
other graces, he subjoins, not "truth" but "exact truth."
For like the hermit, who thought that he had attained
some measure of love or humility or thankfulness, and so,
to burn out any sluggish satisfaction at what he had
attained to, wrote on the side of his cell "fervent love"
"deep humility" "overflowing thankfulness" or the like;
saying, that of these he knew nothing; so, many a man
who would be shocked at being thought untruthful, might
hesitate before he claimed to himself "exact truth." Or
when he says that by Christian principles he means, "[e] a
deep sense of the continual Presence of Almighty God and
of the care which He takes for the welfare of our souls;"
or where "[f] the necessary parts signs and tokens of real

[c] p. 120. [d] Ezek. xviii. 32.
[e] p. 129. [f] p. 165.

Christian repentance," have to be weighed one by one and the like.

The sermons eminently serve that end, which S. Francis de Sales insisted upon, as the characteristic of a good sermon, that they sent the hearers home, saying, " God be merciful to me a sinner," or, " wherein can I better please God?"

Secondary and personal as this is, these sermons have, to many of us, a special interest, as giving glimpses into John Keble's inner life. For in a mind of such intense truthfulness as his, one should be quite sure, that what he wrote, he did not write from mere general knowledge, but had himself known and felt. Thus when he lays down that the duty of one who has the care of others is to "[g] contrive beforehand, how he might order *all* intercourse with them," so as "most to encourage them in duty or check them most effectually in sin;" or says incidentally that "[h] to think, is to be alone with God;" and assigns it as a test of the soul's state whether, "[i] when left to yourself, you naturally begin thinking of heavenly things; whether we find our thoughts returning of their own accord towards Heaven, whenever they have been interrupted by any worldly call or anxiety;" or says, "[k] no words can express the sinking of the heart in the reproof of that in others, of which, *in some way*, he feels himself perhaps guiltier then they;" or the readiness to forgive "[l] because it could not forgive itself its own more inexcusable transgressions towards God;" or that it is hypocrisy even to admit a thought other than people believe of any one; or that ready caustic which he had always at hand

[g] p. 21.   [h] p. 18.   [i] Ib.   [k] p. 37.   [l] p. 38.

against the praise of man, "[m] to remember some one thing which you could least bear to think of;" which he likens to "the sackcloth which they of old wore under the dress belonging to their station;" or when he tells people "[n] we must pray to God day by day that we may"—he does not say "love" but—"fear Him more and more;" or that "[o] the way to be forgiven and heard, is not merely to call yourself a miserable sinner before God, but, knowing yourself to be such, not to be put out, when others treat you as such;" or that "[p] our ears do the devil's work, by listening to our own praises, and the blaming of others," or see his account of a Christian's nightly self-examination[q]; or his long description of varied suffering, mental or bodily, of which he says that, "[r] bitter as they must be to the natural man, they are in the mouth of the believer *as honey for sweetness*, if he can but regard them as signs of his Lord's love, and also as means graciously allowed him, whereby to prove the sincerity of his own love;" or that saying, "[s] Christ is always walking and discoursing in a spiritual inward way with us, as He was with the two disciples, though as yet our eyes, like theirs, are holden that we cannot know Him:" or that suffering from praise, which was such a characteristic of his; "[t] Beware of single sins, beware of depending upon one another's praise, on one or two things which you seem to do remarkably well. Depend on nothing of the sort, but repent of all as well as you can; and *let it be your great care to go down humbly to your grave;*" or that other which was fulfilled too early for us on Good Friday 1866; "[u] To know and feel the

[m] p. 39.   [n] p. 131.   [o] p. 149.   [p] p. 189.
   [q] p. 257.   [r] p. 402. see also p. 166.
   [s] p. 231.   [t] p. 70.   [u] p. 72.

very truth of ourselves, that is humility; and humility will save our souls; for it will bring us to the feet of Christ and He will raise us up."

E. B. P.

CHRIST CHURCH,
ADVENT, 1874.

[The readers of these Sermons are indebted for this selection not to the writer of this advertisement but first, to the Author's nephew, the Rev. T. Keble, Jun., who entrusted them to him, and then to the Editor of some portion of the correspondence of John Keble, so long associated with him, the Rev. R. F. Wilson, under whose careful superintendence they were selected. Other series for Advent and the period from Christmas to Septuagesima will follow, it is hoped, towards the close of the ensuing year, and subsequently, if God permit, volumes for the Easter and Trinity season and for Saints' Days.]

CONTENTS.

SERMON I.
REVERENCE DUE TO HOLY SEASONS.
ASH WEDNESDAY.
S. LUKE ix. 34.

"*They feared as they entered into the cloud.*" pp. 1—11.

SERMON II.
OF NOT RECEIVING THE GRACE OF GOD IN VAIN.
ASH-WEDNESDAY.
2 COR. vi. 1.

"*We ... beseech you that ye receive not the grace of God in vain.*" . . . . . . pp. 12—22.

SERMON III.
SHAME FOR SIN, WHETHER INWARD OR OUTWARD, A MERCIFUL GIFT OF GOD.
PART I.
FIRST SUNDAY IN LENT. 1843.
PSALM lxxxiii. 16.

"*Make their faces ashamed, O Lord, that they may seek Thy Name.*" . . . . . . pp. 23—33.

SERMON IV.

SHAME FOR SIN, WHETHER INWARD OR OUTWARD, A MERCIFUL GIFT OF GOD. PART II.

1843.

PSALM lxxxiii. 16.

"*Make their faces ashamed, O Lord, that they may seek Thy Name.*" . . . . . . pp. 34—43.

SERMON V.

ON FASTING.

FIRST SUNDAY IN LENT. 1856.

S. MATT. iv. 2.

"*When He had fasted forty days and forty nights, He was afterwards an hungered.*" . . . pp. 44—52.

SERMON VI.

DANGER OF TRIFLING WITH GOD'S WARNING CALLS.

FIRST SUNDAY IN LENT. 1850.

2 COR. vi. 2.

"*Behold now is the accepted time; behold now is the day of salvation.*" . . . . . pp. 53—62.

SERMON VII.

CONFESSION. PART I.

1851.

1 S. JOHN i. 8, 9.

"*If we say that we have no sin, we deceive ourselves and the truth is not in us.*" . . . . pp. 63—72.

SERMON VIII.

CONFESSION. PART II.

1851.

1 S. JOHN i. 8, 9.

"*If we say that we have no sin, we deceive ourselves, and the truth is not in us: But if we confess our sins, He is faithful and just to forgive us our sins, and to cleanse us from all unrighteousness.*" . . . . pp. 73—82.

SERMON IX.

CONFESSION. PART III.

1851.

JOSHUA vii. 19. 20.

"*And Joshua said unto Achan, My son give glory, I pray thee, to the Lord God of Israel, and make confession unto Him: and tell me now what thou hast done; hide it not from me. And Achan answered Joshua, and said, indeed I have sinned against the Lord God of Israel, and thus, and thus have I done.*" . . . pp. 83—94.

SERMON X.

CONFESSION. PART IV.

1851.

PSALM xix. 13, 14.

"*Who can tell how oft he offendeth? O cleanse Thou me from my secret faults; keep Thy servant also from presumptuous sins, lest they get the dominion over me; so shall I be undefiled and innocent from the great offence.*"
pp. 95—103.

SERMON XI.

THE PROFANENESS OF ESAU A WARNING TO CHRISTIANS.

SECOND SUNDAY IN LENT. 1848.

GEN. xxv. 34.

"Thus Esau despised his birthright." . pp. 104—114.

SERMON XII.

THE PROFANENESS OF ESAU A WARNING TO CHRISTIANS.

SECOND SUNDAY IN LENT. 1853.

S. MARK viii. 36, 37.

"What shall it profit a man, if he gain the whole world, and lose his own soul? or what shall a man give in exchange for his soul?" . . . . pp. 115—126.

SERMON XIII.

OF ABOUNDING MORE AND MORE.

SECOND SUNDAY IN LENT.

1 THESS. iv. 1.

"We beseech you, brethren, and exhort you by the Lord Jesus, that as ye have received of us how ye ought to walk, and to please God, so ye would abound more and more."
pp. 127—139.

SERMON XIV.

THE WOMAN OF CANAAN.

SECOND SUNDAY IN LENT. 1858.

S. Matt. xv. 27. and S. Mark vii. 28, 29.

"*And she answered and said, Truth, Lord; yet the dogs eat of the crumbs which fall from their master's table. He said unto her, For this saying go thy way: the devil is gone out of thy daughter.*" . . pp. 140—149.

SERMON XV.

THE HARD SERVICE OF SIN.

1854.

Deut. xxviii. 47, 48.

"*Because thou servedst not the Lord thy God with joyfulness and with gladness of heart for the abundance of all things; therefore shalt thou serve thine enemies which the Lord shall send against thee, in hunger and in thirst, and in nakedness and in want of all things.*" . pp. 150—158.

SERMON XVI.

GOD'S REFRESHMENTS FOR PENITENTS.

1844.

1 Kings xix. 7.

"*The Angel of the Lord came again the second time, and touched him saying, Arise and eat, because the journey is too great for thee.*". . . . pp. 159—171.

SERMON XVII.
OUR EVER PRESENT UNSEEN ENEMY.

THIRD SUNDAY IN LENT. 1853.

1 S. JOHN v. 8.

"He that is begotten of God keepeth himself, and that wicked one toucheth him not." . . . pp. 172—182.

SERMON XVIII.
THE WILES OF THE DEVIL.

THIRD SUNDAY IN LENT. 1845.

2 Cor. ii. 11.

" Lest Satan should get an advantage of us: for we are not ignorant of his devices." . . . pp. 183—192.

SERMON XIX.
DEADLY PEACE OF THE UNAWAKENED CONSCIENCE.

THIRD SUNDAY IN LENT. 1850.

S. LUKE ix. 21.

" When a strong man armed keepeth his palace, his goods are in peace." . . . . . pp. 193—202.

SERMON XX.

THE RELAPSED SINNER.

THIRD SUNDAY IN LENT.

S. MATT. xii. 45.

"The last state of that man is worse than the first."
pp. 203—212.

SERMON XXI.

PERIL OF HALF-HEARTEDNESS.

THIRD SUNDAY IN LENT. 1854.

S. LUKE xi. 23.

"He that is not with Me is against Me, and he that gathereth not with Me, scattereth." . . pp. 213—222.

SERMON XXII.

THE DUMB AND DEAF SPIRIT.

THIRD SUNDAY IN LENT. 1847.

S. LUKE xi. 14.

" He was casting out a devil, and it was dumb, and it came to pass that when the devil was gone out, the dumb spake." . . . . . . pp. 223—232.

SERMON XXIII.

OBEDIENCE, NOT PRIVILEGE, THE MEASURE OF BLESSEDNESS.

THIRD SUNDAY IN LENT. 1859.

S. LUKE xi. 27, 28.

"And it came to pass, as He spake these things, a certain woman of the company lifted up her voice, and said unto Him, Blessed is the womb that bare Thee, and the paps which Thou hast sucked. But He said, Yea rather, blessed are they that hear the word of God and keep it."
pp. 233—242.

SERMON XXIV.

TO BE WITHOUT GOD, UTTER DARKNESS.

1852.

AMOS v. 18.

"Woe unto you that desire the day of the Lord; to what end is it for you? the day of the Lord is darkness and not light." . . . . . . pp. 243—252.

SERMON XXV.

SELF-EXAMINATION; ITS SHARP BUT HEALING PAIN.

1852.

PSALM cxxxix. 23, 24.

"Try me, O God, and seek the ground of my heart; prove me and examine my thoughts. Look well if there be any way of wickedness in me, and lead me in the way everlasting." . . . . . pp. 253—259.

SERMON XXVI.

BLESSEDNESS OF THE SOUL CONFESSING ITS SIN
AND FORGIVEN.

1856.

Ps. xxxii. 1.

" Blessed is he whose unrighteousness is forgiven and whose sin is covered." . . . . pp. 260—269.

SERMON XXVII.

THE REPENTANCE OF MANASSEH.

1849.

2 Chron. xxxiii. 12.

" When he was in affliction, he besought the Lord his God."
pp. 270—278.

SERMON XXVIII.

THE REPENTANCE OF NINEVEH.

1849.

Jonah iii. 2.

" God saw their works, that they turned from their evil way, and God repented of the evil that He had said He would do unto them, and He did it not." . pp. 279—287.

SERMON XXIX.

JOSEPH A TYPE OF CHRIST AND A PATTERN TO
CHRISTIANS.

FOURTH SUNDAY IN LENT. 1853.

Hebrews ii. 11.

" He is not ashamed to call them brethren." pp. 288—297.

SERMON XXX.
ISHMAEL'S MOCKING A TYPE OF THE WORLD'S TREATMENT OF CHRIST AND HIS PEOPLE.
FOURTH SUNDAY IN LENT. 1855.

GAL. iv. 29.

"As then he that was born after the flesh persecuted him that was born after the Spirit, even so it is now."
pp. 298—308.

SERMON XXXI.
GOD'S WAY OF PROVIDING FOR OUR BODIES AND OUR SOULS.
FOURTH SUNDAY IN LENT. 1850.

S. JOHN vi. 5.

"Whence shall we buy bread, that these may eat?"
pp. 309—317.

SERMON XXXII.
TIMES OF PENANCE TIMES OF REFRESHING.
FOURTH SUNDAY IN LENT. 1852.

ACTS iii. 19, 20, 21.

"Times of refreshing shall come from the Presence of the Lord, and He shall send Jesus Christ, which before was preached unto you, Whom the Heaven must receive until the times of restitution of all things." pp. 318—327.

SERMON XXXIII.
PERSEVERANCE.
PASSION SUNDAY. 1853.

JUDGES xi. 35.

"I have opened my mouth unto the Lord, and I cannot go back." . . . . . . pp. 328—335.

SERMON XXXIV.
HOW SINNERS MAY DARE TO LOOK UPON THE PASSION OF THE LORD.

PASSION SUNDAY. 1844.

EXODUS iii. 6.

"*Moses hid his face, for he was afraid to look upon God.*"
pp. 336—345.

SERMON XXXV.
CHRISTIAN LIBERTY.

PASSION SUNDAY. 1845.

S. JOHN viii. 36.

"*If the Son therefore shall make you free, ye shall be free indeed.*" . . . . . pp. 346—356.

SERMON XXXVI.
UNBELIEF IN THE PRESENCE OF CHRIST, NOW ALSO, DEADLY SIN.

PASSION SUNDAY. 1851.

S. JOHN viii. 4.

"*If ye believe not that I am He, ye shall die in your sins.*"
pp. 357—366.

SERMON XXXVII.
WORK WHILE IT IS DAY.

PASSION SUNDAY. 1854.

S. JOHN ix. 4.

"*I must work the works of Him that sent Me while it is day: the night cometh, when no man can work.*" pp. 367—375.

SERMON XXXVIII.
THOUGHT OF THE CROSS INTOLERABLE TO THE EARTHLY MIND.

PASSION SUNDAY. 1846.

S. MATT. xvi. 22.

"*Peter took Him, and began to rebuke Him, saying, Be it far from Thee, Lord: this shall not be unto Thee.*"

pp. 376—385.

SERMON XXXIX.
THE UNCHANGEABLE PRIESTHOOD OF CHRIST.

PASSION SUNDAY. 1858.

HEB. vii. 25.

"*He is able also to save them to the uttermost that come unto God by Him, seeing He ever liveth to make intercession for them.*" . . . . . pp. 386—396.

SERMON XL.
SUFFERING THE MEASURE OF LOVE.

FEAST OF THE ANNUNCIATION, FALLING ON PASSION SUNDAY. 1855.

S. LUKE ii. 35.

"*Yea a sword shall pierce through thine own soul also.*"

pp. 397—409.

SERMON XLI.
OUR LORD'S OWN ACCOUNT OF CHRISTIAN FASTING.

1863.

S. LUKE v. 35.

"*The days will come, when the Bridegroom shall be taken away from them; and then shall they fast in those days.*"

pp. 410—419

SERMON XLII.

THE PRODIGAL SON. PART I.

1846.

S. LUKE xv. 11, 12, 13.

" A certain man had two sons; and the younger of them said to his father, Father, give me the portion of goods which falleth to me. And he divided unto them his living. And not many days after, the younger son gathered all together, and took his journey into a far country, and there wasted his substance with riotous living. pp. 420—428.

SERMON XLIII.

THE PRODIGAL SON. PART II.

S. LUKE xv. 14, 15, 16.

" And when he had spent all, there arose a mighty famine in that land; and he began to be in want. And he went and joined himself to a citizen of that country, and he sent him into the fields to feed swine. And he would fain have filled his belly with the husks that the swine did eat: and no man gave unto him." pp. 429—435.

SERMON XLIV.

THE PRODIGAL SON. PART III.

S. LUKE xv. 17, 18, 19.

" And when he came to himself he said, How many hired servants of my father's have bread enough, and to spare, and I perish with hunger! I will arise and go to my father, and will say unto him, Father, I have sinned

against heaven and before thee, and am no more worthy to be called thy son: make me as one of thy hired servants."
pp. 436—441.

SERMON XLV.

THE PRODIGAL SON. PART IV.

S. LUKE xv. 20—24.

" And he arose, and came to his father. But when he was yet a great way off, his father saw him, and had compassion, and ran, and fell on his neck, and kissed him. And the son said unto him, Father, I have sinned against heaven, and in thy sight, and am no more worthy to be called thy son. But the father said to his servants, Bring forth the best robe, and put it on him; and put a ring on his hand, and shoes on his feet: And bring hither the fatted calf, and kill it; and let us eat, and be merry: For this my son was dead, and is alive again; he was lost, and is found. And they began to be merry."
pp. 442—450.

SERMON XLVI.

THE PRODIGAL SON. PART V.

S. LUKE xv. 31, 32.

" Son, thou art ever with me, and all that I have is thine. It was meet that we should make merry and be glad: for this thy brother was dead, and is alive again; and was lost, and is found." . . . . pp. 451—458.

SERMON I.

REVERENCE DUE TO HOLY SEASONS.

ASH WEDNESDAY.

S. Luke ix. 34.

"*They feared as they entered into the cloud.*"

The solemn times of humiliation, such as Lent and Advent, are very trying times to tender consciences, and on that very account, among others, they come with a peculiar trial and difficulty to the ministers and messengers of Jesus Christ.

It is of course our duty, in respect of the great doctrine of Repentance, which especially belongs to such seasons, to set it forth, like every other part of the Gospel, according to the proportion of faith: that is the rule of the Holy Ghost by S. Paul. Now you know what "proportion" means, when we talk of a picture, or a building, or any other work of man. It means that no one part is too large or too small for the rest, but that each of them is kept of the proper measure, according to the size of the whole work. In like manner, the proportion of faith is kept, when the whole of God's message is set forth as He intended, when neither His judgements nor His mercies are forgotten; according to His own solemn declaration by Moses; that "He forgiveth iniquity, transgression, and sin, yet will by no means clear the guilty."

Now in teaching repentance, there is of course a danger of erring on either side of this declaration. One man may speak, or seem to speak, of God's wrath against sinners only; another only of His love and mercy to His redeemed; and even if both be fully set forth, according to their due proportions, both will not always be alike attended to. The hearers will carry away with them, too commonly, only that part of what is said which suits their own temper and frame of mind. The hardened will lay hold of whatever is said in praise of God's great and overflowing mercy; while the bruised and wounded in heart, the tender consciences, will be over-much struck by the severe and aweful part of the doctrine. And thus it will too often follow, that each learner will dwell on just that portion of the instruction, which his own case did not so much require. So it is in reading or hearing the Bible: no wonder, therefore, that so it should be in men's way of receiving the instruction and advice of Christ's servants; no wonder if they often seem to be unduly severe, or overindulgent, when, perhaps, if all they said was attended to, they would be found simply to have repeated God's message. And all this is over and above the errors and imperfections they may fall into, in what they say, or in their manner of saying it.

This, then, is one great danger, whenever we preach, as in Lent we must preach, upon repentance; namely, that the hardened and the tender consciences will often each take to themselves what was properly meant for the other. Another difficulty we are under, lies in a difference which God's Providence seems to have made between one penitent and another.

Even sincere persons, and such as are in earnest anxious to please God, and obtain His pardon, through His Son, at the last day, do not all of them take alike the very plainest and most direct sayings of the Bible. Some appear, even naturally, to require more hope, more joy, more encouragement, than others. As they feel their sins more deeply, so they seem to need more direct offers of pardon. Some cannot bear doubt, it almost seems like death to them; others try to content themselves with it, as part of their ordained penance for a time; and they seem to feel, that it would be a very dangerous thing for such as they are to depend too much on feelings of assurance. Some are like the Prodigal Son, for whom it was best to set out on his long journey, and perform more or less of it, in wonder and suspense, whether his father could ever receive him as a son again; others are like the woman who loved much, to whom our Lord said at once, "Thy sins be forgiven thee."

Now for both of these He has graciously provided, " Who is the merciful receiver of all true penitent sinners." His severe sayings, especially in the Epistles, are enough to keep down too much assurance in the one: His most compassionate dealings with penitents, both in the Old and New Testaments, are the very medicine to keep the other from despair.

Then, lest persons should make a mistake, and apply to themselves that part of His sayings which was not intended for them, or which however, taken alone, does not suit their present condition, He graciously invites them to open their grief to His priests, and receive from them the benefit of absolution, which they are to give sooner or later, as the case may require, and which is the regular ordained mean of assured comfort to broken-hearted penitents. Indeed, it is most deeply to be wished, that such as feel themselves in care and perplexity, from any thing they hear in the Church's public teaching, would make up their minds to speak about it, either to their own pastor, or to some other whom they can trust, in private. It seems the regular and natural way for correcting misapprehensions about their own condition. For "the priest's lips" are to "preserve knowledge," and the people are to "seek the law at his lips, for he is the messenger of the Lord of Hosts." He has also power given him, by our Lord Jesus Christ Himself, to forgive sins in His Name, when truly repented of and forsaken. That blessed ordinance of absolution has indeed a Divine virtue, which many a wounded heart can testify, where it is received in true faith and humility, and followed by persevering obedience; a virtue to calm the troubled spirit, and enable it with hope and comfort to draw near to God's altar. Absolution is like the hand of the compassionate Saviour laid upon a penitent's head, confirming, and applying to him in particular, the good word, "Thy sins be forgiven thee." In a word, absolution, as I said before, is the regular way to that sober assurance of pardon, which even the worst sinners may hope for, truly repenting, and confessing, and amending their ways.

But far be it from me to deny that the Almighty has also other ways of assuring and comforting His people, ways without number, and beyond description, ways which may not and cannot be set down in words, so that it would be exceedingly rash and presumptuous for one Christian to question another's assured hope of pardon, provided that other be really endeavouring to serve God and keep His commandments, and really humbling himself for what has been wrong. The danger is, where people trust to their feelings, without such real practical amendment; or to the disparagement of Church ordinances; or where they insist on such feelings, as a sure and necessary token of forgiveness; or where they are too much disquieted for want of them. In a word, humble obedience for the future is the surest sign of pardon for the past; deep, transporting, overpowering feelings, when they come in aid of this, may be thankfully received as true tokens from above; but without this, they are surely deceitful and mischievous. If men have them, they must not presume; if they have them not, they need not despair.

Now such differences, as I have now said there are, in God's grace manifesting itself in different penitents, this requiring more encouragement than that, one more eager and hopeful than another; such differences will there naturally be, in their way of keeping holy times, such as this present season of Lent. Some will feel deeper compunction than others, will be more inclined to bodily mortification in secret, will feel more earnestly moved towards confession and shewing their deeds: another sort, perhaps, at this as at other times, will have the cheerful hope or sense of pardon more thoroughly awake and alive within them: the Almighty, in His unsearchable Providence, may not have given all the signs and tokens of love; but surely His love is with both sorts alike, provided both agree alike in trying sincerely to hate their sins, and serve their Saviour with all their heart. To both sorts the holy season will be blessed, provided both keep it in the true fear of God.

I say "in the fear of God," that is, in awful reverence before Him, and in a serious sense of His Presence; for *that* is indeed necessary for every one, whether inclined to be hopeful or downcast. No temper, no doings, can be right or safe, without a serious, earnest apprehension of our Creator's eye fixed upon us, of our Redeemer watching to see what love we have to give, in return, for His unspeakable dying love. The very reason why compunction and sorrow are rather to be encouraged in most of us, than undoubting hope, is because our nature, too fond of ease, is apt, in undoubting hope, to forget reverence and godly fear. But if men have that grace, if they are truly serious and earnest, aware of Christ's awful presence, and humbling themselves before it, then they may without danger be encouraged to have joy and peace in believing: they cannot then be other than strict in their conduct, sincere in their obedience, haters of their past sins: whatever courage, and hope, and confidence, go along with the true fear of God, is His gracious gift vouchsafed to make them more perfect and steady in their duty: it helps their repentance, instead of hurting it. Just as, on the other hand, there is such a thing as sorrow and compunction, and that for past sin, without the true faith and fear of God, a sorrow like that of Ahab, or of Judas, mere dread of punishment, or sense of degradation, without love of Christ, or feeling of the cross, without any thought of God as an offended Father; where the heart, though it is pained, cannot properly be called broken or contrite, because it wants the true fear of God, it has not surrendered itself to the gracious influences of the good Spirit, dealing with us as with children.

What a necessary grace this serious fear of God is, at such times as this of Lent especially, you may judge from the account of our Lord's Transfiguration, part of which was read to you as our text: "There came a cloud, and overshadowed them, and they feared as they entered into the cloud." Times of solemn humiliation, like Lent, or of solemn joy, like Easter, are as that cloud, the token of God's presence; it behoves us to fear as we enter upon them.

Consider who the persons were, that had that fear upon the mount. They were the three chosen and most highly-favoured Apostles. If Peter, James, and John feared, surely we ought to fear. S. Peter, the pattern of the Church's true confession, to whom but a week before, the promise had been given, "Upon this rock I will build My Church, and I will give unto thee the keys of the Kingdom of Heaven;" he feared as he entered into the cloud; who then dare presume upon his right catholic belief and true views of doctrine, and thereupon come near to our Lord, and take Christian privileges, without fear? S. James feared, who was to be the first martyr among the

Apostles: we must not, therefore, trust to our own past sufferings, or seeming readiness to endure more for Christ; we must still fear as well as hope, while we draw near the cross; amazed still, and confounded, to think how utterly unworthy is all we have borne or done, as a return for that infinite love. S. John, too, the disciple whom Jesus loved, he also feared as he entered into the cloud: surely, then, we ought to be very jealous of any whisper within our hearts, as though we were especially dear to Him, and might venture to be at our ease before Him. Surely the temper in which we should strive to say our prayers, to keep Lent, to prepare for the Communion, is a temper of serious, thoughtful, anxious dutifulness. Let us look well to that; and the joy and comfort, the peace and hope, will come of itself in God's good time. I say again, if the great Apostles feared, how should not we fear, as we enter into the cloud which is the sign of God's Presence?

Remember that former time, and that other mountain, which the cloud at the Transfiguration must have reminded them of. The Lord came down upon Mount Sinai in darkness, clouds, and thick darkness, and Moses, by special command, drew nigh to the thick darkness where God was. "The glory of the Lord abode upon Mount Sinai, and the cloud covered it six days: and the seventh day He called unto Moses out of the midst of the cloud. And the sight of the glory of the Lord was like devouring fire on the top of the mount in the eyes of the children of Israel. And Moses went into the midst of the cloud, and gat him up into the mount: and Moses was in the mount forty days and forty nights."

"He abode in the mount forty days and forty nights:" "he did neither eat bread nor drink water." That was his Lent: and in what mind did he enter on it, he who was especially favoured by the Almighty, who had found grace in His sight, and whom he knew by name; with whom God talked face to face, as a man talketh with his friend? He said, "I exceedingly fear and quake." Indeed, his own words show how full he was of aweful dread; how the overpowering terror of that time filled his heart, and was never forgotten.

In after-times, whenever the Lord appeared especially in that cloud, we read of His servants, His chosen ones, falling on their faces; so did Moses and Aaron over and over, when the glory showed itself over the tabernacle door; so did Joshua, when the captain of the Lord's host stood before him; so did David, at sight of the Angel standing over Jerusalem, with his sword drawn in his hand; so did Daniel, at the great vision; "there remained no strength in him, he fainted away, and was in a deep sleep on his face, and his face toward the ground;" and this, too, was after Daniel's Lent, after he had been fasting three full weeks.

Remember especially what the New Testament teaches of the fear and trembling of the saints, when even the Man Christ Jesus, the holy and merciful Saviour, appeared to them bodily. S. Paul was struck down, and could not see for the glory of that light, and in that condition, blind, humbled, helpless, fasting, he remained three days. S. John, the beloved one, who had leaned on our Lord's breast at supper, what was his feeling when he had revealed to him the vision of the same gracious Lord in His glory? "I saw seven golden candlesticks," that is, the Holy Catholic Church; " and in the midst of the seven candlesticks one like unto the Son of Man, clothed with a garment down to the foot, and girt about the paps with a golden girdle," that is, our Lord in His Priest's office; " His head and His hair were white like wool, as white as snow; and His eyes were as a flame of fire; and His feet like unto fine brass, as if they burned in a furnace; and His voice as the sound of many waters. And He had in His right hand seven stars,"—the bishops and pastors of His Church;—"and out of His mouth went a sharp two-edged sword: and His countenance was as the sun shineth in his strength." Such was the vision: mark now, how that favoured disciple received it; " When I saw Him, I fell at His feet as dead."

In this respect, you see, the Saints, one and all, were just alike; that they fell down before Christ's glory with the very deepest dread and reverence. Whether He was coming in judgement or in mercy, whether they were penitents or no, whether they had seen Christ crucified or no, made no difference in that respect. All alike received Him with the deepest humiliation and reverence; all alike feared as they entered into the cloud.

Now the same cloud overshadows and covers us. As surely as ever we belong to Christ's Church, and as this time which we are keeping is the holy time of Lent, so surely is that same cloud now over us and around us, whether we choose to believe it, and think of it, or no. It hovers above us, it surrounds us on every side, full charged with the dew of Heaven, with God's pardoning and strengthening grace; but it gives out that dew only to the dutiful, considerate, reverential heart. The blessing of the holy season will come only on those who try to pass it in the true fear of God; to mingle that fear in all their works, especially in all their religious exercises; not to say or do any thing, if they can help it, merely as a matter of course, but to remember all along Whose they are, and Whom they serve. The cloud of this penitential season will be a gracious rain to Christ's inheritance, and refresh it now in its fallen and weary times, if we strive, for our part, to think more and more of His Presence; to chasten ourselves more effectually, even in thought, not giving the reins to any pleasure, be it never so innocent; to understand more and more of our own deep unworthiness, and of His unspeakable love; and thankfully to accept His chastisements, bodily and spiritual, as the corrections of a loving Father.

SERMON II.

OF NOT RECEIVING THE GRACE OF GOD IN VAIN.

ASH WEDNESDAY.

ii. Cor. vi. 1.

"*We . . . beseech you that ye receive not the Grace of God in vain.*"

EVERY person who has read his prayer book with any degree of attention, knows that this season of Lent is appointed by the Church for the especial exercise of repentance; that she intends us to refrain for a while even from the innocent pleasures of the world, that our time and thoughts may be the freer to consider our past lives, to bewail and confess our sins, and so prepare ourselves, with thankful hearts, to acknowledge the infinite mercies of God in Christ Jesus on the great days of His Death and Resurrection.

Now labouring men and poor men are apt to imagine they have very little to do with such times as this: "Fasting and abstinence, humiliation and self-denial, are very well for those who live in mirth and abundance, and, 'fare sumptuously every day;' but we, whose lives are all poverty and toil, had need take all the pleasure we can find, and divert ourselves without fear or scruple, in Lent as well as at other times in the year." And, upon the strength of such excuses as this, too many go on, neglecting their God and Saviour, and burying themselves in thoughts of this world, throughout this holy season, with as little remorse or concern as they have done all the year besides.

But what is the real worth and value of this apology for the neglect of so sacred and useful an ordinance? It comes, when you consider it, to neither more less than this: that they cannot, or will not, govern their own thoughts, and turn them more earnestly than usual towards eternal things, in order that they may be the readier to keep Good Friday and Easter as they ought to be kept. For the reason why fasting and abstinence is good at this season, is no merit or goodness in the fasting or abstinence themselves, but because they are useful helps to us in diverting our thoughts from vain cares and pleasures, and fixing them on eternal things. *That* is what the Church wants; *that* is the use of Lent, for which we shall be called to account at the last day: and if we be too sick or too poor to change our usual diet and mode of living, still we are not the less bound, at this holy season, to do that for the sake of which others are called to mortify their bodies. The poorest man is just as much bounden as the richest, to use Lent for his help, in repenting truly of his former sins. He may turn his thoughts that way more earnestly than he has been used to do; may spend a little more time in his prayers, and strive more incessantly to keep up his attention while he is praying. Surely no one can imagine that such discipline and self-denial as this, carefully persisted in, all through the forty days of Lent, would be of no use in making a man a truer penitent, and a worthier communicant at Easter.

He who desires thus to improve himself, cannot begin better, than by deeply meditating on the weighty and overpowering call to repentance contained in the words of the text. "We," (i. e. the ministers of Jesus Christ) "as workers together with Him, beseech you also, that ye receive not the grace of God in vain."

These words are aweful enough in themselves, and calculated to go deep into every heart which has any sense of God, any natural piety within it. Consider: we stand in the presence of the great and unspeakable God, who fills Heaven and Earth; and not only do we, in common with all His creatures, stand in His presence, but we are likewise objects of His special care; His eye is upon us for our good; we have received favour and grace from Him; we know He means our happiness. Can anything be more startling than the thought, that, after all this, we fail and be miserable? And yet such we see is the case. Nay, not only is the thing possible, but it will surely take place if we are left to ourselves. We have need of exhortation; we want an Apostle to come and beseech us that we receive not the favour of the Almighty in vain.

All this surely ought to make a serious impression upon us, though we knew nothing of the way in which God's favour had been reached out to us. A Gentile might feel it on recollecting His natural mercies, His ways of providence and preservation; the rain He gives us from Heaven and the fruitful seasons, His filling our hearts with food and gladness. A Jew might feel it, when reflecting on the peculiar kindness shewn to the family of Israel; he might reasonably say to himself, "What if I, who am one of God's favoured people, should lose His favour, and miscarry at last by my own fault? will it not be ten times worse with me than it will be with the worst of heathens?"

But if a Jew or a Gentile might talk thus with himself, much more those to whom S. Paul is speaking in the text; much more we Christians. If we would know what infinite reason we have to be very full of anxiety for our own souls, we must look and see what that Grace of God is, which we are here said to have received, and for which, if received in vain, we shall one day find ourselves answerable. We must look back a few sentences in the Apostle's letter, and read as follows: "He died for all, that they which live should not henceforth live unto themselves, but unto Him which died for them and rose again." "God was in Christ, reconciling the world unto Himself." "He hath made Him to be sin for us who knew no sin, that we might be made the righteousness of God in Him. We then as workers together with Him—we also beseech you that ye receive not the favour of God in vain;" the unutterable favour of God in giving His Son to die for you, in reconciling the world unto Himself, in making Him to be sin for us who knew no sin, and in making us in Him, the righteousness of God: that is, joining us to Him by His Spirit. This favour, even the Gift of eternal life, is received by every Christian; but it may be received in vain; in vain, that is, as to the salvation of the particular person receiving it; for doubtless there may be other purposes, unknown to us, which Almighty God accomplishes by making His word known to those who refuse to obey it. But those are secrets of God with which we have nothing to do; what concerns us at present, is to reflect, with all possible attention and seriousness, upon our own awful and dangerous condition. For we have received this grace of God. His Son has died for us, and we know it. His Spirit has entered into our hearts and made us members of Christ. He has poured out for our sakes all the treasures of His mercy; daily and hourly He offers to bestow upon us more and more of His Holy Spirit: and if all this prove at last vain, what can we think or expect? what can we think of ourselves? or what expect from God?

Surely those who have any spark of consideration left, must be roused and animated by such thoughts as these, to examine whether they are not, at this moment, receiving the grace of God in vain. For it is certain that every instance of outward communion in Christian ordinances— every time we read a chapter, or say a prayer, or go to Church, and, most, of all, every time we receive the Holy Communion without being really the better for it, is an instance of our receiving the grace of God in vain. And if we pass our lives in such a course, how can we expect to be the better for that grace when we come to die?

I do not mean that every time we go to Church we must expect to *feel* better than we had done before: but I mean, that if upon fairly examining our own conduct, we do not find, that by degrees we are growing better, the warning of the Apostle comes very near us; and we have great reason to fear for our own present and eternal condition.

When any person is pointed out to us, who never comes near Church, never opens a good book, never even professes to turn his mind to meditation and prayer, we fancy we know at once what to think of that man. We have no scruple in setting him down for one of those to whom the grace of God, which was meant for salvation, will bring no salvation at last, unless a complete change take place in all his principles and ways. And in passing censures of this kind, we are too apt to draw silent comparisons with ourselves, as if, because they are wrong, we are sure to be right.

But perhaps, though we are regular at Divine Service, we feel no real concern, no serious interest in it. Perhaps we are glad when it is over, and pleased to be at liberty to run wild again after the bustle and business of an irreligious world. Perhaps we make no steady effort to keep our thoughts and our words together when we are saying our prayers to God. If such be our case, it is high time for us to leave off censuring others, and take the beam out of our own eyes.

I will make one allowance more. I will suppose that we really do pay something like regular and serious attention to the ordinances in which we draw near to God. I will suppose that for the time we really wish to please Him, and that it would make us truly unhappy and uncomfortable to suppose ourselves out of His favour. Yet the great proof of our sincerity remains to be given; i. e. the amendment of our lives: and that, especially in the following particulars, in which men, endowed with a certain degree of right feeling in religion, are, I think, most apt to go wrong.

First, in the government of our thoughts and imaginations. Men are apt sometimes to fancy, that if they *do* right, they may *think* as they please. But this is surely an inexcusable mistake; for it is supposing God to take no account of their thoughts; of which, as much as of anything else, we may be sure He takes the strictest account; for the order and government of our thoughts proves what we really are, more distinctly than anything else. In thinking, we are alone with God, and the ordering of our thoughts aright is neither more nor less than behaving rightly towards Him.

Consider, then, whether your improvement in this respect has been answerable to the means of grace which Almighty God has mercifully afforded you. Consider whether, when left to yourself, you naturally begin meditating on heavenly things, the Presence of God, the mercies of Christ, the hopes and fears of Eternity: or whether you start aside (like a broken bow, as the Psalmist says), to the vanities and amusements which happen to lie most in your way. To be sure what we think of most, that in our hearts we must love best; and we ought not to be satisfied with our own devotion of heart, till we find our thoughts returning of their own accord towards Heaven, whenever they have been interrupted by any worldly call or anxiety.

Secondly, to know whether we are quite sincere

in receiving the grace of God, we must consider whether we are the better for it in our daily discourse and conversation with other men. Not that we are to be always talking of religious subjects; but since one of the most necessary truths for a Christian to believe, is the corruption of the heart and tongue, it is impossible but that one, who has a true and an increasing sense of it, must be more and more on his guard that he offend not in words. He must be more afraid every day of lying and dissimulation, of violent and reproachful language, of filthiness and foolish talking, of inconsiderate slander and calumny. This will perhaps be the very surest sign and mark by which a sincere man may satisfy his own conscience, that he is really the better for the inestimable love of God in making and keeping him a Christian.

I say, he will be particularly on his guard against slander and calumny in *words;* and for this reason among others, he will watch and stop the entrance of his heart against slanderous and calumnious *thoughts.* He will always endeavour to believe and hope the best that he possibly can of his neighbour's conduct; for if he once give way to uncharitable suspicions within, hardly any caution will enable him to keep himself from doing harm to his neighbour's character, when he comes to speak of him. His real opinion will betray itself, unkind hearers will make the worst of it, and thus our brother's fair fame may suffer more than we can ever repay him, for want of a little seasonable charity in our own deceitful hearts. Therefore as I said before, one of the best signs of our not receiving God's grace in vain will be this: that we have become more mild and charitable in the construction we put on our neighbour's conduct, and always hope the best till we are forced to believe the worst.

Many indeed would reply, that this is out of their power; that they wish indeed to believe the best, but they have been so often disappointed, have met with so much wickedness, that they cannot help growing more suspicious as they grow older. But it is worth their while to ask themselves, whether they have not quite as often found themselves deceived by judging too unfavourably of others, as by thinking too well of them? whether they have not, in very many instances, accounted this or that man wicked and unprincipled, when in fact he was only weak and wavering? If they would examine themselves fairly on this point, no doubt their consciences would teach them, as clearly as their Bibles, that it is their own wickedness, not that of others, which makes them so very keen and acute in putting evil interpretations upon doubtful conduct.

I proceed now to another mark—the last I shall now mention—by which we may try ourselves whether the grace of God, which we are daily receiving, is thrown away upon us or no. Are we daily becoming more industrious, and readier to deny ourselves, for the help and comfort of our neighbour? The more we know of the Gospel, the more we know of God's love to us: how dear it cost Him, how far it reaches, how unceasing and unwearied it is. The more pressing, therefore, is the call upon us, to think nothing too good for our brethren, no sacrifice too costly to be offered for the sake of ensuring their eternal welfare. Every time we draw near to the Holy Communion, we see, by faith, the Cross of Christ, His Body broken and His Blood poured out, to redeem us from eternal death. How then can we avoid reflecting, with the beloved disciple, S. John, "Hereby perceive we the love of God, because He laid down His life for us, and we ought to lay down our lives for the brethren?" "To lay down our lives," says the Apostle; for he lived in constant danger of that extreme trial of his virtue: he knew not how soon he might be called to martyrdom, to confirm the faith of his fellow-Christians. We, by God's mercy, are not likely to have to struggle with such overwhelming temptations, but it is not the less our duty to spend our lives in our brethren's service. In whatever way we are engaged with them, we ought to think much, and patiently, how we may do them most good. I am afraid most of us may find, when our time comes, that we have a more fearful account than we expected to give of our neglect of opportunities of this kind. Commonly we think no more of those with whom we are concerned in the ordinary transactions of life, than how we may deal kindly and honestly by them: but if we had S. Paul's mind, to spend and be spent for them, or the mind of our Blessed Saviour, who went about doing good, we should consider their case more deeply than this; we should contrive beforehand how we might order all our intercourse with them, so as to give them most encouragement in the way of duty, or to check them most effectually in sin. I do not say that we should *tell* them, or any one else, that we are doing thus;

but surely we ought to do so: wherever we are, and whoever is with us, we ought to keep God's watch for the good of our neighbour's soul; and the more regularly and the more quietly we perform this duty, the more reason we have to hope that we are not receiving the grace of God in vain.

This, I say, is a plain duty, and so are all the other tempers and habits which I have now set down as marks of Christian improvement; the right ordering of our thoughts and words, especially what we say and think of our neighbour's conduct. And yet these are points, in which hourly experience shows that it is very possible and very easy to fall short, in the midst of great attention to religious ordinances, and a sincere desire, so far as that goes, of pleasing God.

But none of these marks of real improvement are hard to understand, or hard to try one's self by. Consider then, I beseech you, whether it is not exceeding sinful and dangerous to rest contented in careless doubt about these things, and take for granted that you are going on as well as other men, while it is in your power, by constant watching yourself, to make your eternal salvation sure.

Baptised into the Holy Catholic Church, we cannot deny that we have received the grace of God. "Greater is He that is in us, than he that is in the world:" and whatever temptations we may be thrown amongst, if we die without sincere and timely repentance and amendment, we shall find ourselves answerable for having received His Grace in vain.

SERMON III.

SHAME FOR SIN, WHETHER INWARD OR OUTWARD,
A MERCIFUL GIFT OF GOD.

PART I.

FIRST SUNDAY IN LENT.

PSALM lxxxiii. 16.

"*Make their faces ashamed, O Lord that they may seek Thy Name.*"

WE have in the concluding words of this Psalm, one among the many instances in which the Holy Spirit puts words into our mouth which we should be afraid to have spoken of ourselves, they sound so very severe. After mentioning one after another, the names of many neighbouring heathen tribes, enemies of God and His people, who were then gathering themselves together and contriving mischief against Israel, David concludes with the following prayer: "O my God, make them like unto a wheel or, (as some think it means,) to the rolling thistledown, driven here and there by the breeze; or to the stubble before the wind: like as the fire which burneth up the wood, or as the flame which consumeth the mountains: persecute them even so with Thy tempest, and make them afraid with Thy storm: make their faces ashamed, O Lord, let them be confounded and vexed ever more and more: let them be put to shame and perish." It is the same prayer as in another Psalm, "let them be confounded, and put to shame, that seek after my soul: let them be turned back and brought to confusion that devise my hurt. Let them be as the dust before the wind, and the Angel of the Lord scattering them: let their way be dark and slippery, and let the Angel of the Lord persecute them .... let a sudden destruction come upon him unawares, and his net that he hath laid privily catch himself, that he may fall into his own mischief."

Now, of course, one way in which these fearful verses, and others like them are to be understood, is to let them remind us of the dreadful end of all such as set themselves against God, and His Kingdom. They express the concurrence (if one may so speak) of David and all the Saints—of the whole Church of God—in that unchangeable decree, "Surely thou wilt slay the wicked, O God;" even as the Angels in the Revelation rejoice over the fall of Babylon: and as here, in this Psalm, the Angel of the Lord is His willing minister in scattering and persecuting such as strive against His servants. And in this sense we are permitted and enjoined with deep fear and awe, and without the least uncharitableness, to use these solemn forms of condemnation on the impenitent, as we say Amen, to the curses pronounced in Church against them out of Holy Scripture, at the beginning of Lent. It is not wishing harm to this or that guilty person, but it is acknowledging God's just and eternal judgement against all, whether ourselves or others, who shall at any time persist in such things.

But now these same verses, no doubt have also another and a gentler meaning: according to God's dealings with another sort of people; those who have been against Him, but of whom there is more or less hope of repentance. The Psalmist in the text, shews that even in his severest sayings he was still thinking of such as those, nay, and praying for them with all charity, "Make their faces ashamed O Lord, that they may seek Thy Name," and so in the following verses, when he seemed to have been passing even final sentence on incurable persons; "Let them be confounded and vexed ever more and more; let them be put to shame and perish"—even after this, I say, he speaks words of hope and good wishes for them: "And they shall know that Thou whose Name is Jehovah art only the Most Highest over all the earth." And in the end of Psalm x "Let the heathen be judged in Thy sight. Put them in fear, O Lord, that the heathen may know themselves to be but men." Thus the severest judgements of the Almighty are shewn to be instances of His great mercy towards those who will be taught by them: and it is true charity and tender love to men's souls, to say Amen, to them with all our heart: as it is true wisdom and love to ourselves, to welcome them when they come, and not only to be patient, but thankful for them, as knowing that they are the way to true repentance and everlasting comfort and salvation.

Now hereby we may understand the great blessing and charity of that ancient order of the Church, which, at the beginning of Lent every year, the Prayer Book teaches us to remember, and wish back again. It was, in short, a way to make the faces of sinners ashamed, that they might seek God's Name. The Church had learned out of the New Testament, this plain and simple rule: "confess your faults one to another, and pray one for another, that ye may be healed." She also found by continual and sorrowful experience, how very imperfectly sinners did the work of repentance, as long as it was left to themselves: how apt they were to put off the solemn times of self-examination, to forget altogether many very serious things; to pass lightly over what they cannot help remembering, and to think that the mere length of time which has passed since they committed such and such a sin, to which perhaps they are no more tempted, is a reason why they should make sure of forgiveness.

She therefore encouraged in all ways, as do the Scriptures also, the humble and religious confession of our sins to those with whom Christ has left authority to absolve them. And when those sins were of a grave and public sort, so as to be a stumbling-block to other Christians, then the Church directed that they should be openly and publicly acknowledged, that penitency should be exercised by the offenders either waiting at the Church doors, and asking the prayers of the faithful, or in some other way, such as their brethren might take notice of; and who can tell how many souls such an order as this, may have converted and saved? how many, fearing the shame, were providentially kept from sins which they might otherwise have fallen into: how many were brought to true repentance who would otherwise have been satisfied with a mere passing sorrow, going off like the early dew: how much stricter and truer notions all sorts of men then had of the obedience due to the laws of Jesus Christ, and the holiness necessary for the Kingdom of Heaven.

Now, why this custom has been left off, of men putting themselves to open shame when they were known guilty of shameful sins, I fear no other reason can be given, than that sin has prevailed more and more among Christians, and that the governors of the Church have found it harder and harder to make any kind of effectual stand against it. So much the more necessary of course it is, that every one should be extremely diligent in doing that for himself, which the Church wishes to do for him, but thinks herself for the present unable: so much the more earnest should we be in accusing and condemning ourselves for our own faults: so much the more carefully should we look out for all ways of inwardly shaming ourselves in the sight of God and His holy Angels, for all the shameful things which they know we are too apt to forget: so much the more thankfully should we take all the circumstances and events, little and great, which are from time to time befalling us, by God's merciful Providence, apt to call our sins to remembrance, and to make us loathe ourselves in our own sight.

It is of this sort of inward and silent discipline that I now wish particularly to speak. I shall try to mention some of the ways in which all of us, who will but open their eyes, may discern God's fatherly Hand laid on them, to bring them down as it were on the knees of their hearts, to humble them, though not before men, for those many sins of theirs, which men either know not of their committing, or if they do know or guess them, pass over them far too lightly. In this way, by God's help, we may each of us learn to do some kind of penance inwardly in our hearts, to make up for the want of what is outward, and not let this holy season of Lent pass away without benefit to our sick souls.

For example, no one I should think could come to Church regularly, and attend to what he hears and reads there, without feeling sometimes struck with it, as though it were said to him particularly: as if he were being reproved by the Almighty before the congregation for his own secret sins. Verses in the Psalms, or in the Sermon on the Mount, or in S. Paul's Epistles, or in the Proverbs, or in some severe Prophet, will suddenly flash over us like lightning, seeming to dart into the hidden and most shameful corners of our heart, and to make us feel as well as acknowledge, that God's eye is upon them. Sometimes, what is even more aweful, it will be more than a single verse—a whole chapter or course of reasoning, the whole history or character of some person or other, will keep on reminding us of ourselves. Sentence after sentence will seem to say to us, as Nathan to David " Thou art the man." How miserable, how humbling, should it so happen that this sort of confession is forced from us by some of those histories which are most frightful, of those characters which are most hateful to God and man! Yet this will be most frequently the case, if we are at all true and impartial in our thoughts of ourselves. Thus to most persons it would be a shocking thought, that they should themselves resemble Cain—that he should be the Scripture character whose history reminds them of themselves. Yet if we will let our conscience deal truly with us, must not a great many of us own that the beginning of his horrible sin was but what they have been daily practising for many years, perhaps are not yet cured of? They have been out of humour, and have had sullen looks, because they saw some brother or neighbour more prosperous, more favoured in some respect, than they were. They come to Church, and hear or read in their Bibles, "Cain was very wroth, and his countenance fell." If they mark it, they cannot but feel that the words are spoken of them, as well as of him: with them, as with him, the voice of God expostulates, "Why art thou wroth? and why is thy countenance fallen?" They are made to feel that their beginnings are the same with those which led him on to bear malice, and murder his brother, and called down a curse from the Almighty on his person and name: and is not this a shameful and a startling thought? They feel it to be so: every sullen envious person, if he attends, must perceive his own likeness in the dismal description of Cain. Now, it may be, more than words can express, may depend on his way of dealing with this thought, when the Almighty has presented it to his mind. He may turn carelessly from it, he may put it aside as uncomfortable; then of course it will do him no good. Or he may compel himself, however unwilling, to attend to the fearful lesson thus brought home to him; he may dwell with shame and alarm on the thought, that he has already made a beginning with Cain, he has gone a certain way in his sin, and who knows how far he may go hereafter, who knows how much farther he might have gone already, but for shame and fear of man, or God's restraining Providence, or for some other reason, the credit of which is in no way due to himself. He whose conscience tells him that he has been envious and sullen, is self-convicted of being so far like Cain; and the very shame of such a likeness, one may hope will cause him to shake off his bitter feeling, and clear up his discontented brow, when he is next tempted by the same evil spirit.

Again, it may be, there are persons who when they read or hear of Balaam, falling with his eyes open, falling into deadly sin though he knew the knowledge of the Most High, are forced to own to themselves too truly, that this is their own history too: that they too knowing right from wrong, according to the measures of the New Testament, and not daring in certain matters to do wrong, have yet permitted themselves wilfully to wish that they might do so, and to take pleasure in imagining, what, if they were to indulge themselves? and so they have brought upon themselves the curse of those who lust after evil things, and then lust has more or less effectually conceived, and brought forth sin, and now it only remains for their sin, if they repent not, to be finished, and bring forth death. It is God's especial mercy to such, to let them read or hear the history of Balaam, or of any other among the many, who, knowing the truth, and not daring openly to gainsay it, have yet gone hovering as near the forbidden borders as they dared. Well may they feel shame, bitter agonizing shame, when they reflect what Balaam came to, and how near

God he was at first. He began by wishing that it were lawful to curse God's people for money—he durst not do it, he only wished it were lawful, and indulged the wish: and he ended with teaching their enemy how to corrupt them, how to lead them by sensual lust, to the worship of idols. Well-instructed Christians begin by wishing in like manner that it were not sinful to indulge this or that sinful thought: God in His anger gives them the opportunity of indulging it: they give way, and go on from bad to worse, sinning all the while with their eyes open. Then God in His forbearing pity puts such examples as Balaam's before them, they shudder inwardly to think how near they have been venturing to the edge of destruction, as though the flame had already laid hold of them: and, His grace helping them, they draw back. But to make their repentance complete and safe, they must not shrink from again and again contemplating the danger they have been in. They must pray to have their consciences kept tender, and the remembrance of their sins grievous. They must keep their minds open and awake to the many indirect, and seemingly accidental reproofs, which they will hear continually, out of the Scriptures of God. The word hypocrisy, with our Saviour's many and grievous woes pronounced against it, ought especially to startle them; for although we might not, of regular purpose, intend to deceive others, yet in such measure as we have indulged any evil thought, maintaining at the same time a fair character for godliness, so far we have been more or less like hypocrites, and the endeavours of our whole remaining life after true inward purity, will not be too much to prepare us for receiving Christ's gracious absolution at last.

I cannot conclude without taking notice, what a striking instance the lesson for this Sunday—the first lesson in the morning—is of the way in which grievous crimes recorded in Scripture may practise us in wholesome shame. We think ourselves far enough from the utter lawlessness of those miserable persons on whom the Lord rained down fire and brimstone from Heaven, but have we never felt and spoken as they did, when in answer to Lot's interfering with their wickedness, they said, "This one fellow came in to sojourn, and he must needs be a judge?" Surely this is a temper of mind, and tone of words, which we often fall into—we are angry and vexed when those who are beneath us, those who we think have no right to do so, seem in any way to reprove or check our faults. Now then we see to what kind of people this temper properly belongs: it is the temper of the accursed people of Sodom.

Again, we read, Lot, speaking of the ruin that was approaching, "seemed as one that mocked," unto his sons-in-law: and is it so very uncommon for serious remonstrances, warnings of the Day of Judgement, to be treated as if the utterer of them could not be in earnest?

By such plain examples as these my brethren, you may discern, how the worst sins recorded in Holy Scripture, may serve to put us to shame, and make us do secret penance; far enough as we may seem from them, we shall many times find some secret agreement between our own behaviour, and that of the miserable ones who are so set forth for an example in God's word: we may discern in ourselves the beginning of such crimes as Cain's or Balaam's or Judas Iscariot. It is dreadful to think of; but let us not lose sight of it: rather let us pray God to keep it ever in our hearts, that humbling ourselves by the thought of our likeness to those wicked ones, we may by degrees become utterly unlike them, and recover that gracious Image of God, to which He restored us at Baptism, but which we have so sadly defaced.

SERMON IV.

SHAME FOR SIN, WHETHER INWARD OR OUTWARD, A MERCIFUL GIFT OF GOD.

PART II.

Psalm lxxxiii. 16.

" Make their faces ashamed, O Lord that they may seek Thy Name."

PERHAPS it would be not untrue to say, that the great difference between a truly religious and an ordinary sort of person is, the one being always ready and watchful to take hints from Almighty God, while the other only acknowledges His Presence when it can hardly be overlooked. A dutiful child watches his father's countenance, and rejoices to be guided, as the Psalmist says, by his eye: whereas that son or daughter, who only wishes to be so far dutiful, as to avoid blame from others, waits to be told loudly and clearly, what he must do and what leave undone. Now a penitent is one who having fallen, is learning and trying to be truly religious again : and therefore if we are sincerely penitent, we shall be always trying to walk by this rule to gather both from God's Word and from His Providence as many silent and indirect hints as we can, as to what we are to think of the past, and how to order ourselves for the future. One way of using God's

Word to this purpose I have before pointed out, i. e. to take notice how sadly the beginning of great sins recorded in Holy Scripture such as those of Cain, Judas, Balaam and the like, answer to what our own consciences tell us of motions and tendencies of our own hearts towards sin : how the envious man should humble himself and be alarmed, seeing that he is setting out towards his brother in the same way as Cain towards Abel: the lover of evil thoughts, on finding himself a follower of Balaam ; he who takes little liberties with his neighbour's goods of any kind, on perceiving that he is entering on the very course which was the ruin of Judas Iscariot. Fearful indeed it is, and humbling, to have such thoughts of ourselves, but far better, surely than to go on in such ways with no fear, no distressing self-reproach, until matters are too bad with us to be mended. Who would not gladly be made afraid and ashamed, to feel how near he is come to the everlasting burnings ; if so, by God's mercy he may draw back in time, and be saved finally, yet so as by fire ?

I shall now speak of another way in which the Almighty and Merciful One would " make our faces ashamed that we may seek His Name". He is continually causing things, little or great, to happen in the course of His Providence, such as may remind a sincere penitent of the evil of his past ways, the particular sin or sins, which he knows in his heart must have been written down against him in God's Book, and of which his conscience is most afraid. Most persons who have gone wrong, and have come at all to serious thought, are, I suppose in something like this state of mind : there is some particular sin or sinful habit, or very likely more than one, which hangs with peculiar weight on their souls; concerning which they feel on reflection that it stains, corrupts, infects, their whole life: it has been the kernel, as it were, and core, around which other sins have from time to time been gathering: if it had been away, they feel that they should have been quite different persons from what they have been and would have led quite different lives. When the grace of God has touched a man's heart so far, as to make him tender and uneasy about any thing of this kind, it is wonderful how almost every thing that happens will in some way or other be turned into a remembrancer of it: just as if we have pain or weakness in a particular limb, every posture almost, and every motion, will cause us to feel it more or less, and not let it go quite out of our memory. Whichever way we look, our sin will be ever before us. For example, we hear a person reproved, perhaps for something wrong in the very same kind: presently the thought arises in our minds, "If the reprover knew, he would address the same words to us: surely we have deserved this and more, considering all we knew of our duty: we have deserved it for indulging bad thoughts and wishes, even though a gracious over-ruling Providence (no thanks to us for it) may have kept us from scandalous and notorious sins." I say, when words spoken to others, awaken such thoughts as these in our consciences, we do well to consider them as a message from God to ourselves: they are tokens what God and His Angels and Saints, what all the Court of Heaven is judging of us: they are reproofs to make us ashamed, that we may seek His Name. Especially when, as frequently happens, it has become our own duty to address the like reproofs to other men: as when parents have to tell children, or masters scholars, or pastors those committed to their charge, of some dangerous and deadly fault, while conscious all the time that they are themselves guilty before God in the same way; possibly, considering their opportunities, more guilty. It is not hypocrisy in them so to reprove, it is their duty to do so, but it is a very sad duty: no words, I suppose, can express the sinking of the heart which comes over a person of a tender conscience, when, like Solomon in the Book of Ecclesiastes he has to reprove that in others, of which, in some way, he feels himself perhaps guiltier than they.

Sometimes the matter is brought more immediately home. People suspect or know some harm of us, and an opportunity occurs for their telling us so, more or less rudely: this is a direct trial of the truth of our repentance, for if, upon this, we permit ourselves to be affronted, and say, as persons too often do, "we have repented of that long ago, you have no right to bring that up against us:" or, "it is true we sinned so and so, but you are not the persons to reproach us with it:" any such answer as this is a token that our repentance is at least very imperfect: we have not yet got the broken and contrite heart, which is thankful to have its sins kept before it in this world, that God may hide His face from them in the next: we make use of that which our heavenly Friend intended as a reproof from Himself to make us seek His Name—this we use as a pretence to take us farther away from Him.

It very often happens that the reproofs and rebukes of man take a wrong direction concerning their brethren: a man is suspected, for example, of drunkenness, when it is some other secret sin which perhaps makes him guilty before God. In such a case, we are too apt to turn all our anger on our reprovers, quite away from our own faults. But a person who will be wise for his own soul, will humbly acknowledge in his heart, "This is God's rebuke, though not for the particular sin of which I am by mistake supposed guilty, yet for this or that other one, which I know to be quite as bad in His sight, and which too surely, He has seen me commit many times, He whose eye is on my heart." Thus when David was called a bloody man and a man of Belial, as though he had been disloyal to Saul, with whom he had ever dealt most loyally, and had feared to lift up his hand against him: instead of being angry at the false and malicious reproach, he took it as a call to repent of the sins, no less grievous perhaps, which he could not deny. "Let Shimei curse, for the Lord hath said unto him, Curse David." That was a noble, a self-denying repentance, which could well forgive other people their calumnies, because it could not forgive itself its more inexcusable trangressions against God.

It belongs to the same mind, to be truly and really pained when men give us praise: feeling sure, as we may, how very different their sentence would be of us, could they but know all: so that we really seem to be in a manner imposing on them, and playing a sort of hypocrite's part, if we at all accept their praise, or gladly receive such kindness at their hands, as we know they would not pay, were they aware what we really are. Yet often we cannot undeceive them: and it is a very fearful thought to such as reflect what the Holy Scripture says of the end of undeserved praise. "Woe unto you when all men shall speak well of you:" and, Herod accepted the shout of the people, and immediately the Angel of the Lord smote him. He who is praised, then, can he possibly be too earnest in giving God all the glory, as in other ways, so in humble confession of his sins? Well and comfortable will it be for him if circumstances allow him to have one friend or Pastor at least, who may know the hidden wound of his soul, and help him to afflict himself for it in secret, whenever he is praised: so turning that most dangerous snare into a help for seeking God's Name. But if you have no one to whom you can well make such confession, at least protect yourself against the praise of men by some such rule as this: to have always ready in your thoughts the remembrance of some one or other of the most shameful actions and circumstances of your life, and such as you can least bear to think of: to have it, I say, always at hand, wherewith to put down any satisfaction, which you might be otherwise inclined to feel when your brethren treat you partially: as penitents in ancient times wore sackcloth to vex themselves, under the dress that belonged to their place and station, fearing lest they should not enough remember their sins.

And men may the more easily keep up these humbling thoughts, as very often the outward circumstances of their past sins are such as they are being continually reminded of. They have transgressed, perhaps, miserable thought, under the shadow of their own home, or, still worse, of the Holy Church of God: in the midst of pure, true, holy, charitable, affectionate examples, they have been in some way or other wilfully impure, false, profane, unkind, or unthankful. There are sights and sounds all around them, which remind them of their disgrace and danger, as often as they look or listen: as S. Peter is said to have been reminded of his denying our Lord whenever he heard the cock crow. The words, looks, and actions of those among whom they live, even the nearest and kindest and best-beloved, may secretly reveal, in a way frightful to think of, moments of which they are now utterly ashamed: which they would give the world's treasures to blot out of their lives, if they could. When earthly good befals them, it is saddened by the thought, how much better and more perfect it would have been, had they no evil memory like an unwholesome feverish taste rising up as it were within them, and spoiling their enjoyment: and when God's visitations fall upon them, or upon those who are as part of themselves, how are they embittered by the too reasonable fear, that they have brought it all upon themselves, by their inexcusable breaches of their holy baptismal vow. Especially, when, as very often happens, the affliction is of such a sort, that any person, knowing of the sin, would at once say it was a punishment for it: as when one who was a disobedient child is tried as a father with undutiful children: in such cases no one can fail to acknowledge the affliction or disappointment to be a real judgement, although to the rest of the world it may not appear so: and what should he do, but secretly bow himself under it, and turn the hidden shame and anguish to a real, though hidden, exercise of repentance?

Evil thoughts darted we know not how into our minds, and mixing themselves, it may be, with our very prayers, with our holy readings and endeavours to do good: these are another set of shameful and humiliating, yet, if so it please God, wholesome ways, by which past mischief may be rooted out, the work of repentance helped, and the sinner's face, as the text says, "made ashamed." Evil thoughts coming in this way are not always a sign of past sins: we know not what permission the wicked one may sometimes have to tempt and perplex with them even God's most innocent servants. But where sin has gone before, there we must surely consider such thoughts as part of our punishment, and of the trial of our repentance. They are permitted to make us ashamed, to humble us more and more for what cannot be undone, and to cause in us more and more of godly fear lest our repentance prove imperfect. They must be put away to the best of our power, and the sins of which they are the relics, must be more throughly repented of. As far as they are simply painful, we must bear them patiently, and humbly pray God not to lay them to our charge, mingling as they do with a sad pollution and disturbance among our best and holiest things. And although we cannot but be distressed and alarmed, at finding that the Evil spirit has power so to interfere with our very devotions, to call up the remembrance of what we would most wish to forget, when we are on our knees perhaps before the Altar of our Lord and Saviour, yet no man need despond therefore. The mischief that comes into a man's mind will not be imputed to him for sin, if he consent not to it, if he take no sort of pleasure in it. If it make him more earnest in prayer, fuller of penitence for the past, more watchful and devout for the future, then, instead of making his burthen heavier, it will turn to his profit, and be counted among the instances in which, by the good help of his God, he has got the better of his spiritual enemy.

In any case whatever, we must have shame, sooner or later, for our sin. Adam could not eat of the forbidden tree, without his eyes being opened, and his knowing himself to be naked: and it was the greatest of mercy to him and to us, that when he would have hidden himself, God called him out, and brought him to confession and repentance. Let us take comfort as well as warning from him. If God in any way makes our faces ashamed, let us take care that the shame do its work upon us; let it lead us to seek His Name. If He put us to open reproach before men, let us take even that thankfully, hoping that it may save us from confusion in the day of judgement. If our shame be but in secret, occasioned by the bitter and tormenting recollection of our past and secret sins, let it render us the more humble, the more circumspect, the more self-denying: but in any case never let it drive us to any sort of sullenness or despair.

But as we think deeply of our sin, and pray for grace to acknowledge it as we ought, and to loathe ourselves for it in our own sight: so let us keep continually before us the mysterious hope of our possible forgiveness and recovery. Well may it seem too high and hard a saying, for such as know the evil we know of ourselves, ever to think of such deliverance as the blessed Gospel holds out the hope of: entire purity, the presence of God, seeing Jesus Christ as He is, and becoming more and more like Him. It is more than we can conceive, yet by His mercy we may hope it, and we may be doing some little, every day and every hour, towards having it fulfilled in ourselves. All days and all hours we may be offering ourselves before God, as the leper in Capernaum did; "Lord if Thou wilt Thou canst make me clean;" or as the woman of Canaan, "Lord help me, for even the dogs eat of the crumbs." And He Who has recorded in His Gospel such gracious deeds for our encouragement, will not be wanting to us, when we are cast down by His severe warnings and judgements. Between the shame and penance He lays on us, and the comfortable examples He sets before us, we shall be abundantly helped towards that blessed place, which our sins have so nearly forfeited. Only we must make up our minds not to shrink from the inward shame, any more than from the outward affliction—which at any time He may send. We must submit humbly and hope courageously: and then, although as long as our life here lasts, our confusion may one way or another cover us daily, the sweet hope will still be ours, of wakening up one day in the Presence and Likeness of Christ, and feeling that we are freed from sin and shame for ever and ever.

SERMON V.

ON FASTING.

FIRST SUNDAY IN LENT.

S. Matt. iv. 2.

" When He had fasted forty days and forty nights, He was afterwards an hungered."

FORTY whole days and nights He went without meat and drink, and instead of wasting away and perishing, as a mere man left to himself, of course must have done, long before the end of that time, He was not, it should seem, even hungry, until the end of the days. Then the pangs of hunger came upon Him; until then He lived on in the body without meat or drink, and without pain at the want of them.

Surely brethren, to the poor the Gospel is preached, in this as in all other parts of it. Surely this history of our Lord's fasting is one very striking instance of His unspeakable love and condescension, in so ordering what He did, and what His Evangelists should write of His doings, as should most especially make Him known, as He is, to the poor of His flock.

For the very first foundation and corner-stone of

His Gospel is this: that God the Son made Himself Man, perfect Man, in all but sin like unto us, that He might be our Redeemer, and the Author of everlasting life: continuing all the while perfect God, One with the Father and the Holy Ghost, "over all blessed for ever." This is the foundation of the whole everlasting Gospel: for if our Lord had not been made Man, He could not have died and suffered for us, nor have risen again, nor ascended into Heaven, nor would He have had any Body for us to receive, and thereby through His Holy Spirit, to be united to Him. I say, the Incarnation of Christ is the foundation of all our hope and comfort: and how could this glorious Incarnation be more effectually preached and witnessed to the poor of the flock, than by the account of His divine and wonderful fast? The forty days continuing without food by His own power,—this sheweth His Almightiness and Divinity: His bearing the pangs of hunger at the end of the time no less certainly sheweth Him to be true Man.

And who can sufficiently admire and love His wonderful sympathy and charity with poor fallen man, that He, the Most High and glorious God, Who made the earth and bringeth food out of it, should endure the same inward pain and sinking of body as any one of us sinners on being left a certain time without food. Thus He began His ministry, for this miraculous fast, as you know, was the very last step in the preparation He made, before going forth on His great work of overthrowing Satan's power, and working our deliverance openly in the sight of angels and men. After He had fasted and had hungered, He was tempted, and after His temptation He straightway began to preach the Kingdom of God and to heal diseases. His ministry —His suffering ministry began with hunger, and ended with thirst: thus every way, He would have us behold in Him a true Son of our Father Adam, one who can be touched with a feeling of our infirmities. He began with hunger, by voluntary and willing hunger, which we call fasting—thereby teaching us how to overcome the bodily appetite which led our first parents wrong. They sinned by eating, He overcame sin by fasting—They began to yield to the serpent by longing after the forbidden tree, He began to bruise the serpent's head by abstaining from food in itself lawful and innocent. He began, I say, with hunger, and He ended with thirst, for one of His three last words on the Cross was, "I thirst," the fever which goes before a painful death was strong upon Him, and He complained of it, not to have it relieved,—for He knew that they would give Him nothing but vinegar to drink —but partly to fill up the measure of His sufferings, that the Scripture might be fulfilled, partly to give one more token of His true partaking of our nature and entire sympathy with all our infirmities.

He began with hunger and ended with thirst: so far those can best understand His mercy, who best know what thirst and hunger are: and who are those? generally speaking, of course not the rich, but the poor. The poor, by their very situation in life sometimes going without food, sometimes having but a scanty allowance, can best judge by actual feeling and experience how great the love must have been which induced our Saviour to fast for our sakes forty days and forty nights, knowing what pangs of hunger He was bringing on Himself. Thus the Gospel of His Incarnation is especially preached to the poor.

And herein is another great token of His love for the poor of this world, whom He hath chosen, we know "to be rich in faith, and heirs of the Kingdom which He hath promised to them that love Him"— I say it is a very particular token of His love for them; (would to God they would think more of it;) that by His willing hunger He encourages and helps them to bear their ordinary low diet thankfully, as a kind of sacrifice to Him. They must live hard, that they cannot help, it is their appointed portion in life, but their privilege as Christian poor is, that if they take their hunger and thirst, and other denials of that sort, with cheerfulness and patience, for Christ's sake, He will account it an acceptable offering to Him: He will bless their bread and their water, as He did the spare low diet of Daniel and his companions, and it will do them ten times more good, both in body and soul, than all the delicate and abundant meals would, which they are tempted to envy in their rich neighbours. For as it is in sickness and pain, men must endure it when God sends it, be they ever so restless and unwilling, but He graciously gives them this privilege, that their pain being patiently endured, shall be accounted to them for a kind of martyrdom, and they will have some portion of the reward of those who not only believe, but also suffer for His sake:—so it is in this matter, men are permitted (as the saying is) to make a virtue of necessity, if they will be willing and obedient, they turn their enforced fast into a devout service, most acceptable to the Lord; and He, by His good Spirit, will put into their loving hearts, other ways of saintly self-denial: and whereas looking at their station, you might think they had nothing to give up, they will secure to themselves, by loving quiet patience, a part in that highest promise, "A hundred fold in this life, and in the world to come life everlasting."

And there is another thing, a great thing for those poor men who wish to live in the fear of God, and dare not trust their own hearts. If you learn from our Lord's example to make much of your hunger and thirst, as special helps to bring you nearer to Him, this by His grace will effectually keep you from that which of course is one of your greatest dangers, the devil will in vain tempt you to take his advice how to get your bread. This we know was the way in which he tempted our Blessed Lord in His Hunger, "Command that these stones be made bread," as he might come to any of you in low circumstances, and whisper, "Here is this or that portion of your neighbour's property within your reach: cannot you turn it into money or money's worth to keep yourself and your family from starving?" Thus has the Evil one before now, spoken craftily to many a poor man's heart and seduced him into the deadly sin of dishonesty; but if that poor man had been well trained in our Lord's school of fasting, if he had made up his mind to cast all his wants, and the wants of his children, upon the Lord, Who hath promised to nourish them, if he were used to present their hunger and thirst patiently borne every day, as a kind of

On fasting. 49

sacrifice to Jesus Christ: then their want would be no temptation to them; they would answer him as our Saviour did, Man need not steal or cheat or take wrong liberties in order to live: God can and will keep him alive, by any means that He may judge best: and so the poor honest Christian with a holy stubbornness, will be enabled to hold his own against the strongest temptations to dishonesty.

But if by God's mercy the constrained fastings of the poor may be turned into so great a blessing to their souls, the like blessing will not be denied to the voluntary fastings of those who are better off in the world—who might eat their fill, but decline doing so, because they understand it to be God's will, and know it to have been Christ's and His Saints' practice, and feel it too, good for their souls, often to leave out or to lessen one or more of their meals. You know what the Holy Scripture says of fulness of bread. It is mentioned along with pride and idleness, as having brought about the ruin of Sodom. "pride, fulness of bread, and abundance of idleness, were in the midst of her." That was the beginning of Sodom's iniquity: fulness of bread; i. e. eating and drinking without stint or scruple, was the beginning of sins which brought fire and brimstone from the Lord out of Heaven. So it had been from the beginning; the very fall of Adam, as I said just now, was brought about by ungoverned appetite. So Esau in keen hunger, sold his birthright for a little broth, and became a proverb to express the madness of Christians selling their immortal souls for earthly trifles. So the children of Israel in the wilderness longed after the flesh pots of Egypt; they lusted for flesh, and God in His anger sent them meat for their lust, and while it was yet in their mouths His heavy wrath came upon them, and they fell down dead by thousands. But the most awful instance of all is the rich man in our Lord's parable "who was clothed in purple and fine linen and fared sumptuously every day."

Many might say to themselves, "of course being rich he would do so: any one else would do the same:" nay my brethren; but mark the end: "in hell he lift up his eyes, being in torments." Why? because his continued sumptuous feasting, among other things had hardened his heart: he repented not towards God, and took no notice of the poor man at his gate: if he had denied himself a little for God's sake and the poor's in those costly banquets of his, his end, in all likelihood, would have been very different.

But if fulness of bread, abundant, continual feasting be indeed so very dangerous, what is to become of rich persons, of those who have enough and to spare and never know any want compelling them to fast? Fasting, religious fasting, is the regular remedy; just as religious silence is a remedy against sins of the tongue, and religious watching against slothfulness. And this is no fancy of ours: our Lord in the Sermon on the Mount, as you must all know, most distinctly warrants our fasting, "When ye pray, says Christ, be not as the hypocrites:" "when ye give alms, do not as the hypocrites:" "when ye fast be not as the hypocrites." By which you may plainly understand, that a Christian man cannot go to Heaven without fasting, any more than he can go there without prayer, or without alms. And in another place our Lord distinctly appoints that His disciples should fast during the days when He should be away from them: the days of Lent and of the Holy Week; and so the Church, almost all of it has practised, ever since the Apostles' times. And scattered up and down both in the Old and New Testament are histories, many more than can be now mentioned, shewing all of them how great favour God is used to bestow upon such as religiously deny themselves. There is the history of Esther, who saved her countrymen and her own life, by an earnest and long continued fast, obtaining God's blessing on the petition she was about to present unto the king. There is the King of Nineveh with all his people, making so good a confession before God in their fasting with sackcloth and ashes, that "God repented of the evil He thought to have done unto them, and He did it not." In the New Testament again; the greatest mercies are connected with fasting: I will mention one case only in which we are all greatly interested. S. Peter and Cornelius were each of them fasting, when the message came from God separately to each of them, to seek out the other, which led to the Gospel being openly preached to the Gentiles. In short you will hardly find a holy person in the whole Scriptures, either of the Old Testament, or the New, who was not in some part of his life greatly profited by devout fastings.

People sometimes appear to be surprised at the slow progress we make as a Church; saying so many good prayers as we do, they wonder so many of our brethren should be still sitting in the darkness and shadow of death; so many by Baptism Christians, but in heart unconverted. They wonder again and are sorely disappointed at themselves and others for their very great imperfection: they try, they say, and have long tried to do better, yet they can give no such good account either of their prayers, of their alms, or of any part of their duty as considering the time they ought to be able to give: it is all dead and dull and lukewarm: all so very much wanting in love. May not part of the reason be, that with all their good intentions, too many of them greatly neglect this evangelical duty of fasting? Humbly and discreetly used—fasting has a great blessing to open the mind and heart, to make men self-denying and charitable in other ways: watchful to do their neighbours good, and ready to take the lowest and most inconvenient place.

Some no doubt there are, weak in body who cannot fast, and ought not to try: some few who are hurting their souls as well as their bodies by unadvised endeavours in the way of fasting. I do not now speak to such: God will provide for them in His own method: but I speak to those who are in ordinary health and strength, and I beseech them to consider whether they are really trying to use such abstinence as our Lord taught and practised.

Be sure of it: the Bridegroom, Christ, expects us to fast in the days while He is taken away out of our sight, i. e. in these days; only let us take care not to be as the hypocrites, seeming religious in order to be praised of men: and as surely as they miss their reward, as surely will He help us, by His mercy to find ours.

# SERMON VI.

DANGER OF TRIFLING WITH GOD'S WARNING CALLS.

FIRST SUNDAY IN LENT.

2 Cor. vi. 2.

"*Behold now is the accepted time; behold now is the day of salvation.*"

You heard in the first lesson this morning, how that while Lot lingered on his way out of Sodom, the angels whom God had sent to deliver him laid hold of his hand, and of the hand of his wife, and of the hand of his two daughters, the Lord being merciful unto him, and they brought him forth and set him without the city. Here two things are very remarkable: one, that Lot lingered; the other, that God's messengers would not suffer him to linger.

He lingered and loitered; he was unwilling to get fairly out of the place, and yet the word had been most express, "We will destroy this place; the Lord hath sent us to destroy it; arise lest thou be consumed in the iniquity of the city:" the words were plain, and he could not doubt their truth; for they had been just confirmed by a great miracle. The men who had tried to lay hold on Lot had been smitten with great blindness, so that they wearied themselves in vain to find the door of his house. And besides after the frightful sin, sin not fit to be named, which the whole city had just made itself guilty of—old and young, all the people from every quarter, one would think that a just and righteous man such as Lot was, would make haste to get out of the place. Nevertheless he still lingered, of course he had made up his mind to go, but he lingered and hesitated about taking the first step. We may fancy him, lingering in the room where he was used to sit: at the door of the house which had so long been his home: at the end of the street where that house was still in view: we can easily imagine how hard it was to him to part with all the familiar places— the furniture—the neighbours, the very marks in the street—. It is but too plain to us how naturally he might stop and linger, and keep on turning round for one more last view of this thing or of that, although he had been told that his very life depended on his making the best of his way out of the place. We understand it but too well, because we know how apt we are ourselves to delay and loiter, and not set about our duties at once, as soon as we know them to be our duties.

But let us also understand what the consequence must be of our doing so. If Lot had gone on lingering until sunrise, he would undoubtedly have been destroyed in the tempest of fire and brimstone which came pouring down on Sodom and Gomorrah from Heaven. It would have done him no good though he had pleaded ever so loudly, "I only lingered and loitered a little time, just to take a last look; to say farewell to the places, things and people which had been so long familiar to me." He might have cried out "spare me, I did no more than was natural, no more than others would have done in my place," but the brimstone and fire would not have minded his words; they would not the less have come showering down upon him, and have swept him and his excuses away for ever.

But here comes in the other remarkable thing, which, as I said, we find in this moment of Lot's history. He would have lingered, but he was not suffered to linger. There were those with him who cared more for him than he cared for himself: and they laid hold of his hand, and urged him on, in spite of himself, till they had set him without the city. It seems that for all their warnings they could hardly have got him off in time if they had not laid hold of his hand. This is the remarkable, the most comfortable thing; namely, God's exceeding love for us, in that He not only warns us beforehand of our souls' danger, but is also at hand, even at the very time, to urge us onward and say, "Escape for thy life."

The same lesson is repeated in the Epistle for the week "Behold *now* is the accepted time, behold *now* is the day of salvation." All who have any experience know, what an important word this one word *now* is in matters pertaining to this life. There is scarcely anything of consequence which people do, in which all does not turn on our seizing the proper moment. Ask those who are skilful in any art or trade, ask the soldier, ask the farmer, or the gardener, whether the welfare of the crop does not depend on people's making use of the favourable weather when it occurs. They must avail themselves of it to-day, while it is called to-day. They must not wait till to-morrow. Ask those who speak in proverbs about "making hay while the sun shines": about "striking while the iron is hot," and other familiar sayings. We indeed apply them to common and ordinary things; too common and ordinary, some may think, to be properly spoken of in this holy place; but as our Lord condescended to make even the games of children playing in the street into a parable, so may we reverently use such every day sayings to remind us of our souls' good.

Or to speak of that which is most important in this life, i. e. bodily health, who knows not how much depends in medicine, on our not letting the exact moment pass by? So the wise man, "there is a time to kill, and a time to heal." How often may physicians be heard saying, "you have called me in too late; I can do no good now: some time ago I might have been of service, but now the time is gone by, and the disease must have its course." It is just the same in regard of the soul's sickness; if we could read the hearts of men, and know their true spiritual history, we should be more aware than we now are how very dangerous it is to let occasions of good pass. We should know better than we now do, how that every soul on its way to Eternity has its appointed times and seasons of good, which if they be allowed to pass away, shall never never return again. Though the person be not lost, yet the innocence, the heroism, the saintliness may be. I will put the matter in another point of view: kings and great persons on earth, fathers and mothers in their families, masters and mistresses among their servants, have their times to be favourable and gracious; times in which they may be approached with more than usual hope of obtaining whatever one desires of them; so Holy Scripture plainly teaches that God Almighty has His own times and seasons which, if we let them pass, will never more return again.

Of course, if one could know those times, every one who has common sense would make haste to draw near before his own time was gone by. But we cannot ordinarily know those times, as our Lord Himself told His most favoured attendants. "It is not for you to know the times and the seasons, which the Father hath put in His own power." He spoke it of the great times of His Providence which affect His whole Church, the times of ignorance, the times of the Gentiles—the day of Jerusalem, the days of the Son of Man, the day of the Lord, the times of refreshing, but it is true also in respect of His dealings with each man's soul. The Father of all has kept to Himself the knowledge of those particular times, after which it will be impossible to approach Him with good hope of obtaining His blessing; which if we let pass, the blessing will go away for ever, or at least be greatly diminished. In His wisdom and mercy He has not told us of those times. He has not told us when we shall die; that we all know: but neither does He tell people beforehand when it is His purpose to shorten their time of trial in other ways besides death, as by taking away their reason in whole or in part—or (more fearful) by withholding His calls and His grace, hardening their heart, whatever that may mean. And one reason why He has hidden them from us, we may well believe is this: that we may improve to the best of our power the present time, and the present season, whatever it be—not knowing but it may be our last. "Behold now is the accepted time, behold now is the day of salvation." This verse read in the Church is as an Angel from Heaven saying to each of us, "say your prayers as well as you can this evening, because we cannot at all know whether we shall ever wake in the morning to say another prayer." We must, each time that we may come to Holy Communion, try to communicate as worthily as ever we can, because we do not know whether we shall ever have a chance to communicate again. We must lose no opportunity of doing good to the souls and bodies of those whom God's good Providence has put under our care, because if we miss it by our own fault, it may never again be allowed us; the persons whom God intended us to profit may be taken out of our reach, may be taken into another world before they come in our way again. Such recollections as people grow older are indeed very sad. Why did David so mourn over Absolom? because being come to true repentance himself, he felt the horror of his son's dying in his sin, and that he had not done the best for him. One may be reminded of that text so worthy to be a watchword in all pastoral and missionary work, "walk in wisdom to them that are without, redeeming the time, because the days are evil;" and the more if the days are evil—the world or the Church, or at least the neighbourhood degenerate, and so the chances of going good, fewer and further between. And so of all other spiritual privileges; all other parts of a Christian's duty—if we are but as wise for our own souls,. as any farmer, tradesman, or labourer is in the most ordinary part of his daily work, we shall ever remember that *now* is the accepted time—now, not by and by—now this very day and hour, is the hour and the day of salvation. *Now* must be the time; for who can assure us that to us there will be any hereafter? But mark another great mercy, although, as I said, in a common way God does hide His times from us, yet He appoints signs, symptoms, forebodings for one spiritually wise to make use of: as the prophecies, for all believers: as His providential warnings of every kind, decay, sickness &c., and in a different way deliverances &c., and eminently the time of youth: which is indeed to every Christian an accepted time. "Remember now thy Creator in the days of thy youth." Blessed words but aweful in that they tell us of a chance which once gone is gone for ever: which may be compensated but cannot be recalled. And if the time of youth is especially an accepted time, so are God's own holy seasons, and if it is inexcusable to trifle with any time, yet more profane and dangerous, surely, shall we find it, if we venture to trifle with God's own sacred times, with the seasons in which He vouchsafes to declare and shew us that He is drawing nearer to us than usual.

For undoubtedly there are such seasons. This very time of Lent whenever it returns, is such an one. Our Lord at this time draws near to us all, as any one of His priests might outwardly and visibly draw near to any one of us. He draws near to remind us of our sins, to invite us to Confession, to offer Absolution and Communion. We if we choose may look another way. We may listen to other voices, rather than the voice of our Saviour. But it will be at our souls' peril.

Lent, as well as other Church seasons, is an accepted time, a time of salvation, to all of us alike if we will so take it; and there are besides to each one of us, our Lord's private and personal warnings. Did you never hear some word of Holy Scripture, some sentence in a sermon, or saying out of a good book, which seemed at the moment to suit yourself so exactly, to come so straight home to you, that you could hardly help believing the speaker or writer was thinking of you? Now whether he was so thinking or not, God Almighty, God your Saviour, you may be quite sure, was thinking of you. The word came from Him: it was He who put the thought in your mind. And the time when the thought came, you may also be quite sure was an accepted time; a favourable time for you to draw near to Him. If you refused to do so, you have cast away such a time. Take care how you do so again: the next trial may be the last. Now, this moment, resolve that by God's grace you will act upon that warning whatever it was. Lift up your heart to Him in silent prayer, that He would touch you again, and that the next time He touches you, it may not pass away as in a dream. Watch religiously for the next chance of doing good or of overcoming temptation, which He may put in your way. When it comes, make much of it. Consider that it is the very time that God has prepared for you: that it will soon be over like former times; and who can say whether it or any thing like it will ever return? Who can say how deeply, how grievously God Almighty may be offended, if you let it pass, taking no account, making no endeavour to improve it?

Let no man say in his heart, these times of the Lord are for grievous sinners, I am no murderer or adulterer or thief, why need I be so careful to turn every thing into a warning? How do such thoughts agree with the love of God? If you love Him in earnest you will be on the watch for whatever may help you to love and serve Him better. Some sins to be sure you have; in some duties to be sure you are imperfect; whatever that sin or neglect be, to go on with it after special warning must needs make it very serious. If you use yourself to make light of warnings, for ought you know you may be at this moment living in some deadly sin; what if you should die before you have truly repented of it? what if you should be struck down suddenly, and depart into the next world without any time to recollect it and mourn for it, much less to repent and make amends? What if God, justly displeased at your making so light of His former visitations, should visit you the next time as He did Dathan and Abiram, allowing you no time at all to repent in? What if you should lose your senses? or be so full of pain of body, or anguish and perplexity of mind as to be unable to think and turn to God? Surely no one of us can say that he is in no danger of any of these things? None of us can say that it would be any thing so very surprising, any thing so very much out of the ordinary way, for himself to die suddenly, or to lose his senses, or to be incapable of a regular confession. Now, now is the time, now is the moment for one and all of us to prevent the evil day, amending our lives, and watching our hearts in earnest, before the power of doing so is taken away.

Think in earnest my brethren of the Day of Judgement. Do you suppose that in that hour any one of us will repent himself as though he had not made the most of life, having turned to God sooner or more heartily than he need? My brethren we all know better than that, we all know that the most a man can do will seem to him nothing in that hour. At least let us lose no more than we can help of the short time that yet remains. Let not this Lent be added to our list of neglected warnings. It is here now: it will very soon be gone: God grant the memory of it may be a joy to us all for ever!

SERMON VII.

CONFESSION.

I.

1 S. John i. 8.

"*If we say that we have no sin, we deceive ourselves and the truth is not in us.*"

ONCE more the time of Lent is come; in one year more the Holy Church has cried aloud in our ears and spared not. She has lifted up her voice like a trumpet, declaring as you heard last Wednesday, the sentences of God's wrath against impenitent sinners, who are such, how accursed they are in this world, and what their end must be in the next, if they do not betake themselves in time to their only Saviour. All this has sounded in our ears, every one of us, for indeed we are all concerned in it: it is a serious time for us all. Not for a few notorious sinners only, such as are called reprobates, and pointed at in all the neighbourhood; not for such only is this time of Lent appointed, but for all and every one of us. For Lent is a time of penitence, and all have need of penitence, or as the Commination Service calls it, of Penance. Look at a little child of a day old, even that has need of penance, i. e. of God's corrective discipline. For it is a sinner in the sight of God, and subject to His wrath, having in it, that seed and spark of original sin, which has been born with each one of us, ever since the fall of Adam. And we may well believe that in some mysterious way the pains, and especially the death of little children may serve as a penitential medicine to heal the sore and foulness of that birth sin, which though it be forgiven as to its eternal mischief, continues within them, even after they are baptized. But this is one of God's secrets. With regard to elder persons it is quite certain, that "if they say they have no sin they deceive themselves," were it only in respect of the sin which they inherit from Adam. We ought to think of that original mischief more, and more gravely than we too commonly do. For only consider what your feelings would be, if you were made aware that you carried about with you the seeds of some dangerous and tormenting disease, which would soon become incurable if you were careless about it. Would it not make you very watchful, very much on your guard not to do anything that would strengthen the complaint, or bring on an attack of it? Would it not come into your mind along with your morning and evening prayers, and help you to feel how feeble and powerless you are, so long as you are left to yourself: how entirely in the hands of your Lord for life or death? Well now, such as would be your feelings concerning your body if you knew you were subject to a bad and dangerous sickness, such ought to be your feelings concerning your soul, which you know for certain to be infected with the most miserable fatal pestilence of sin. We ought never to forget it, we ought never to go on for a moment as if we had no sin. But alas! it is the hardest thing in the world to keep up to this rule, plain as the rule is to every man's common sense. It is the hardest thing to watch and pray always: yet who can doubt that there is no other wise and safe way, since Hell is always open to devour us, the devil always lying in wait to thrust us into that horrible pit, sin always lurking hidden in our souls, to beguile us to the very edge of it.

Thus watchful, thus earnest ought our lives to be, even though we had no sin of our own, but were only partakers of Adam's sin, how much more now that all who get beyond infancy, have also sins of their own, more or less grievous, to answer for! For as the wise man asks, "*Who can say I have made my heart clean, I am pure from my sin?" In the way of temper, in the way of proud imagination, in the way of thoughts and desires, greedy, selfish, unclean, or otherwise irregular, who that really considers, does not feel that he has a great deal to answer for? But most alas, or at least very many, must make a worse confession than this, if they speak the truth to God and to themselves, they must own themselves guilty of grievous deadly sin; for every thought indulged, word spoken, and deed done, against the known and remembered will of God, is indeed deadly sin: it makes a wound such as will kill the soul for ever, unless the proper remedy be applied. And the proper remedy is penitence, or penance. I say it again, there are few of us, I fear, grown beyond the estate of children, who do not stand in need of penitence, in respect of known and wilful sins of

* Prov. xx. 9.

their own. If any say that it is not so with them, there is surely great reason to fear that those persons are guilty of some dangerous deceiving of themselves. Observe only what S. John says in the text: "If we say that we have no sin, we deceive ourselves," we; that is, Christians in general. I, you, all for whom I am writing this Epistle, whoever we are, we have sinned, "and if we say that we have no sin," we do but deceive ourselves. Now, my brethren, if S. John said this, the Disciple whom Jesus specially loved, and who leaned on His breast at supper, if even he was obliged to say for himself, and for all other Christians "If we say that we have no sin we deceive ourselves:" much more must the same be owned concerning such as we commonly are: and if we do not really feel that we are sinners, if our sins do not really trouble us, we may be sure there is some dangerous mistake. See how the Church teaches us all to confess our own condition to God: "We acknowledge and bewail our manifold sins and wickedness, which we from time to time most grievously have committed, by thought, word, and deed against Thy Divine Majesty, provoking most justly Thy wrath and indignation against us. We do earnestly repent, and are heartily sorry for these our misdoings; the remembrance of them is grievous unto us, the burden of them is intolerable." These are indeed very heavy, very sorrowful words. No person is fit to use them who thinks lightly of his own sins. No person is fit to come to Holy Communion in our Church of England, unless the remembrance of his past transgressions has become indeed grievous unto him, and the burden of them more than he can bear.

Otherwise if he does come with a careless easy heart, making little of what is past, if he take up with those common excuses " Such an one is far worse than I am." " I am as good as the generality"—"I am as good as my fathers before me"—what can we say of him, but that he tells a lie to God—he knowingly, and deliberately professes before Him that seeth in secret, that which is not true; and what should you think must be the end of such behaviour? Plainly then the Church in the Prayer Book makes it a necessary part of true religion, that men should have a very deep and sorrowful sense of their own sins. If they have no such feeling, the Church would have them stay away. For she knows and is sure that their religion is vain,—it is an empty thing, a shadow without substance. As S. John goes on to say "The truth is not in" such persons. They are in an unreal state, in a kind of dream. And only think, my brethren, how miserable, how fearful it must be when the shadows pass, and the reality comes on, when they are wakened up from their dream, their soothing flattering imaginations of their own goodness—to find that it was but a dream. The Holy Spirit in the Psalm describes their sad disappointment. "[b] O how suddenly do they consume, perish, and come to a fearful end! Yea even as a dream when one awaketh so shalt Thou make their image to vanish"—the pleasing condition in which they fancied themselves to be, proves to be just nothing at all. "[c] It shall even be as when a hungry man dreameth, and behold he eateth, but he awaketh and

[b] Ps. lxxiii. 18, 19.   [c] Isa. xxix. 8.

his soul is empty, or as when a thirsty man dreameth, and behold he drinketh, but he awaketh and behold he is faint, and his soul hath appetite."—These words of the Prophet Isaiah may give us some faint notion of the bitter shame and anguish with which, as may be feared, too many will wake up in the other world.

For example, what if any among us should be leading a decent but irreligious life, quiet perhaps, and affectionate in his family, honest and civil towards his neighbours, decorous and inoffensive before men in his personal conduct, but negligent alas, or at least very lukewarm towards Him Who is more than friend, neighbour, or family: passing by as though it were nothing to him that his Saviour were hanging on the Cross; impatient of Church services, and of devotional exercises, glad when they are over, contented to think of other things while they are going on, seldom or never at Holy Communion, and very jealous of any who seem to be more devout, and self denying than the rest, caring little for the Church of God, and not very willing to offer of his substance for the carrying on God's work of converting the world. Such an one we may be almost sure, will be well thought of by others, and their praise and good opinion will too commonly encourage him to go on even to the end, praising and thinking too well of himself. What if he should fall asleep in confident hope, and wake up in miserable despair, finding himself without a Saviour in the other world, because he is satisfied to remain at such a distance from Him in this world?

Or again, what if there be here and there a person whose life is in most respects correct, and his heart even deeply touched as far as feeling goes, with religious impressions; but in some one respect he is keenly tempted, and gives way in secret: from time to time reproaching himself, and wishing he had a heart to stand firm, but as often yielding when the temptation comes? like the shallow ground which made a fair show for a time, but lacking moisture, caused the corn very soon to wither away. This person too will not be unlikely to die in good hope, easily forgiving himself, because he is so well spoken of by his neighbours. But what saith the Scripture of such an one? "[d]Whosoever shall keep the whole law and yet offend in one point, he is guilty of all." Though you seem to yourself as well as others, to keep all the commandments but one, yet if you knowingly and habitually break that one, you do in effect scorn them all, for you show, that you would break all if you were in equally strong temptation to break them. Therefore praised as you may be among men, and buoyed up even to the end, by an inward secret trust in yourself, (which you may think is trust in God!) you too, will have a sad awakening. You will find that you were against Christ, while you thought you were for Him. You will knock, as it were, at the door of the festive chamber and say, "[e] Lord, Lord open unto us!" and when He from within, shall answer and say, "I know you not whence ye are," you, perhaps, hardly yet understanding, will, in a manner plead with Him," Lord, Lord, have we not done great things in Thy Name?" but you will hear nothing comfortable; " I tell you, I know you not; depart from Me, all ye workers of

[d] S. Ja. ii. 10.   [e] S. Luke xiii. 25, 27.

iniquity."—Ah! what a sorrowful case will that be! what a mourning for the good Angels! what a triumph for the evil spirits! what a disappointment to our Pastors! and to the whole Church and people of God, to see one secret bosom sin, one unknown piece of mischief, leavening and cankering the whole of a man's character, otherwise very noble and amiable! What a grief, if I may so speak, even to the ever-Blessed Son and Spirit, to see Their seals thus wantonly defaced, and Their gracious purpose towards us made void: as if you should open a precious perfume and find it spoiled, as the wise man says, "*by one dead insect," corrupted and corrupting. The whole must of course be thrown away. If you would escape such a miserable ending, I say to you my friends, Beware of single sins! beware of depending on one another's praise—on one or two things which you seem to do remarkably well. Depend on nothing of the sort, but repent of all as well as you can; and let it be your great care to go down humbly to the grave.

It is but too possible for careless persons to go down to the grave in absolute forgetfulness of every great and deadly sin committed, it may be, many years ago—they cannot repent of it, because they have fairly forgotten it; and how then can it be confessed and forgiven? will it not meet the man in the Day of Judgement? and how will he then look it in the face? his only chance is to try so earnestly to recall all his sins to mind, and to pray so devoutly "Cleanse me from my secret faults" that the merciful God for Christ's sake, may pardon that which, if the penitent

f Eccles. x. 1.

knew or remembered, he would surely have confessed.

Neither must we forget one great sin to which we are all of us but too prone—the sin of under-rating our privileges, and so thinking too little of our failures. We do not consider, nor lay it to heart, what the Church so plainly teaches us, that we are indeed members of Christ, born again, of water and the Holy Ghost, and therefore we cannot say that it is out of our power, to keep the commandments, to be holy and good, if we will. We owned this in words, a little less than a twelve-month ago, we many of us set our names to it in writing, for if you remember we petitioned our Bishop that no one might be allowed to contradict the Prayer Book, by teaching the contrary of this in our Churches. We owned it in word and writing, have we been owning it ever since in act and in deed? Have we really and truly humbled ourselves for our many failures, with the thought that surely we might have done better, that we were sinning against the Blessed Spirit who was at hand to help us? Nay! too often we have failed in this; too often we have passed over our faults lightly and easily, saying to ourselves we are but like other men, we are not saints, that we should resist every temptation. Has it not been so, my brethren? do I not speak the truth? can any man deny it?

For all these reasons then, for the stain of the first sin abiding in all of us; for the actual sin of all who are old enough to sin; for the grievous deadly transgressions of too many; for our want of religion when we seem to be going on decently; for the single sins whereby, not a few have spoiled and thrown away the goodness of the rest of their lives; for the sins which we have forgotten; for our great abuse of privileges, and sad trifling with the grace of our Baptism; for all these reasons, and many more as sad as these, I beseech you, brethren, let us now and for ever leave off saying and thinking that " we have no sin : " let us take God at His word, and be quite sure that we have many sins, if we would but find them out : let us find them out as well as we can, holding the candle of the Lord, the light of God's Spirit and of prayer to the inmost parts of our conscience and memory, not shrinking from the shame and pain. For this let us watch and pray; let us strive and labour above all things, to be real and true. For to know and feel the very truth of ourselves, that is humility, and humility will save our souls, for it will bring us to the feet of Christ, and He will raise us up!

SERMON VIII.

CONFESSION.
II.

1 S. John i. 8, 9.

"*If we say that we have no sin, we deceive ourselves, and the truth is not in us: But if we confess our sins, He is faithful and just to forgive us our sins, and to cleanse us from all unrighteousness.*"

LAST week I spoke of the disease, the fearful disease of sin: how it lurks deep in the very constitution of our souls—what symptoms of it we may all find every one of us in himself, and those not least, who from outward and general decency might seem to themselves and others in the best spiritual health. I besought you, now in this time of consideration, to think deeply of these things: to search diligently, and as it were with candles, into your own heart and soul and memory: to pray that you might not be allowed to forget your old sins, as too many do: and above all things, to be quite true and frank and honest in your dealings with your own conscience, and with your God. And now, having said so much of the disease, it is time to consider the remedy: but first I would say one word more, for the more perfect understanding how grievous the complaint is.

And the word I have to say is this: we ought to make up our minds that there is sure to be a great leaven of sinfulness even in the best and wisest of all our works. It mingles unawares with our charities and our devotions—with all that we do that is best and purest either towards God or man. It haunts us in our prayers: it taints all our holy desires. The more people watch themselves, soberly and in earnest, the more certain will they be of this. At a distance, and on a rough passing view, and in comparison with others, they may be tolerably self-satisfied: but look more closely into the mirror, examine yourselves more truly, and you will find all the beauty disappear. So that it may seem nothing extreme, but just plain fact, plain common sense, which was once asked by a wise and holy man in our Church, "If God Almighty were to promise to forgive all our sins, upon condition of some one act being done, quite free from sin, by one of the fallen race of Adam, could any one such act be any where found?" For only think how apt we are, as soon as by God's grace we have done a right thing, said a good word, thought a good thought—how apt we are to begin praising ourselves for it in our hearts. Think, how shamefully little selfish ends mingle with our kind and devout purposes: how, while we are denying ourselves in one way, we contrive as it were, to take out our recompense by indulging ourselves in another way. Think how badly we say our prayers. Which of us can remember having ever said a single prayer from beginning to end quite as he ought to have done,—with entire humility and devotion? So that not only in our lives taken generally, but in each particular portion and act of our lives we may with too much reason take up the Apostle's word, and say, If we say that we have no sin—nothing amiss either in doing or leaving undone—we do but deceive ourselves and the truth is not in us.

This is our sad, our imperfect condition. But we are not left in it without hope or remedy. The same Holy Spirit which tells us of our misery tells us also, and that immediately, of the perfect cure which He has provided. "If we say that we have no sin, we deceive ourselves—" sin hangs about us, we cannot yet be free from it; but we may, by His mercy, be in a sure way to be free: and how may that be? the Apostle teaches us in the very next verse. "If we confess our sins, He is faithful and just to forgive us our sins, and to cleanse us from all unrighteousness." You see, confession is set down here as the way to complete deliverance. For what is complete deliverance from sin? Does it not consist in two things, forgiveness of the past, and cleansing for the future? now both these are promised in the text to confession of sin. "If we confess our sins, He is faithful and just to forgive us our sins:" that is one thing: He will blot the past out of our account. And more than that: He will "cleanse us from all unrighteousness:" His grace will take away the stain which past sin has left in our souls: it will heal the sores, and strengthen the weakness, which our sad transgressions and backslidings have engendered. We might think it a strange thing that so simple a process, as confession appears to us, should produce so great an effect, work such miracles of grace. We might think it strange, but we cannot doubt it, for here it is set down in so many words. Confess, and you shall be forgiven and cleansed. Christ's own beloved disciple, taught by the Spirit of Christ, tells us so: we must not, we dare not gainsay it.

But indeed when we come to consider it, there is something in this great benefit of confession not so much unlike what we are used to in other things. Suppose any one ill in body in pain and distress, lying awake at night, refusing his nourishment or finding that it does him no good, his spirits low, his heart full of anguish, feeling as if all his good days were gone, and not knowing what to do, what medicine to take, how to live in order to obtain health and strength again. What are men used to do when such trouble as this comes upon them? Finding they cannot cure themselves, they go to some one whom they think more likely to cure them. They go to the physician: and having come to him, do they leave him to find out what is the matter by merely looking at them, or do they tell him their case themselves, and answer all his questions? Of course they tell him: it is their only chance to be cured: for how else is he to know what is the matter with them? and if he do not know, how can he prescribe for them? as then the way of bodily cure is to tell one's case fully to the physician, so the way of spiritual cure is to confess our sins to the physician of our souls: that is, to Almighty God, for He only can heal the soul.

Let no man say, what need to confess to God? what can I tell Him that He does not know already?

Of course He does: He is always and everywhere present: whatsoever your sins were, He was by at the committing them. He was even in your heart, watching the bad thought which you were cherishing: His ear heard your words, of falsehood, blasphemy, unkindness, presumption, or in whatever way your tongue has been sinning: His eye beheld your evil and corrupt doings, from the very first beginning to the last end: He knows it, far better than you can: He knew it from the beginning, and He never can forget nor mistake. He knows it, yet it is His will that you should confess it to Him: just as it is His will that you should pray, though He knows beforehand what you want: As our collect says, "He knows our necessities before we ask," and yet He will have us pray to Him: something, perhaps, in the same way as parents insist on their children asking respectfully for what they would have, though the parents themselves know perfectly well what that is. And in the same kind of way we know that our Heavenly Father would have the Jews remind Him at the Passover every year of the great things He had done for them in bringing them out of Egypt. Had He forgotten those deeds? of course not: to Him all things are present: but He chose to be so put in mind of them. And to speak of what is yet more solemn; it is the Father's will that we should continually put Him in mind of His Only Son, His well-beloved, by the offering of that Bread and Wine which He declares to be His Body and Blood, in the Sacrament of the Holy Communion. Can He then forget His Son, His Only beloved? Nay: but in His mercy and wisdom He hath so ordained it: and by that Holy Sacrament we must plead before Him His Son's death, else He will not remember it for our good.

As we are taught thus to put our God in mind of our needs and His mercies, in prayer, and in Holy Communion, so are we enjoined to confess to Him the sins which He too well knows: one by one we are to acknowledge them: not in the mass only, as when we say in the general confession at the beginning of daily service, "we have left undone those things which we ought to have done, and we have done those things which we ought not to have done:" not so, but specially: "thus and thus have I done: at such a time I told a lie, at such another time I stole, at such another time I was too angry" and the like. This is how we must own our transgressions to God: as we would describe our complaints to the physician.

And there is great encouragement in Scripture to do so: not only in this express promise by S. John but in other sayings both of the Old and New Testaments, "*whoso covereth his sins shall not prosper, but he that confesseth and forsaketh them shall find mercy." That is the saying of the wise king Solomon. And you know the Psalm, the thirty second Psalm, provided so many years beforehand to be a Christian Hymn, to help in Christian confession. "Blessed is he whose unrighteousness is forgiven and whose sin is covered. For while I held my tongue my bones consumed away through the voice of my complaining. For Thy hand was heavy upon me day and night, and my moisture was like the drought in summer."

* Prov. xxviii. 13.

Here you see the sad comfortless dreary condition to which sinners are reduced, who have not yet opened their hearts to God. But in the next verse comes relief: "I will acknowledge my sin unto Thee, and mine unrighteousness have I not hid. I said, I will confess my sins unto the Lord, and so Thou forgavest the wickedness of my sin." And see what joy and gladness ensues: "Thou art a place to hide me in, Thou shalt preserve me from trouble, Thou shalt compass me about with songs of deliverance." Such is special confession to God, as taught in the Psalms and Proverbs. It is also taught in the Law more especially by what was appointed for the cleansing of a leper. Who was to be the judge of leprosy? not as you might have expected, the physician, but the priest. And when a man was thought to be leprous, he was to shew himself to the priest. The priest looked well all over him, and then pronounced him a leper or not, according to the signs which the Law had particularly mentioned. So when a grievous sinner is moved to confession when he begins sitting at home and keeping silence, he will do well to be as particular in his confession as ever he can. He should confess all, that he may be forgiven all. The promise of pardon is to what we confess, not to what we wilfully abstain from confessing. As to what we leave out, but not wilfully, (since none can remember everything) He will mercifully forgive that too: but we must in each following confession try, as we can, to supply what was unintentionally left out in the last. Do this honestly, and He who is not a hard Master, but a loving Father, He, be sure, will allow for your infirmities: He will forgive and heal you, entirely, partial and imperfect as your confession must needs be.

It may help us to dutiful thoughts of our Lord's dealing with us in this matter, if we consider how those of us who are parents, or in any way entrusted with the care of others, proceed in pardoning the faults of those under their care. Suppose there has been something wrong: what do people expect from the children who have offended? from their scholars, from their servants, from all concerned in the mischief? of course they expect an honest confession: without that they cannot forgive with any profit to the penitent: if he confess not honestly, what good will the absolution do? People expect and take trouble to bring it about, that their children's or servant's confessions may leave out nothing particular. They know it perhaps all, themselves, beforehand: but they do not less encourage the penitent to repeat it. As I said, it is very like this when grown up sinners are making their confession to God. He knows all, yet He expects them to tell all. As we read in the Book of Joshua, when a certain man named Achan had been secretly taking part of the spoil of Jericho, and had been the cause of sad trouble to the people of God, for, because of that act of his, Israel had to turn their backs before their enemies: by and by, upon Joshua's prayer, God made known by casting of lots who it was that had committed the sin, and although he could not be forgiven in this world, yet Joshua advised him what he should do, as the only right thing, having it perhaps in his heart, that on his so doing, he might be spared and forgiven in the world after death. And what did Joshua advise Achan? "My son, give glory to the Lord God of Israel and tell me what thou hast done," and Achan's heart was touched, (as we may believe) and he said, "indeed I have sinned against the Lord, and thus and thus have I done:" and with that he told Joshua exactly how he was tempted, what he had stolen, and where it was then hidden: and although Achan by God's commandment was stoned to death for his grievous sin—he could not, as I said, be forgiven in this world—we may well believe that he was in some unknown way, the better for the true and humble confession which he made: God in some unknown way might be merciful to him, as to others, who sinned and repented before they could know of Jesus Christ. But however it was with Achan, we are sure by what was said to him, that God accounts it giving Him glory, when sinners confess what they have done amiss, and put themselves to shame before Him: when in the bitterness of soul we go over our transgressions, the sad and shameful story of that too large portion of our lives, when we perhaps were turned away from God and altogether taken up with helping ourselves in secret to the accursed things of the world, the flesh and the devil—He would have us do this, not once only, when we first turn to God, but from time to time, at solemn seasons especially, and most especially at this season of Lent. He would have each one of us set apart some leisure hours, before we come to the Lord's Table at Easter, to sit alone and keep silence, renewing before God the sad memory of the years of darkness, of which

G

we are now ashamed. It should be done in the way of prayer, as to God, and in His especial Presence: it should be done with care and fear, that we sin not by delighting unawares in the thought of any sin, even while we are confessing it to God: it should be done in a way of great thankfulness to Him Who has so far opened our eyes, and in loving hope, that He will by His grace make the future better than the past: and when this our confession is over, and it is time to go into the world again, let the holy sadness so far remain on our spirit, that we may be kept humble and resigned, not allowing ourselves to go on being angry, however ill we are used; nor fretting and repining, how badly soever things turn out; since we are the persons who have just had to make so miserable a report of ourselves to the Judge of all. Thus the sweet savour of our sacrifice of confession will spread over our whole lives: the house will be filled with the odour of the ointment: sin will be hated: holiness most earnestly sought for: our Lord will be glorified, and our souls by His mercy, saved.

SERMON IX.

CONFESSION.
III.

JOSHUA vii. 19, 20.

"And Joshua said unto Achan, My son give glory, I pray thee, to the Lord God of Israel, and make confession unto Him: and tell me now what thou hast done; hide it not from me. And Achan answered Joshua, and said, indeed I have sinned against the Lord God of Israel, and thus, and thus have I done."

SIN is the disease of the soul, the mortal disease, common to every one of us; and the Blood of Christ is the only cure; and that Blood can be applied no way, but only by true Christian penitence; and Confession is a necessary part of that penitence, as you heard last Sunday from our Lord's own beloved Disciple: "* If we say that we have no sin, we deceive ourselves, and the truth is not in us; if we confess our sins, He is faithful and just to forgive us our sins." You heard also, that Almighty God expects this our confession to be a particular or special one. We are not to make it lightly, and after the manner of dissemblers with God: i. e. we are not to confess as the hypocrites do. How is that? why you know,

* 1 S. John i. 8, 9.

brethren, or if you consider a moment you will know, what a power we have in some respects over the thoughts of our hearts. We are to a great extent able to attend to things or to pass them over, to throw our minds this way or that as we please. A person who wants to be humble and penitent has it in his power by God's assistance to think over his old sins, and the many infirmities which he carries about with him : a person who wants to please himself, has it no less in his power to puff himself up with thoughts of the matters in which, as he imagines, he has done well, and of the praise and good opinion which he fancies he has earned for himself among his fellow creatures. Well then, one who is afraid of not repenting well enough, has it in his power to turn his mind steadily away from the vain proud fancies, away from all self pleasing thoughts : and to dwell in his secret heart upon what he can remember against himself. We may, by God's help, every day of our lives, place ourselves in thought before the Judgement seat, and imagine what will be read out against us, in the hearing of all, when we shall really stand there. For you know that God keeps a Book, in which all that we say, do, and think, are regularly set down; and all those sins of ours, of which we have not truly repented, will be then rehearsed out of that dreadful Book, in the hearing of men and angels. But if we have judged ourselves before, we shall not be then judged of the Lord. There is nothing hid which shall not be revealed : all our most hidden sins must one day be known and come abroad : but if we have truly and really confessed our sins here, and taken the shame of them on ourselves, we shall be delivered from that reproach at the Last Day : it will not turn to our *everlasting* shame and contempt. This then is the use of special confession to God, that by it we go the best way to prevent the sad overwhelming confusion, which in that hour shall come suddenly upon the wicked ones who have kept up a decent appearance before men : upon those who have dealt with their own consciences lightly and after the manner of dissemblers with God. We must make our acknowledgements of sin to Him as special and particular as ever we can, and thereby prove ourselves quite in earnest in our repentance: so may that gracious word be accomplished in us, which the God of mercy has promised the truly contrite: "All his transgressions which he hath committed, they shall not be mentioned unto him; I will cast all his sins behind My back."

Now in pressing this point, how necessary it is that our confession of sin to Almighty God should leave out none of our wilful sins, you may perhaps remember, some of you, that I mentioned the case of that unhappy Achan, of whom we read in the book of Joshua : whose history has always seemed to me a sad type of unfaithful and wicked Christians, their, secret sins, their certain shame and exposure, their miserable end. It may help us in making a good confession this Lent, if we go more particularly into that mournful history.

When Joshua and the children of Israel had come over Jordan, the first city which they had to take was Jericho; and before they took it, Joshua, in God's name, gave order that no one should seize for himself any portion of the spoil of it. All the persons were to be killed (except one family who had turned to God by faith) and all the property was to be holden as accursed: it was either to be burned or brought into God's treasury: if any person took any of it for himself, that man would make himself accursed, and would bring a trouble and a curse upon the camp of Israel. (This was for a token that God's people should renounce thoroughly the wicked world and the vanities of it; and that if any Christian still goes after the world, he brings a curse upon himself, and trouble upon the whole Church.) This proclamation then being made, the Israelites proceeded to take the city: and they took it, not in the usual way, but in a very wonderful manner, by a special miracle. "They made a procession round the city, the ark of God with all the armed men and seven priests sounding trumpets; this they did six days in silence; and on the seventh, they shouted with a great shout, and the wall of the city fell flat on the ground, and the people went up into the city, every one straight before him, and they took the city." Could there be a greater miracle, a thing more apt to fill men with alarm and awe, and make them humble themselves in the dust before our terrible and holy Lord God? And yet at that very time, one was found among God's people, with no more faith and love, than to commit the sin which he had just heard cursed by God's prophet. A certain man named Achan committed a trespass in the accursed thing: he took privately some of the spoil, a goodly Babylonish garment, and some silver and gold, which ought to have been destroyed or put into God's treasury, and instead of destroying it, he hid it in his tent under ground. And then, I suppose, Achan took his place among the rest, and went on as if nothing particular had happened to him. But what was the consequence? In a mysterious way, that sin of Achan's affected the whole congregation of the children of Israel. The next time they went to battle against their enemies, they were beaten back, and some of them slain; although the enemy was a very poor and insignificant one: Joshua in great distress called upon God and the Lord's answer was, "Israel hath sinned, and they have transgressed My covenant: they have even taken of the accursed thing, and have also stolen, and dissembled also, Therefore the children of Israel could not stand before their enemies, but turned their backs before their enemies, because they were accursed: neither will I be with you any more, except ye destroy the accursed from among you." Take good notice of this, my brethren, Achan's sin was a single, private, personal sin: yet see what effect it would have had upon the whole congregation, had it not been dealt with according to holy discipline. It would have forfeited God's blessing, and not only Achan would have been accursed, but Israel would have lost the promises. But God would not so forsake His people. He instructed Joshua how to find out the guilty person, they were to cast lots, and the Lord would cause the lot to fall first upon the tribe, then upon the family, then upon the particular house, then upon the very person which had to answer for this sin. This was done and the lot fell upon Achan and so it was known, God Himself being witness, that Achan was the guilty person, but it was not known what he had done. Then what was Joshua's advice to him? this is what I wish you, my brethren to take particular notice of; for in this answer of Joshua's to Achan we do, in effect, find God's answer to the question, what we ought to do, when we have inexcusably sinned, and forfeited the blessing given to us in holy Baptism. What was Joshua's advice to Achan? you heard it in the text, "My son, give glory I pray thee to the Lord God of Israel, and make confession unto Him and tell me now what thou hast done." This was the Lord's advice by Joshua : it was simply, Confess. Do not make a bad matter worse by denying and hiding it. Confess: I make no promises: I do not say that you will be forgiven; but I say, Confess, because that is the way to give glory to the Lord. Well, Achan did confess; he told the Lord's messenger exactly what he had done—what garments, gold and silver he had taken, and where it was hidden— Joshua sent and found it all just where Achan had told him, in Achan's tent : so Achan was stoned to death, and the Lord left off being angry with Israel.

Now I say, that this history shows us, in a very remarkable way, what is the best thing we can do, when any one of us has unhappily fallen into serious sin after Baptism. For as I mentioned before, this sin of Achan, being the first serious sin which is mentioned as being committed in Israel after they had come into the Holy Land, answers in some respect to the first great sin in any one of Christ's baptised. It is a token and type of Christian people wilfully falling away after Baptism. For in that they are Christian persons, they have heard the warning against the wicked world, as Achan heard that against Jericho, how that the world passeth away and the lusts thereof, and they that profanely take of it, shall perish with it: and yet they have gone on helping themselves to the accursed thing. They have done it, most likely, as Achan did, in secret. They have seen something which they coveted, and they have not resisted the temptation. They thought to themselves, no one on earth will know it, and by God's mercy I shall live to repent, and no harm will come of it in the other world. And then too often men have gone on, and committed uncleanness and other sins with greediness, keeping up all the while, perhaps, a fair character among men. This was like Achan's taking the precious spoil, and hiding it, though he knew the will of God concerning it.

And see what the consequence has been. The whole Christian world is fallen and decayed in a very sad and fearful way. The Almighty has more or less withdrawn His grace and presence from us: as He declared to Joshua, I will not be with you any more, except ye remove the accursed thing from among you, so it is when Christians sin. If it be but one single Christian, committing but one deadly sin, in the most private and least scandalous way: it spreads in a mysterious way over the whole Christian Body: as it is written, when one member suffereth, all the members suffer with it, and when one member is honoured, all the members rejoice with it. And again, however people may think to indulge themselves in one single sin without being the worse for it in their general character, in practise they find it far otherwise, were it only because the consciousness of their one sin weakens their hearts and hands sadly: they are afraid and ashamed to be forward in well-doing:

like David, who was never the same man after his sin in the matter of Uriah the Hittite. How many are there, who like David, feel as if it was not for them to keep their families in order, and set a good example in their neighbourhoods, and speak out boldly for God, because they have hanging over them the sad memory of something very wrong in their youth! And then, how much encouragement, more than we know, is given to the evil spirits, aware no doubt very often of the sins men commit in secret, and made all the bolder to put fresh temptations in their way: and the holy Angels are grieved and depart from us: and so, worst of all, does the holy and Divine Comforter Himself, until we have in earnest sought to Him by true repentance. So mischievous and so dangerous will prove, though it be but one sin, like Achan's, not to the doer of it only, but to the whole host of Israel, the whole camp and people of God. Surely my brethren, we can never think enough of the sad and dismal effects, which in God's just judgements, are ordained to follow upon any one deadly and wilful transgression in a Christian. Now and then the veil is drawn up, as in this case of Achan, and the just Judge shews us what comes of one single sin. For only think, my brethren, had nothing been done to remedy this, how entirely it would have intercepted God's plan of miraculous mercy for the establishment of His people in Canaan. Israel would have gone on turning their backs before their enemies, and the heathens and unbelievers would have seemed to have their own way in the world. And yet it was a very simple, ordinary fault—I mean according to the vain thoughts of sinful men it would seem to be little more than a sin of infirmity. How do you know but any thing you do, in known disobedience to any one of the great commandments, may by God's righteous decree bring after it as long a train of mischief as Achan's? If any such remembrance is upon your consciences, will you not, if you may, make all haste to clear yourself of it?

And how may you do this? Hear what the Lord by Joshua said to Achan. "My son, give, I pray thee, glory to the Lord God of Israel, and make confession unto Him, and tell me now what thou hast done." He calls upon him to confess, to make a double confession—one to God, and another to him. "Give, I pray thee, glory to the Lord God of Israel and make confession unto Him." You see he bids Achan confess to God, although God not only knew the whole already, but had proved him guilty before the congregation, for He had taken him by casting of lots. In His great mercy God counts it giving glory to Him, when we sorrowfully acknowledge our transgressions, however well known they may be before. Much better, no doubt, it would have been, had the unhappy man found it in his heart to give glory to the God of Israel by a true confession, before the lot had fallen upon him, which seemed in a manner to leave him no choice. How much he would have gained in the favour of God, we know not, but we are sure that he would have gained very much in the way of present relief and comfort. He would have escaped all those miserable feelings, which he must have experienced while the lot was being cast. Think what agony it must have been to him—how like fresh torture coming gradually on—when the first lot was given forth, and the tribe of Judah was taken—and then the second lot, and the family of the Zarhites was taken: and then the third, and fourth, and so it came on to himself—nearer and nearer —till he found there was no escape. All this Achan would have avoided, had he come forward manfully at once, and confessed, I am the man. But even when he had missed that chance, still you see he is pressed to confess, and his confession would be taken and received as a good work, as giving glory to the Lord God of Israel. And so will ours be, as many of us as have sinned grievously after Baptism. "If we confess our sins, He is faithful and just to forgive us our sins, and to cleanse us from all unrighteousness." Confessing our sins, as we see by this place about Achan, is not merely calling ourselves in a general way, miserable sinners, but it is going over our own sins in our own hearts, as sadly and as distinctly as we can, as in the presence of Almighty God, it is carrying about the remembrance of them, wherever we go, all our lives long—humbling our hearts, and subduing our tempers, and teaching ourselves patience and the fear of God, with the recollection that we are the people who have done such and such intolerable things,—who have been so foolish and so wicked. This is confessing our sins to God: and we understand by the words of Joshua to Achan, as well as by many other places of Scripture, that it is a great part of true repentance—a thing which ought to be practised by all God's servants, who have unhappily fallen into grievous sins.

And there is also another confession mentioned

by Joshua at the same time : a confession to Joshua himself, over and above the confession to be made to Almighty God. He says not only, make confession unto the Lord, but also, "tell *me* now what thou hast done—hide it not from me." And then Achan tells Joshua also the chief particulars of his sin, what he had put by, stealing it from God and where it was to be found. Clearly it was right of him to do this: even as we always think it right in the unhappy persons who suffer the sentence of the law for murder or other great crimes, to confess the crime before they go out of the world. It was right in Achan to confess his sin to God, though God knew it already: and it was right in him to confess it to Joshua, and give Joshua all help towards exposing it more thoroughly, and putting him more entirely to shame. And Achan as I have said is the type and figure of such Christians as have broken their Baptismal vows, and not kept themselves from the accursed thing.

Accordingly the Church plainly teaches, that it is good for those whose consciences are troubled with any weighty matter, to make special confession of their sins, and so to obtain absolution from the Priest; even as our Lord promised, "[b]whose sins ye forgive, they are forgiven unto them." In old times, sinners used to come forward publicly in the face of the Church, and acknowledge their faults, and submit to "open shame, that their spirits might be saved in the day of the Lord:" but in our days the Church rather recommends that the penitent should open his grief to the Priest, in private, as the sick man would to the physician : and many Christians, by

[b] S. John xx. 23.

God's mercy, have found in this holy ordinance very great help and comfort to their souls. I speak this to those among you who ought to feel that they are concerned in it—alas ! I fear too many—who have weighty matters, i. e. serious sins, upon their consciences—I invite all such, in the name of our gracious Saviour, to come quietly and open their griefs : according to His own merciful and encouraging call, "Come unto me all ye that labour and are heavy laden." The Church recommends it, the Scripture warrants it, many and many have tried it and found it most blessed. It is an excellent way for helping souls to awaken themselves and shake off the sloth which is too apt to grow upon us all. He that makes a good confession, must first have examined himself thoroughly : and he that examines himself in earnest, cannot but be in earnest humbled, and he that is humbled, is drawing daily nearer to Christ. Therefore sincere and lowly confession of sins, to God always, to the Priest if need so require, is Christ's own blessed way for bringing us to Himself. Why should Christ's people fear to walk in Christ's way? why should the sheep fear to commit themselves to the Good Shepherd? Achan confessed, with all humility, though he knew it would not save his life—he committed himself, so far, in his sad condition, to our merciful God: how much more ought we to trust ourselves to Him who has distinctly told us, "ᶜHe that confesseth and forsaketh his sins shall have mercy."

ᶜ Prov. xxviii. 13.

SERMON X.

CONFESSION.

IV.

PSALM xix. 12, 13.

"*Who can tell how oft he offendeth? O cleanse thou me from my secret faults; keep thy servant also from presumptuous sins, lest they get the dominion over me: so shall I be undefiled and innocent from the great offence.*"

I SHOULD hope that enough has been said, this Lent, to make all of us who are inclined to good thoughts, aware, how very necessary it is, that in confessing our sins unto the Lord we should be as particular as we well can be; not saying simply, I have sinned, great is my sin, but as Achan did, Thus and thus have I done. It is very plain that unless we are thus particular, we shall hardly ever come to be as sorry for our sins, and as humble before God, as we ought to be, in order to obtain full forgiveness. Neither shall we know how to order either our lives or our prayers afterwards, so as to avoid falling again into the same condition, or a worse. On every account it is needful, as the Church says, that we should do much more than own ourselves sinners in a general way. To be forgiven and cured, we must "examine our lives according to the rule of God's commandments, and wherein soever we perceive ourselves to have offended, either in will, word, or deed, there we must bewail our own sinfulness, and confess ourselves to Almighty God, with full purpose of amendment of life." That is, we must use particular special confession.

But in order to do this, it is plainly necessary that a person should know what sin is, and whether or no some sins are worse than others, and what it is that makes them so: otherwise we shall not be able to judge ourselves, that we be not judged of the Lord. As to what sin is, all persons think they know *that:* all persons nearly will tell you, if you ask them, that they know right from wrong. But indeed, my brethren the more experience we have of ourselves, and of one another, the more reason shall we find to fear that many men are greatly and inexcusably blinded on this matter. You or I might think it strange that any body here in England should go on stealing or committing adultery without scruple, not once dreaming that it is sin: and yet I fear it is too certain, that there are hundreds and thousands in our great and crowded towns, who not only live in such deep corruption, but really know no better. What if you or I too, brethren, should be going on in some course or other, of thought, word, or deed, which is as bad or even worse for us, as stealing or adultery for those poor ignorant outcasts? what if it should be only our own carelessness, which prevents us from knowing that we are in deadly sin—condemned already by the holy law of God. Would it not be most miserable to die in such a state of conscience?

Then let us lose no time, but begin this very night to examine ourselves as seriously as we can in regard of those commandments which we know, and to pray Him as seriously as we can for light to understand those which we do not yet know. Let us beseech God to light His candle in our hearts, that we may be able to search out all their innermost and darkest corners. And let us, if we can, read our Bibles and our Prayer books, and other good books which His Providence may put in our way, for this special purpose, to know which *are* God's commandments. What He really and truly would have us to do, and what we must on no account do, if we would keep any reasonable hope of Heaven. Those who cannot read, let them use the same care to know God's will, which they would use to know the will of a master or employer or friend whom they wished to please. Let them go regularly to Church, and listen there as attentively as they can; let them inquire of those who are likely to know better; and especially of God's trusted and appointed messengers, the Clergy, and above all, let both sorts, those who are scholars and those who are not, be very diligent in doing that part of God's will which they know already: for, so doing, they have a promise from Him, to inform them sufficiently of what they do not as yet know. For unto him that hath, shall more be given.

The very simplest of us all, when he sets himself thus earnestly to learn God's will, by doing it, will presently find that he knows already a good deal more than he thought, and is in a way to improve in that knowledge continually. He will understand that as sin in itself is something contrary to God's law and will, so, to each person, that is sin, which he knows, or ought to know, to be displeasing to God: according to S. James' aweful saying, "ᵃTo him that knoweth to do good, and doeth it not, to him it is sin." Again he will understand that this account belongs both to sins of commission and of omission: right things left undone, as well as wrong things positively done: as we confess to God in Church every morning and evening: "we have left undone those things which we ought to have done, and we have done those things which we ought not to have done, and there is no health in us."

But you will say, who is sufficient for these things? What man, what created being, is able to notice, remember and acknowledge all his departures from the will of the Most High? Who can tell how oft he offendeth? Who indeed? not one of us all: and it may be that some persons, considering this, neglect confession altogether, and are content to own themselves miserable sinners. But this is a great and grievous mistake. For suppose you had a piece of work to do to a pattern, would you give it quite up, because you found you could not at first come quite up to the pattern? would you not try and do it as well as you could, especially if you were quite sure that you had a kind master, who would make every allowance for you? So it is in this matter of confession: we cannot remember all, far from it: but our merciful Lord's purpose will be answered if we take care to remember and confess the principal things. And what are the principal things? First, any single acts of ours which we knew to be very wrong at the time and which we clearly

ᵃ S. Ja. iv. 17.

see to be contrary to the plain Commandments of the Lord— murder, or adultery, or fornication, or wilful uncleanness, or theft, or false witness, or blasphemous words spoken against God. Next any bad or irreligious habit or custom into which we have allowed ourselves to fall, especially if we went on with it in spite of reproof or the warnings of our own conscience: such as angry thoughts, angry words, greedy ways in eating and drinking, carelessness about speaking the exact truth, inattention in prayer, hard and unkind thoughts and words about other people. I say no person who means and wishes to confess his sins truly and religiously will leave out such things as these: and he will greatly help his confession, if he will consider with himself *how* bad his practices have been: as for example, if a man has ever given way to the love of strong drink, when he comes to repent he will acknowledge distinctly how far the temptation prevailed against him, how many times he was overtaken in the course, say of a year, a month, or a week, whether he went out of his way for it, whether it was against warning, whether it made him wicked in other respects, dishonest to his employers, unkind to his family, negligent of his devotions, or the like. And so in respect of other sins, it is well that we should not only confess ourselves guilty of such sins in general, but acknowledge also in the bitterness of our soul how far, how often, how sadly they have prevailed against us, and what miserable consequences *we know* them to have drawn after them; besides the many other evils, secret to us, which are sure to have arisen from every wilful sin.

By observing such rules as these, we may hope to do God's work in making a good and religious confession of our sins: we may hope to obtain His special grace, so far as to leave no mortal or deadly sins unconfessed and unrepented of—with a special and particular confession and repentance. I say, no mortal or deadly sin: for that there is a real distinction, a real difference among sins, some being mortal and deadly, some lighter and more easily cureable, Holy Scripture plainly teaches, and it is of great consequence to us that we bear it in mind. When I say, some sins are mortal and deadly, I mean that any one of them is enough to kill the soul, that is, to separate it from God, and break off saving communion with Jesus Christ, so that if a person died with the full guilt of that sin upon him, he never could enter into Heaven: such sins e.g. as wilful murder, or adultery—and when I speak of certain other sins being lighter, and in comparison more pardonable, I mean that although being truly sins, they offend God and deserve His anger, and ought as far as may be to be confessed and repented of, yet each one of them is not in itself so bad as to separate between us and our God; and by itself to ruin the soul, such things I mean as giving way unduly to anger, speaking untrue words, judging harshly of others and other such as I mentioned just now. And yet even these if indulged and persevered in, and permitted to grow into a habit, and that in spite of warning, and contrary to the misgivings of conscience, will grow and multiply into deadly sin, even as grains of sand, which are simply of no weight that can be felt, if you heap enough of them together, will sink a vessel.

This is the difference between deadly sins, and sins of infirmity; and it is a difference which Holy Scripture plainly teaches. Our Lord Himself in His sermon on the Mount, speaking of sins committed against the 6th Commandment gives us to understand that it may be broken, and that in the way of deadly sin, by many acts short of murder: and that it also may be broken in a lighter and more excusable way: though any breach of it is bad enough. He says a man who is angry with his brother puts himself in danger of the judgement, i. e. he sins, and incurs *some* penalty. If without cause he say Raca, i. e. if he utters a scornful word, then he is in danger of the Council, i. e. of a severer judgement than the former, which wants special consideration before it can be passed. But if without cause he say Thou fool, i. e. if he deliberately utter a spiteful word, calling the other person a reprobate, he is in danger of hell fire—such words, repeated and made habitual, it is to be feared, will prove the ruin of his soul. This place surely makes it evident, that in His sight Who will come to be our Judge, some sins equally wilful, are far worse than others. Another place in Scripture where the like distinction is made, is the latter part of S. John's first Epistle, where you will find mention made of a sin unto death. And holy David teaches us the same in the text: which is a most earnest prayer to be brought to true confession and amendment. "Cleanse Thou me from my secret faults: keep Thy servant also from presumptuous sins, lest they get the dominion over me: so shall I be undefiled and innocent from the great offence." You see we are first in danger of secret faults—sins of infirmity, surprises, which come suddenly on us, in the way of hasty anger, or idle words, or looking where we ought not: such are sins not unto death, provided they are not knowingly indulged, nor suffered to grow into a habit. Next we pray to be kept from presumptuous sins, i. e. from known, wilful, deliberate, breaches of the Commandments. From these we pray to be kept altogether, from the other only to be cleansed: it being by God's mercy quite possible and the bounden duty of each one of us, to keep entirely away from presumptuous, i. e. from known wilful deliberate sins—while from secret faults, surprises, sins of infirmity, we can hardly hope to be quite freed in this world: it is enough if we repent of them, watch against them as well as we can, and pray earnestly to be cleansed from the guilt of them. In this way, though no one is sinless, yet every one may if he will, through God's special grace, be undefiled and innocent from the great offence—from all serious, wasting sin.

Thus plainly does the written word of God acknowledge the difference between the degrees of sin; that some sins are mortal and deadly, others not so: and that even the same sin may bring much more guilt upon one than upon another, we are taught over and over: to mention only one place, "[b]He that knew his Master's will, and prepared not himself, neither did according to His will, shall be beaten with many stripes; but he that knew not—i. e. knew not so well, and did commit things worthy of stripes, shall be beaten with few stripes." And the Church's Litany instructs us in this difference of sins: bidding us pray

[b] S. Lu. xii. 48.

to be delivered from "fornication, and all other deadly sin:" whereby we are clearly given to understand that some sins, such as fornication, are deadly—kill the soul themselves, if not cured—and others are not so.

Now, brethren, I say that this notion of their being such a thing as deadly or mortal sin, ought to be borne in mind continually, that in all our behaviour we may be very much on our guard, and more especially that in our self-examinations and confessions we may deal *truly* with our God and with ourselves. Let no man deceive himself, nor deal with his Judge as if he could deceive Him. Nature indeed is frail; God is very merciful: and there are such things as secret faults, sins of infirmity, and which are not unto death: but God is just as well as merciful, and there are also open and notorious sins, grievous sins, sins mortal and deadly, sins, any one of which, unrepented, will be "unto death." These in the first place we must fear: against these we must fight and pray. Pray humbly, fight sincerely, especially against the particular sin (be it what it may) which your frail heart most inclines to: pray humbly, fight sincerely, confess to God unreservedly, and you will not fight nor pray nor make your confession in vain.

SERMON XI.

THE PROFANENESS OF ESAU A WARNING TO CHRISTIANS.

SECOND SUNDAY IN LENT.

GEN. xxv. 34.

" Thus Esau despised his birthright."

LAST Sunday, the voice of God uttered a fearful warning, in our ears, to those who sin by despising His threatenings, and refusing to think of their latter end. The fruitful land made barren, Sodom all smoking with fire and brimstone, all that dwelt therein overthrown, she who did but once look back turned into a pillar of salt: all these things our merciful Lord has made a sign and token to Christians of the fearful ruin of the Last Day: and He causes us all to hear of it in the beginning of Lent, that we may lose no time in escaping for our lives. And now, this second Sunday, the same merciful voice is again heard, putting us on our guard against another grievous sin, of which we are in extreme danger, as many of us know by sad experience: God speaks to-day to those especially, who sin by despising their own spiritual privileges, and refusing to consider how near they are to God. He speaks to all such by the example of

Esau, as He spake last Sunday by the example of the Sodomites to the ordinary sort of unbelievers.

The history of Esau is shortly this. He was the elder of the twin sons of Isaac and Rebekah, and in the ordinary course of such things, would have succeeded not only to the better part of his father's property, but also to the glorious promises, made first to Abraham and afterwards to Isaac, concerning our Lord, Who should one day be born of their race, "In thee and in thy seed, shall all the families of the earth be blessed." Esau by his birth, was in due time to be head of the holy household, to which the especial offer had been made, "walk before me, and I will be thy God."

Of course then, if Esau had any religion, any love of God in him; if he were in the least like his fathers Abraham and Isaac; he would have treasured up this promise as they did, and would have thought it more valuable than all his earthly possessions. But see how he behaved. One day when he came in from hunting, quite faint with weariness and hunger, his brother Jacob was seething pottage, i. e. he was preparing a mess of broth; and Esau took a fancy to it, and asked for some: "Feed me, I pray thee, with that same red pottage, for I am faint." Jacob moved by a secret Providence, said to him, "sell me now thy birthright." He said the words, not aware perhaps of their deep and very serious meaning: perhaps not at all expecting that Esau would really do such a thing: but Esau willingly caught the words up, as if he were even glad of an opportunity to shew how little he cared for God's blessing. "Behold

I am at the point to die, and what good shall this birthright do me?" A strange way of speaking when he was only a little more tired and hungry than usual. But to punish him, he was taken at his word, and really and seriously made that foolish bargain, and confirmed it by oath. "He sold his birthright unto Jacob; and Jacob gave Esau bread and pottage of lentiles, and he did eat, and drink, and went his way." Well may the holy writer go on and say, "thus Esau despised his birthright." He could not hold it more cheaply, than to part with it, wilfully and knowingly, for a dish of broth.

Having thus satisfied his appetite, Esau, it appears, went his way, and thought no more about it for a long time. He was far indeed from understanding or really considering what he had done. Time passed on, and the two brothers pursued their several ways of life. There was nothing, so far as we read, to put either them or their acquaintance in mind of the strange bargain which had passed between them.

But by and by, as you heard in the lesson this morning, Isaac having grown old, and desiring naturally to bless his eldest son, i.e. to make a division of his property in Esau's favour before he died, things were so ordered and contrived, not without God's secret Providence, that Esau should lose the blessing, and Jacob receive it, and be chosen, he and his family, to be God's own peculiar people, while Esau and his seed were cast off, and compelled to take their place among the outcasts and heathen. Then at last Esau found out what he had really been doing in his behaviour with regard to his birthright. Then he cried out with an exceeding loud and bitter cry, "Bless me, even me also, O my father," but it was too late. He had cast himself out, and could not be restored to his place as the eldest son. He could never more be reckoned among the holy nation: and the name of Edom, which was given him in remembrance of what he had done, continued ever after to be the name of his family and nation: a token of their sad condition, and a warning to us.

I should not wonder if some persons thought it hard, when they read or hear of Esau's behaviour about the pottage being so severely punished: just as in daily life, in schools and families and parishes and kingdoms, it will sometimes seem hard when people are punished on doing something which may seem little in itself, but which is indeed great, because it is a part and an instance of a regular course of bad behaviour, such an instance as shews that the man is thoroughly impenitent, and resolved to go on in the sin. He may go away perhaps and complain, how hardly he was used, how he did but take such a liberty, which by itself may seem trifling and excusable, and presently he lost his place, or was otherwise punished: he may complain, but all considerate people understand that in such cases a man is punished not for that one act only, but for being such an one as that act shews him to be. Just so it was in this case of Esau. Holy Scripture in the Epistle to the Hebrews tells us expressly why he was punished: it was for being a thoroughly *profane* person. "Take heed," it says, "lest there be among you any fornicator, or profane person, as Esau, who for one morsel of meat sold his birthright^a." Profaneness: that was Esau's sin. What is it which we properly mean by profaneness? It is when people know in their hearts that a thing is holy, and ought to be treated with religious reverence, and yet they treat it as a cheap and ordinary thing. It is different from the sin of Sodom, and in one respect perhaps it is worse: as our Lord Himself seems to intimate, when He says to wicked Christians, "^b It shall be more tolerable for the land of Sodom in the Day of Judgement, than for you." The sin of Sodom was unbelief: they knew not God, and would not believe what He told them by His messengers. Esau could not say, he knew not God. He had been bred up in Isaac's family, which was blessed as Abraham's had been, because the master of it not only kept God's holy commandments himself, but commanded his children and his household to do the same. Esau therefore could not be ignorant how great and good a thing his birthright and inheritance was, and how near he was to God, so long as he kept that inheritance. To trifle with it, he could not but know, was trifling with God Almighty, making light of His blessing and favour. Yet he did scorn and make light of it, in the way just mentioned. He took a sort of pride in shewing how little he cared for it. It could be but in mocking and scorn, in the way of what men call "braving out" a thing, that he parted with God's blessing as he did for a little broth. It was an insolent way of bidding people take notice that he did not care for God or his blessing at all. So far then he was worse than the Sodomites, as he had been better instructed and

^a Heb. xii. 16.   ^b S. Matt. xi. 24.

brought up, and knew more of Him whom he was sinning against. And in Esau's punishment there is this fearful circumstance, over and above what happened to the Sodomites, that he was cast out of God's kingdom and near presence, they were hurried away by His judgement before they had ever entered in. To all his other grief and agony was added this sad circumstance, that he could remember when it was otherwise, as the evil spirits remember their first glory.

See now, my brethren if this profaneness of Esau does not answer but too well to the behaviour of many Christians, in respect of the high privileges which God has made them partakers of.

We are all bred as it were in Isaac's family: we know our God from our youth up. Ever since we could speak, we have been taught, the greater part of us, that we are children of God, as being members of His Son, made such in Holy Baptism: "ᶜand if children, then heirs; heirs of God, and joint heirs with Christ."

As Christ then is the First-born, so is each one of us. Every child newly baptized is in God's sight as an eldest son: and his birthright is, the Kingdom of Heaven. All this we have been taught, as many of us as have learned our catechism: we have known it as certainly as Esau knew the promises made to his father Isaac, and the share which he as the firstborn had in those promises. Have we, or have we not, despised this our birthright? are we, or are we not, in God's sight, guilty of profaneness like Esau's? alas! I fear that most of us have too much reason to tremble on putting such a question as

ᶜ Rom. viii. 17.

this to themselves: but it is better to tremble now before your Saviour, than hereafter before your Judge, when it shall be too late. It is better to be strict in trying yourselves, now in Christ's accepted time, in His own forty days of trial and amendment, than to wait until you shall be tried by the fires of the Last Day. Consider then this matter of profaneness; whether it ought not to lie heavy on your conscience, partly in respect of your whole course of life, and partly in respect of particular sins which you have committed, and habits which you have got into. It is too clear that many are profane in their whole course and habit of life: in that, knowing about about heaven and hell, knowing the great things which God has done for them, and from time to time owning it all in words, they nevertheless slight it and turn away from it, and are impatient of being put in mind of it, in their ordinary doings. Their practice speaks for them continually, much in the same tone as Esau spake: " behold, I am at the point of losing this or that worldly good: and what good shall this birthright do me?" They care not even about the Kingdom of Heaven, they feel as if it could never make them happy, if they cannot have so much money, or enjoy such and such a pleasure, on which they have set their childish earthly hearts. Therefore they are impatient of God's promises, and treat them scornfully, as the Sodomites did His threatenings: and what is this, but the very sin of Esau?

It is the sin of Esau over again, when young persons on first setting out in life, turn away from their gracious God and Saviour, and refuse to give themselves up to His service and obedience: why? because they have already set their heart on this poor miserable world, so soon to pass away: and they know that in order to serve God truly, this evil inclination must be overcome, and they have no will as yet to overcome it. Is this an uncommon case? Nay, let us only remember, as almost all of us may more or less, what usually takes place among us when the Bishop gives notice of a Confirmation. Once in every three years, you know, we are tried in this way. Once in every three years a certain number of young Christians are solemnly called on to choose between God and the world, and to seal their choice, in the most aweful way, by partaking or declining to partake, of their Lord's own Body and Blood, in the Sacrament which He appointed. By God's especial mercy, we trust that that holy ordinance is never without its fruits: yet in each instance how many are there, who fail to present themselves because they are not in a mind for any thing so serious! how many again who will go a certain way, will offer themselves to receive the Bishop's blessing, but will not go on to sacrifice themselves entirely, in soul and body, to their Saviour in the Holy Communion! They will not communicate, believing that if they do, they must hereafter live to God and not to the world. That is, they despise their birthright. They refuse to turn themselves with all their heart towards God. They have asked the way to Zion, they have turned their faces thitherward, but they will not take the next needful step on the road: they have entered in, they think, at the straight gate, but they will not walk along the narrow way. They will find this, by and by to have been the great original sin of their lives: viz. that they neglected, now in their young days, to devote themselves once and for ever to their Saviour in the only effectual way; He called, and they would not answer: thus they sinned the sin of Esau, and before long, without timely repentance and amendment, Esau's bitter cry will be heard from them; they will not find their birthright again, though they seek it carefully with tears.

But over and above this profaneness, running through the whole course of men's lives, they are tempted continually to repeat the sin of Esau: they do so in fact, as often as ever they knowingly commit any grievous sin, against the warnings of their own consciences and the godly motions of the Holy Spirit within them. The pleasure or the profit of the sin is as Esau's mess of pottage. Esau's birthright is the shadow of that hope of Heaven which they rudely scorn and trifle with: Esau's thankless and insolent words, "what profit shall this birthright do to me," are but too exactly, alas! the thoughts of our foolish hearts, when we sin with our eyes open, against warning, and remembering, it may be, the very words of our Lord and Judge, telling us of the miserable consequence of that very sin. It makes no difference whatever, in this respect, what the sin is. It may be uncleanness in thought, word or deed, persisted in even although God's good Providence, at the very same time, recal to a man's mind that saying, "If thine eye or thine hand cause thee to sin, cut them off and cast them from thee: not to be cast into hell, where their worm dieth not and the fire is not quenched [d]." It may be covetousness or unkindness to the afflicted, in which a person has gone on, though he knew Christ's sentence, "[e] If ye did it not to the least of these, ye did it not to Me." It may be that he wilfully lied, with the full knowledge, that all liars shall have their part in the lake that burneth with fire and brimstone. Your sin may have been either of these, or it may have been something different from either of them: but whatever it were, if it were committed with a high hand, if scruples were overpowered, if it was done in a resolute way, as though a man should say to himself, "Come what may, let the Bible say what it will, let our Lord's warnings be never so express, I will enjoy this profit or pleasure:" I say, whenever a man sins in this mood of mind, recollecting eternity but making light of it, he is a profane person, as Esau was: and every word which Holy Scripture speaks concerning Esau ought to come home to the heart of that man.

Now then, now in the accepted time, now while the day of self-examination and repentance lasts, let us bring this aweful matter home to ourselves: let each one ask his own heart as seriously as possible, am I not also guilty of Esau's sin? am I not a profane person in one way or another? either in neglecting to offer myself up, soul and body, with purpose of heart, in Christ's Holy Communion to serve Him truly all the days of my life: or else in going on after some evil desire, when the Holy Comforter within said, "stop: for if you go on, you forfeit God's blessing." Were an angel to go

[d] S. Mark ix. 43. [e] S. Matt. xxv. 45.

round any Christian congregation and engage persons one by one, truly to confess what is upon their consciences, how many, think you, would be found, free from profaneness in both these kinds? how many, who had never wilfully trifled with God's grace, and their own immortal souls?

It may be, that as you hear this, you do not feel particularly alarmed, your own heart does not accuse you of being profane. If it be so indeed, you are happy: but take care: this is a matter in which it is easy to deceive one's self: and if you should be wrong, the forfeit is very dreadful. Remember, Esau went on for many years as if nothing particular had happened: he neither thought himself, nor did others think him, so great a sinner: yet it appeared in the end, that he had lost his birthright by profaneness, and that irrecoverably. O let us pray with all our hearts, that if there be any such thing against us, the merciful God may open our eyes to see it, and our hearts to repent of it, ere it be too late. And that we may find grace truly to repent of the past, let us watch against all profaneness for the time to come. Let us above all things beware of saying in our hearts, "I care not," or "it must take its course," when the question is about ruining or saving our souls, pleasing or displeasing Him who died to save them.

SERMON XII.

THE PROFANENESS OF ESAU A WARNING TO CHRISTIANS.

SECOND SUNDAY IN LENT.

S. MARK viii. 36, 36.

" What shall it profit a man, if he gain the whole world, and lose his own soul ? or what shall a man give in exchange for his soul?"

AWEFUL questions indeed, whoever might ask them of us, how much more aweful, when we consider that *He* asks them, Who alone of all beings can know the entire value of a soul. He alone knows what eternity is, what heaven, and what hell. What unspeakable heights of glory He hath prepared for the bodies which He Himself formed out of the dust of the earth, and for the living souls which He Himself breathed into them ; and what deeps of misery. He Who made your souls and mine, and every living soul of man, He also made heaven and earth, and He knows how to weigh one against another ; and He distinctly tells you here—O my brethren will you not believe Him ? that the price of the whole earth is nothing to set against the loss of one soul ; and that once lost there is nothing which man can give whereby it may be redeemed. His words contain a kind of parable taken from our notions of loss and gain. He supposes a kind of commercial transaction; a man has set his heart on something or other, and he has to consider whether the cost is too great; he is invited to join in some speculation or adventure, and he has to compare the profit with the risk ; the possible future advantage with the immediate and certain hazard. What would a sensible man, but unskilful, do in such a case ? would he not, if he could, seek out some one of knowledge and experience, some one also who dearly loved him and would be sure to advise him for his good ? and having found such an one would he not do well to abide by his counsel, whatever his own fancy or that of others might say against it ? Well here is an Adviser who loves you so well as to have given His life for you, One Who knoweth the end from the beginning, what will be good for you, and what evil, for ever; how all your works will turn out; and He speaks plainly and says, this is good and this is evil ; this is life and this is death ; this is blessing and this is cursing. I have set them before you ; therefore choose life. And besides this plain truth He has set you a plain example. It was but last Sunday that He invited you to go up with Him in spirit into a high mountain whence could be seen all the kingdoms of the earth, and the glory of them. What He did when the devil offered Him all, if He would only fall down and worship him, He invites you and me to do, as often as the like question comes before us. You may say perhaps, "Nay, but that never takes place ; my temptations are in little every day matters; I have nothing to do with the kingdoms of the world, and the glory of them." Well my brother: but have you never met with something which seemed, for the time, as if it were the whole world to you; some profit, or pleasure, or companion, or life-long habit, which you felt as if you could not do without? And on the other hand were you not aware of the plain voice of God in His word and in your own conscience, telling you that you *must* do without it, or lose your own soul? I beseech you, put your mind to this: think well of it: is it not the plain truth? Aye indeed, it is so plain and simple, that we have most of us heard it over and over, and gone away thinking of it as a mere matter of course. But what if each time an Angel was at hand listening, and putting down in the un-erring book what was then read or said to you, and how you took it? what if it should prove hereafter that every time you have had this choice, and chosen amiss, you were doing that very thing which our Saviour here and always, did so earnestly warn His disciples against: preferring this world, or something in it to your own soul? What would have become of you if you had died that moment?

To make this thought the more serious, observe another most aweful truth, plainly implied in the first of our Lord's two questions, "what shall it profit a man if he gain the whole world and lose his own soul?" If you heard this for the first time, could you help saying to yourself "a soul then *may* be lost, after all that has been done for us?" And when you came to read or hear afterwards of one unhappy person, concerning whom our Lord said, "good were it for that man if he had never been born," could you help feeling that such loss would be for ever? O my brethren fix these sayings in your heart, for they are the sayings of love unutterable, to keep you from casting yourselves away, now that He has died and liveth to save you. Lend no ear to the cruel tempter when he would flatter you that after all there may be repentance and forgiveness in hell. Believe your good Saviour when He warns you, and love Him the better for warning you so plainly.

And you may take it as an additional token of His loving care, that we are taught these same lessons to-day, by way of type or parable, in the story of Jacob and Esau. That history was no doubt meant as a help to us, towards fixing in our poor weak unstable minds, how precious our souls are, and how incurable their loss.

It consists of two parts, first, Esau selling his birthright to Jacob in a kind of jest, then God Almighty confirming the sale in very sad earnest, in the matter of Isaac's blessing. The first of these, Esau selling his birthright is meant to be a type and pattern to us of what Christian persons really do, when for any temptation whatever they commit such sin as God has told them will be the death of their souls. The other, Esau seeking vainly his father's blessing, of which you heard in the first lesson just now, is the type and pattern of what will befall wicked Christians when the day of grace shall be past, and they shall find too late, that never again may they hope to be accounted children of God.

The beginning of the mischief, the loss of the birthright, seems not to us, perhaps as we read it, so very shocking. That a person coming in hungry from hunting, should part with his privileges as the

elder son, to his younger brother, for a little broth
or pottage; wild and foolish, and over childish it
may well appear, but why should it be so grave a
sin in the sight of God? The reason is this: the
birthright in that family was a great religious privilege.
It carried with it not only a claim to the
larger and better portion of the father's property, but
also a great blessing from God; the very blessing of
Abraham and of Isaac: God's promise, to be their
God; a God unto them and to their seed after them.
Selling this birthright, then, was in a manner selling
God: it was as if one of us should in some way sell
his own baptismal privilege, as if according to some
ancient stories, a wicked spirit should invite a man
to sign a paper parting for ever with his portion in
Jesus Christ, and the man should accept the invitation.
And the manner of selling it proved but too
clearly how little Esau cared for holy things. For
what was the seeming consideration which induced
him so to part with that which was indeed his all?
Just a little pottage, a little broth, which seemed to
him particularly good when he came in faint and
weary from the field. "'Feed me, I pray thee,
with that same red pottage, for I am faint." Jacob,
moved no doubt by a secret instinct from the Lord,
said to him, "Sell me now thy birthright." Instead
of being shocked at such a thing, Esau said to
himself, "Behold, I am at the point to die:"—not
surely that he would have died for want of all food,
had he missed that which he just then had a fancy
for: no, as faithless persons do, he thought only of
the short time of his own life, and said to himself,

^f Gen. xxv. 30.

what good shall this birthright do me—this promise which cannot be fulfilled until after I am dead? I will give it up, for it is nothing in fact to me, and will just enjoy myself for the present. "I will eat and drink for to-morrow I shall die." Jacob, no doubt again by providential instinct, to draw Esau's attention to the seriousness of what he was doing, calls on him to confirm the bargain in the most solemn way, by swearing to him, calling God to witness; and Esau does not even shrink from that. He is not afraid to call God to witness, that he willingly and knowingly gives up God's blessing, for a little broth which pleased his appetite. And so, as the holy book goes on to tell us, "Jacob gave Esau bread and pottage of lentiles, and he did eat and drink, and rose up, and went his way: thus Esau despised his birthright."

Are you ready to cry shame upon him? Do you stand amazed at his irreligious trifling with his God? well you may: but consider my brethren, whether your next thought should not be to cry shame on yourselves—to be amazed at your own trifling, in times past, perhaps even down to this very hour, your own irreligious trifling with God's best gift to your souls, your birthright as a *Christian* bestowed on you in Holy Baptism. For of this you may be quite sure, that in every instance in which you have knowingly and purposely broken any one of God's plain commandments, upon any earthly consideration whatever, you have committed the sin of which Esau's was but a shadow; you have done despite unto the Spirit of grace, and deserved to forfeit your baptismal privileges. It does not signify what the sin was: the wilful deadly sins of Christians are in that respect all alike, that each of them is selling our birthright as cheaply as Esau sold his; for the whole world and all that is in it, is no more in comparison of our souls, than Esau's mess of pottage was, in comparison of the blessing which he parted with.

All our grievous sins are so far like one another, and like Esau's; but perhaps the likeness to Esau's is most visible in what are called sins of the flesh. The drunkard, the glutton, the impure, what has each one of these to shew for his bargain, when the pleasure of a few moments is over? what will he think of it by and by, when from the other side of the grave he looks back upon his foul and shameful satisfactions, and begins to count the cost of them? Esau seems to have been a man for present enjoyment, such a man as is sometimes called "nobody's enemy but his own," and so far, indulgence in carnal sin may appear to answer most exactly to his ill behaviour. As the Epistle to the Hebrews intimates, saying, "g Take heed lest there be among you any fornicator or profane person, as Esau, who for one morsel of meat sold his birthright."

But yet there may be Esaus in regard of other sins too, as when a person is undutiful, or steals, or slanders, or satisfies his spite or envy towards another, though he knows it is grievous sin; the little brief indulgence is more to him than the fear of God, the love of Christ and the hope of Heaven. Is not this too selling one's birthright for a morsel of meat? and so in short is all behaviour which Scripture

g Heb. xii. 16.

teaches us to call "profane." Esau is the proper type of all "profane" Christians.

In this again, which of us, alas, will venture to say that he himself has never been in any respect an Esau, that he has never wilfully made light of his own high calling and hope, never knowingly trifled with his baptismal vow, for something which even at the time he knew to be of small consequence? for example, how many an one has deliberately told a lie lest he should be laughed at, lest he should miss some amusement or pleasure, which at most would last a few hours, lest he should undergo some little punishment which would do him no real harm. Whenever we sin, the gain really is to the loss, no more than as a mess of pottage to Esau's birthright: but this profane temper of which we are speaking actually accepts it *as* a mess of pottage; "I dont care," it says: "at all events I will please myself for the moment: I will crown myself with rosebuds before they wither; let good books and holy men, the Bible and the Church, say what they please: I know all *that*, but I will not let it daunt me : I will let Eternity take care of itself: I will have my own way for the present, come what will."

Esau was not really starving, nor did he think himself to be so. But he scorned the promise because he should have to wait long for it—because the better part of it would only come after his death, and we have seen that it is much the same with all *Christians* who deal profanely with their God, who trifle with baptismal vows and gifts, and with their own precious souls; with all who, being warned, make light of holy obedience, and amuse themselves, as it were, with sin. What shall it profit them, to gain a whole world of such amusement and satisfaction as this, and in the end to lose their own souls? What shall it profit them? It is our Lord Himself Who asks the question—who can answer it?

But perhaps you will say, "It is not for long: I mean, before I am many years older, to repent; I have heard that to such as repent God is very merciful, and that He has promised to remember their sins no more." Perhaps you say, or rather indistinctly think, "I hope to have my soul saved at last, though I do indulge for the present in what our Lord has told me will ruin it." But listen, I beseech you, to our Saviour's second question, and attend to the second part of this sad history of Esau. Our Saviour having stated first, that the whole world is nothing to compare with a man's soul, goes on to ask, supposing that soul once lost, what ransom can any man offer, what can he find to give in exchange for it? We know that all souls were once utterly lost, and no *man* could find or give any ransom. God Himself found one, the Sacrifice of His own Incarnate Son, but man could never have found or contrived any. But now that we have been once ransomed, if any of us wilfully lose ourselves again, who will be our ransom a second time? The answer of Scripture is very plain and very alarming, "[h] If we go on sinning wilfully after that we have received the knowledge of the truth, there remaineth no more sacrifice for sin, but a fearful looking for of judgement." Now this is your very condition, whosoever of you put off your seriousness and your repentance to a more convenient

[h] Heb. x. 26.

season. You are still sinning wilfully, after that you have received the knowledge of the truth. *If you die such as you are now, you are lost.* True, you are yet on your trial, and so still have a chance, but at present the trial is going against you, and your chance lessening every hour. What are you to do, if while you are thus lingering the Bridegroom should appear, and your time of trial be over? Remember the conclusion of Esau's sad history. By and by, when he perhaps had forgotten his profane bargain, or as the manner of some is, remembered it only to make mirth upon it, God in His Providence caused him to miss the special blessing of his father Isaac, on which he had now set his heart. He sought a place of repentance; such repentance as would put him again in the condition of the first-born which he had forfeited. But he found no such place, though he sought it carefully with tears. He was quite in earnest, then; at least so far as the worldly portion of Abraham's blessing was concerned. He greatly desired that his family should rule over Jacob's family, even when he should be dead. But he found it too late. The blessing had passed over to Jacob, and could not be recalled. So will those who go on deferring their repentance, find, some day before they expect, that their trial is over, their time of repentance is past. They will knock at the door, but the Bridegroom will say, I know you not. Having passed their years *here* in despising their birthright, they *may*, when they come *there*, they *may*, and they *will*, cry out as Esau, with an exceeding loud and bitter cry; but they will never really repent, any more than Esau did. And that he in that distress, did not truly and fully repent, we are sure; for what was his comfort in the great disappointment? Why, he comforted himself touching Jacob with a purpose to kill him. So far, surely, he was impenitent, and his tears had been tears of vexation, not of contrition. We may hope and believe, from what we read in Genesis, that his anger turned away, and that he did a long time after, really repent of his unbrotherly mind, and forgive his brother. But there was no place for such a repentance as might win him back his birthright: and in this he bears the mournful image of Christians, who have lived and died profanely. There is no hope at all for them: they have no ransom for their own souls, and have rejected Him Who is the true and only Ransom.

Perhaps some such, on coming to their latter end, feeling themselves to be on their death-bed, tried to repent, they sought place for repentance, and that earnestly, as it seemed to those around them. So far, there is hope for them; but it must be more or less an uncertain hope, a fearful and trembling hope: not such a hope as one would wish to feel, both in dying, and in waiting upon the beds of the dying. But alas! the far greater part, apparently, of those who trifle with their God as Esau did, come at the last to no better a repentance than Esau's.

Whatever you do then, dear brethren, my younger brethren especially—avoid profaneness. Put away irreverent reading, loose thoughts, irreligious companions. Above all, put away lust and uncleanness: as for other reasons, so especially for this, that it tends so to make men utterly profane. Never sell your soul for a morsel of meat; or if you have unhappily done so, make haste and redeem it by laying hold of Christ as a penitent, whilst you are yet in this world, whilst you are yet so far happier than Esau, as to have your Lord still within reach, still offering you place of repentance. This, thank God, is our condition—yours and mine—at this present moment. To this end hath He spared us to see another Lent, that we may consider how we have hitherto dealt with our glorious birthright; that, on our knees, in the bitterness of our soul, we may by His help remember and confess our secret sins especially; the many times that His Spirit has whispered, "O do not this abominable thing," and we have gone on and done it; that submitting ourselves humbly to His chastisements and clinging to His Cross, we may ask His pardon with all our hearts and be absolved, and wilfully sin no more. Amen. So be it, O Lord, through Him Who alone can obtain it for us, Thy Son Jesus Christ our Saviour. To Whom &c.

SERMON XIII.

OF ABOUNDING MORE AND MORE.

SECOND SUNDAY IN LENT.

1 THESS. iv. 1.

" We beseech you, brethren, and exhort you by the Lord Jesus, that as ye have received of us how ye ought to walk, and to please God, so ye would abound more and more."

IF any one wishes to see, what it is to begin well in Christian faith and practice, and, at the same time, what care should be taken not to depend too much upon mere beginnings, however praiseworthy, he cannot do better than examine carefully these two Epistles of S. Paul to the Christians of Thessalonica.

The Apostle seems hardly to know how to say enough of their faith and charity, or of the noble and self-denying way in which they had received the Gospel. They had received it, he says, in much affliction (being persecuted by Jews, and Gentiles too, the moment they were seen to favour it), yet with joy of the Holy Ghost; joy, that is, poured into their hearts by the Holy Spirit of God; and thus they became ensamples and patterns to all the Christians of those countries; and having so received it, they continued in it, not failing at all either in their faith towards God, or in their affection to

S. Paul himself. This was such a delight to him, as can only be expressed in his own affectionate words. "[i] Brethren, we were comforted over you in all our affliction and distress by your faith: for now we live, if ye stand fast in the Lord. For what thanks can we render to God again for you, for all the joy, wherewith we joy for your sakes before our God; night and day praying exceedingly that we might see your face?"

There could not well be more promising converts; and yet the very next words show how anxious he was that they might not trust in their first promising conversion, "Praying exceedingly, that we might see your face:" to what purpose? not for his own pleasure, but "to perfect that which was lacking in their faith." The same feeling runs through the whole of the letter; his joy in what they *had* done is everywhere tempered by a real and serious anxiety, lest they should stop short, and begin to think they had done enough. Both are shown together, in the verse which begins the Epistle for this day: "We beseech you, brethren, and exhort you by the Lord Jesus, that as ye have received of us how ye ought to walk, and to please God, so ye would abound more and more." "As ye have received of us how ye ought to walk;"—that is an acknowledgment of their having begun well: "we beseech and exhort you by the Lord Jesus, that ye would abound more and more;"—that is a call, as serious as the heart of man could imagine, not to stand still, not to suppose they had done enough. And with reason is the verse chosen by the Church for one of her Epistles

[i] 1 Thes. iii. 8, 9, 10.

proper for Lent; since one indispensable mark of true repentance is a daily, unwearied endeavour to improve. This I shall first endeavour to shew, and then add some remarks on the sinfulness of neglecting such endeavours, the danger we are in of doing so, and the most effectual way of guarding both ourselves and others against that danger.

Now, with regard to the absolute necessity of continual improvement, it appears, in the first place, from this circumstance, that if we rightly value the first good beginning, we must, from the very nature of the case, go on from one degree of holiness to another. Men may very well do something which looks like repentance upon poor imperfect worldly reasons, and may deceive themselves and others into a notion that they are true Christian penitents; as, for example, intemperance may be left off for health or character's sake, or a quarrel may be made up with a view to our worldly interest, or the fear of approaching death may drive men against their will to long-neglected ordinances of religion; and it is no wonder if such a repentance as this very soon begin to stand still: if, having reached such and such a point, the man imagine himself good enough, and take no more pains to be better: but this is quite contrary to the nature of true repentance upon Christian principles.

By Christian principles, I mean first a deep sense of the continual presence of Almighty God, and of the care He takes for the welfare of our souls. Consider this peculiar presence deliberately and seriously, and let it prevail with you to change your ways in earnest, and begin to turn from the sin, whatever it be, to which you feel yourself most inclined. When you have done so, you will still perceive in your heart exactly the same reason, why you should go on and repent yet more perfectly, and serve and obey your all-seeing God, yet more affectionately and sincerely : and so on from day to day, through every degree of repentance and obedience. Remember only in earnest that God is watching you, and you can never, surely, be quite satisfied with yourself; you can never think you have thought, said, and done, virtuously enough, to be fit and worthy to stand in His sight.

This, I say, would be the natural consequence of considering God's presence in a Christian manner. I say, "in a Christian manner," because, if we considered it apart from what the Gospel teaches, it might naturally (though not reasonably) lead many of us to despair, instead of endeavouring to improve. Men might say to themselves, "When we have done our best, there is no standing before this Just and Holy God; therefore we may as well give it up, and enjoy ourselves while we can." Such was the impiety of many, before the Gospel was made known. Let us hope that there are none among us, who are even now guilty of the like blasphemous thoughts; for indeed they are most blasphemous and inexcusable in every one who knows what Christ has done and suffered for us, and what grace and assistance His Holy Spirit is always waiting to bestow upon us. We are sure now, how feeble soever we may find ourselves, that whatever we do sincerely, in the way of goodness, is sure to tell; we dare not therefore despond, and we have no excuse whatever, if we do not carry on our first good beginnings, and repent better and better every day of our lives.

This is yet more absolutely necessary, because, if men do not improve, they are, in practice, sure to go back. They cannot stay where they are; they must either grow worse or better. For it is the nature of all strong impressions to act vehemently on the mind at first, and after a little time to fade away as it were, and gradually become weaker and weaker. Thus the fear of God, and the dread of sin and punishment, in which repentance usually begins, if we do not, resolutely and on purpose, endeavour to keep them up, are sure to lose their force on our minds. We must pray to God, day after day, that we may fear Him more and more; or else, as the world continues close to us, and we cannot avoid being tempted, we are sure, in fact, day after day, to fear Him less and less. We must without any delay set about *doing* right, and not trust in any degree to mere right *feeling*, however earnest and sincere. The feeling of its own accord will grow weaker and pass away; but we shall be no losers by that, if we take care to strengthen ourselves in the habit of doing what is right and religious. S. Paul, no doubt, was more overpowered at first with remorse for his sins, and the terror of God's presence, immediately after his conversion, than he was in after years, when the truths of the Gospel had become familiar to him. But he was improving, nevertheless, all the time; because, what he lost in intense and passionate feeling, he more than made up by his fixed, habitual piety. But if he had allowed the one to abate, without serious and constant endeavours to cherish and advance the other; if, when he waked from his trance of fear and astonishment on his conversion, he had taken no particular pains to become a better Christian, who does not see that even *his* good impressions would by degrees have died away, and he would, naturally and of course, have lost the benefit of God's gracious invitation to repentance?

Just so will it turn out with any one of ourselves, who may be so presumptuous as to imagine, that he can by any means stand still in his course of piety and virtue. Suppose, for instance, a man possessed with an evil spirit of covetousness, or pride, or malice, or any bad desire, in which he may have gone on for many years; and suppose some illness or misfortune to take place, which causes him, for a while, to have serious fears of his own everlasting condition. As long as those fears last, he will seem to himself and others, perhaps he will really be a better man than he was. But the illness goes off; the misfortune is remedied; and the emotion of fear and remorse is blunted by time, or overpowered by newer and probably more enticing passions. Is not this man in the greatest possible jeopardy? Must he not watch and pray, form deliberate resolutions, and deny himself dangerous liberties? In short, must he not spend his whole life in steadily and considerately trying to become less and less proud, less and less covetous, less and less dissolute? And if he neglect to do so, will he not of course, and without any effort, fall back into a worse condition than he was in before his partial recovery? An Apostle has taught us what to think of this. "ᵏ If after they have escaped the pollutions of the world through the knowledge of the Lord and Saviour Jesus Christ, they are again entangled therein and overcome, the latter end is worse with them than the beginning. For it had been better for them not to have known the way of righteousness, than after they had known it, to turn from the holy commandment delivered unto them."

Consider what has been said, and you must perceive that the only reasonable and the only safe way is, having once begun the work of religion, to be always labouring to "abound more and more."

And, over and above this, we are to recollect what our Blessed Saviour has clearly intimated, that there are degrees of glory in the world to come; and those who have made the best use of their time and talents shall receive the highest reward. No man can ever know for certain that he himself has done enough, considering his privileges and opportunities of various kinds, to make his salvation sure if he were to die this moment. But if he could be certain of this, still reason, and conscience, and wisdom, and gratitude, would urge him to lose no time, but press forward and forward to obtain as much as ever he could of the inestimable joys of eternity. Too many of us, up to this time, have been sadly perverting the mercy of God, in leaving it unknown to us how far He is pleased with us at any time. He meant that the uncertainty of our spiritual condition should urge us on to continual improvement; that we should never dream we had done enough. We take it as if we might indulge ourselves more freely

ᵏ 2 S. Pet. ii. 20.

in doubtful things; as if we had done quite enough for ourselves, when we are not quite *sure* that we are in a bad way. Let us be persuaded henceforth to try and have better minds.

It may help us, in judging more truly of our duty in this respect, if we put ourselves, as nearly as we can, in the place of these Thessalonians, who had learned Christianity from the lips of S. Paul himself. For, indeed, we are very nearly in their place; we, like them, have received of the Apostles how we ought to walk and to please God. The only difference is, that they received this knowledge by word of mouth, we by reading the Apostolic letters and listening to the Apostolic Church. Now what sort of a spirit and temper should we have judged these Thessalonians to be of, if we found that as soon as their teacher was gone away to Athens, they had become careless about his instructions, thought much of what they had done already, and took no pains whatever to improve? Whatever censure we pass on them, we must acknowledge surely to be due to ourselves, in such measure as we neglect the duty of amending daily, because our Teacher is out of sight.

Yet this is what we are sure to do, if we be not constantly exhorted and reminded of it; nay, there is great reason to fear that all exhortation may prove in vain. For, first of all, having been bred up from our cradle in the *knowledge and understanding* of our Christian duty, we are apt to fancy ourselves familiar with the *practice* of it too. We are convinced in our minds that we *know* it well enough; and this of itself inclines us to be too soon satisfied with our accustomed way of doing it. Let us recollect ourselves a little. Have we not, up to this day, very many of us, been saying good words over and over so often, and so inattentively, that it might seem as if we imagined good thoughts and good actions would come after them of course, without any particular effort or trouble on our part? We grow tired of watching, of prayer, of self-denial, simply because it is the same thing over and over again: and so it must of course be, as long as the temptations are the same which we have to resist. But they will not be the same : they will be stronger and stronger, if we give way to this feeling of weariness. And, on the other hand, if we patiently strive against it; if we *force* ourselves to attend to great and eternal truths, however often we have attended to them before, our task will not perhaps seem easier to ourselves, but our reward will be surer in Heaven, and we shall stand higher in the favour of God. We shall, though we may not feel it, gradually become holier and better men, by the mere effort and anxious endeavour not to become in any degree worse.

Again; a sincere Christian will be on his guard, that he make no dangerous comparisons between himself and his neighbours. It will never do to take it for granted that we keep our place in respect of piety and goodness; that we are no worse than we were, in fact;—because we are no worse in comparison with them. It may be that all around you are gone astray from GOD, and in the way to everlasting ruin. If such turn out to be the case, you may excuse and flatter yourself now, that you are no worse than they; but it will be little comfort to you in the day of account, when you find that your condemnation is as bad as theirs. Obvious however as these reflections are, very few Christians indeed have courage to bear them practically in mind. We look to see what our neighbours are doing, instead of applying ourselves, with all our might, to the performance of God's will as soon as we know it; and thus throw away, one after another, our best chance of improvement and perfection. Each time that we give way to bad example, our transgression seems more natural and easy to us, till at length it comes as a matter of course, and we hardly reckon ourselves the worse for it. There is no such enemy to real amendment, as a too anxious regard either to the opinions or example of others.

These are some of the many temptations which beset us at every moment of our lives, and are the cause why too many Christians, instead of seeking to abound more and more, go backward in goodness as they draw nearer their latter end; temptations, great, and near, and powerful; it is impossible, do what we will, to remove ourselves quite out of their reach. They must be met and overcome, for they cannot be avoided.

And how are we to meet them? By true principles and steady purposes; by a deep mistrust of ourselves, and as deep a confidence in that Almighty Spirit, who is always at hand to help us. The Apostle, in three words of the text, has pointed out to us what we should do. "We beseech you, brethren," says he, "and exhort you, by the Lord Jesus." That Name once mentioned, enough is said to awaken, in any considerate Christian, a fixed resolution to improve daily, and a comfortable hope of grace to do so.

For we are not to suppose that S. Paul introduced the sacred Name of our Saviour merely to strengthen his own expression, and make the Thessalonians more attentive. There is more in it, a great deal, than this comes to. It was as if he had said, "Do you believe in good earnest that the Son of God died on the cross, to save you from your sins? then remember that you must be conformed to His death, or He will have died in vain for you; that the Lord Jesus Christ, our Saviour and Redeemer, is now and ever present with you, by His divine power and Godhead; that He seeks your salvation now as anxiously as when He prayed for you, hanging on the Cross; that He feels all your wants and infirmities, knows exactly where your weak places are, and is prepared to strengthen and assist you the moment you seriously ask Him? Can you believe this, and lie slothfully down, not caring whether you please or offend Him; whether you are growing better or worse?"

Again, when S. Paul calls on us to abound more and more, by the Name of Jesus Christ, it was as if he had said, "Do you believe what the Gospel tells you of our Blessed Master's pure and perfect example? that He spent His nights in prayer and His days in charity? that He 'went about doing good?' that His worst enemies could find no fault in Him? that He laid down His life for His betrayers and murderers, and died praying to His Father for them? Do you indeed believe this? Then how can you be contented to live as you are living? to die as you are likely to die? so very imperfect in your faith, your purity, and charity; so very unlike your Holy and Divine Redeemer. How can you be at rest a single moment, without trying at least to come a little nearer His example, before your time of trial is over?"

Again, the Name of our Lord is here used to put us in mind to Whom we are accountable; as if it were said, "In the Name of Him Who will come to be your Judge, I charge you to be careful of every moment of your time, every talent of your mind and body. I charge you, make the most of them all; for you know not how soon you may be called to answer for all, in a world where it will be too late to think of improving."

Lastly, the Name of Christ is used to remind all who have ears to hear, of His awful warnings concerning those who are too soon contented with their own imperfect repentance. "When the unclean spirit is gone out of a man, he walketh through dry places, seeking rest." The evil one being driven out of our souls and bodies, either by Baptism or by true and sufficient repentance, will not rest until he have obtained a lodging in one miserable person or another: and if he possibly can, he will return to the same again. Beware of him: for if he find the house empty, he will not return alone, but with "seven other spirits more wicked than himself." They will "enter in and dwell there:" there will be little or no chance of their being ever any more cast out: "and the last state of that man will be worse than the first;" by how much he has abused greater grace, and become more like a fallen angel.

"I beseech you therefore, brethren, and exhort you by the Lord Jesus;" by His Cross and Passion; by His continual Fatherly Presence; by His gracious and perfect Example; by His severe threatenings against the unprofitable ; and by His coming again to be our Judge :—I beseech you, "that as ye have received of us how ye ought to walk and to please God, so ye would abound more and more."

SERMON XIV.

THE WOMAN OF CANAAN.

SECOND SUNDAY IN LENT.

S. Mark vii. 28, 29.

"And she answered and said, Yes, Lord; yet the dogs under the table eat of the children's crumbs. He said unto her, For this saying go thy way: the devil is gone out of thy daughter."

WE heard just now in the Gospel, the history of the woman of Canaan, how she came begging of our Lord to cast the unclean spirit out of her daughter, how He kept her long waiting, and made as though the mercy could not be granted: and how at last as one even wondering at her faith, and as if He were unable to resist such prayers, He said, "Be it unto thee even as thou wilt." A most beautiful and touching history it is, most full of comfort to all loving hearts, when any belonging to them are in affliction or in sin, and they kneel before God to pray for them; full of comfort to fathers and mothers offering up their supplications for their little ones when they cannot pray for themselves: full of comfort to us all, when our hopes, as must often be the case, are deferred and we feel sick at heart, with waiting so long on our God, and wondering whether or no He will grant us the desire of our soul. I think there is something practised continually in this and other Churches, which may well remind us of this history. We are continually asking your prayers, my brethren, the prayers of the Church for this or that sick person, for this or that portion of our fellow Christians, on whom the Lord seems to be laying His afflicting hand. Day after day, week after week, month after month, nay often year after year, the same names are repeated, the same objects of intercession recommended to you, before the Litany, and also before the Holy Sacrifice and Sacrament of our Lord's Body and Blood; and I dare say the thought at times crosses many of our minds, why should we go on so long mentioning the same objects? is it really worth while? Now, my brethren we do not mean it so, but this is at the bottom an unbelieving thought. If the prayers of the Church were good for a sick man or for one in trouble a twelvemonth ago, they are just as good now, supposing the grief or sickness to go on. Ask the poor man himself: if he have true considerate faith, he will not wish the Church to leave off praying for him. You would not in his place: do then as you would be done by: try to remember in earnest each one of your brethren who so asks your prayers, however often he may have asked them before. Perhaps one hearty prayer more is the very thing God is waiting for to bestow on him some great comfort or blessing.

But now I go back to the history of the woman of Canaan. Besides the comfort it offers to a Christian at prayer; I want to shew you how it is very particularly a Lent lesson; how it may help us in the spiritual work of this holy season in particular. In the first place it helps us to war against the devil. Last Sunday the Gospel, as you know, was the account of our Lord's Temptation shewing us each one how to resist that wicked one when he attacks us in our own proper persons. To-day's Gospel shews us how to fight against him when he seems to be having his own way with some one whom we are bound to care for, whose soul we are bound to care for. You have a son or a daughter, a brother or a sister, a friend or companion, or some one committed to your charge: and that person we will suppose is unhappily living in some grievous deadly sin; he is in such a condition, that if he died this moment, there is no help for it, he must perish for ever. What are you to do? you have spoken to him over and over, but he will not hear, you have tried all ways you can think of with him, and it still seems to do him no good: well then, this Gospel tells you that if you can do nothing *with* him, at least there is one thing which you may do *for* him. You may cast yourself down as Moses did, forty days and forty nights praying for his stubborn unbelieving countrymen, you may do the same this very Lent, for any one belonging to you, who seems to be going the wrong way. Every day you may add to your prayers a short petition for your friend whose soul is in danger: and who knows but that petition may be answered even before you have got up from your knees? Put the case which our Lord's words most especially put us in mind of, the case of unclean, impure behaviour. The woman's daughter "was vexed with an unclean spirit." Poor creature! she was like thousands more who grow up and go on in uncleanness, till they are really quite possessed with it, as with a bad and fallen angel. They feel as if they could not help themselves, so entirely subject have they become to sinful lust, "the law in their members warring against the law of their mind." They are such as the Apostle describes: "Having eyes full of adultery, and that cannot cease from sin." God help them, poor creatures! against the great enemy! May God touch and turn their hearts! for vain is the help of man. But then, the less you can do for them, the more you should pray for them. The woman of Canaan could of herself do nothing for her child, but this one thing she could do, she could find out Jesus, and pray to Him: and this she did with all her might. She prayed and prayed, and by and by came the answer. Will you do the same for any friend or kinsman of your's, whom you believe or fear to be living in uncleanness. Try; it will be the very least you can do, but it will prove a great thing if you try in earnest.

But I must warn you, that you will not try in earnest to pray for the soul of one sinning by impurity, unless you be deeply convinced of the guilt of impurity in your own soul, in your own life and heart, so far as you have ever given way to it. If you think it a trifle yourself, you will never pray as you ought for your friend or child to be delivered from it. A mother may be really anxious to have her daughter steady, a father may make a great point of his son's keeping out of bad company, but it may be merely on account of the inconvenience and discredit it will bring upon you in this world, and then neither their advice, nor the prayers which they seem to themselves to make, will be likely to do their children much good. If they in their young days have sinned at all in the same kind, O let them make haste to repent of those sins, deeply, bitterly, with all their hearts, and then they may hope to have their prayers heard, when they come to our Blessed Lord and ask Him to cast the unclean spirit out of their son or daughter. But if in your secret heart you think it a matter of course for young persons to sin more or less in that way, and so feel little troubled at the remembrance of your own sin; it will be a wonder if such evil ever depart from your house. You will not be able to keep your children steady, for you will not pray as you ought that the unclean spirit may go out of them.

Now this woman in the Gospel will teach you if you will mind her, how to repent both of your lusts, and of every other transgression which stains your conscience. That is the other Lent lesson which you may learn of her, though she was not even an Israelite, and you are a Christian. This poor woman was at the beginning far from Christ in every sense: she was a Greek, a Heathen or Gentile, living out of the Holy Land in the coasts of Tyre and Sidon; she was far from Christ in her home, and far in her religion, not however so far perhaps as too many of Christ's own people have made themselves by their sins. Perhaps you are amongst them: then hear what she did, and do you go and do likewise. First she watches for her Lord and Saviour, she found out when He came nigh, she would not for the world lose the chance which His coming afforded her. She went out to meet Him, and as it seems, did meet Him first on the road, and there applied to Him, and when He made as though He did not hear her, when He answered her not a word, she did not leave off, but still kept calling upon Him "have mercy on me, O Lord, Thou Son of David; my daughter is grievously vexed with a devil." So persevering was she, and in such an agony did she pray, that the disciples had pity on her, and hinted to our Lord that it would be well to give her what she asked, that she might leave off troubling them. "Send her away for she crieth after us." Then when He had gone into a house seeking to have no man know it, He could not be hid: she found him out, and still her prayer and her cry was the same. My brethren, when shall we be like this poor Gentile woman, in seeking from the Son of David that we and those belonging to us may be quite freed from the evil spirit? when shall we return to our prayers again and again, as she did, and take no denial, nor ever be contented until He has really cast out the evil one, made us whole of whatsoever disease, whatsoever bad custom we are living in? we who instead of seeking Him out, too often rather avoid Him, and draw back on purpose from where we know Him to be, who shut the book, or cut short the conversation when we see it is going to be edifying: in whose ears is the sound of the Church bell, and we cannot think why it should go so often: who put off holy things, the seeking of Christ, until the world has turned its back upon us, or we have lost the power of enjoying it. O be wise, be dutiful, be grateful in time,

L

seek out your Lord while you yet have a choice, while you have some little to give up for Him, lest He refuse to be found of you at all: for why should the great King, our God and Saviour condescend to be the happiness of those who fall back upon Him as it were, because they can find nothing better?

But this believing woman has discovered Him in His hiding place and lo! she is again at His Feet. She worships Him crying "Lord help me!" He, still trying her faith, makes answer in a tone of something like reproach, "it is not meet to take the children's bread," i.e., My mercies are to be yet for awhile granted to the Israelites only, who are children in Christ's family; not to the Gentiles who as yet are no better than dogs. And then comes her answer, that remarkable answer which caused even Christ to wonder, and makes her a very special example to all who come to serve God. "Truth, Lord, yet the dogs eat of the crumbs which fall from their master's table." The reproach of being classed with dogs did not in the least affront her. She only made it a fresh occasion of prayer. To be sure, I and the like of me, are but as dogs, we pretend to no better: but even the dogs under the table eat of the children's crumbs. O rare combination of entire faith and true humility! nothing could make her leave off prayer, nothing could tempt her to think well of herself and of her prayers. And see how great and rare her reward! not only the immediate healing of her daughter, but the especial praise of our Lord, "O woman great is thy faith: be it unto thee even as thou wilt." And moreover to have her saying put into the Church's Liturgy:

those of you who are communicants will remember it, just before the Consecration of the Bread and Wine to be His Body and Blood. For there we are taught by the Church to confess, that we are not worthy so much as to gather up the crumbs under His table, and yet at the same time to pray for the highest, blessing He can give. " That our sinful bodies may be made clean by His Body, and our souls washed through His most precious Blood, and that we may evermore dwell in Him and He in us."

This untiring faith, this unfeigned humility, the woman of Canaan practised for her child's sake, but our Lord's Will is that we His servants should practise it, each one for his soul's sake. He wants you to come to Him one by one, crying out and saying, "Have mercy on me O Lord Thou Son of David! my soul is grievously vexed" with the devil of lust, of malice, of what not. He wants you to know the plague of your own heart, and to seek your cure, where only it can be had, from Him. He wants you to come praying to Him, not once nor twice, but as a regular thing, without which you cannot be comfortable. He wants you to keep on praying, not to give up because He seems to hide Himself from you, always to pray and not to faint. Above all, He wants you to be very humble, to think very lowly and meanly of yourself, and to go on doing so, all along, even when you may have good hope that by God's grace you are in some measure reformed, and that He has forgiven and is forgiving you. Every day you call yourself a miserable sinner: take care that you mean what you say: do not come before God, as the Pharisees did, with a lie in your mouth.

Shall I tell you how you may judge yourself, whether you are committing this great sin or no? Watch yourself in your daily life and conversation, how you take reproof and ill usage from others. It stings you of course, it is unpleasant, it cannot be otherwise. But the true penitent puts down those angry feelings, saying to himself, it is no more than I deserve, if not for this, yet for some other part of my behaviour, some secret which God knows and I know. He will say like the contrite thief on the cross, I indeed suffer justly, for reproach is the due reward of my deeds, though in this matter I may have done nothing amiss. Is this your way, when you are reproved or affronted? or do you fall into a passion, and turn away your mind from your own sin, thinking only of the affront you have received? If such be your mind and way, depend on it you are not yet a real penitent in God's sight, not yet one of those to whom the merciful promises are made. You are not yet like the woman of Canaan. For what was the very point which so recommended her to Christ's special blessing? Not simply her perseverance in prayer, but her taking reproof and hard words as she did. Which of us would not be ready with an angry answer, or at least with an angry bitter thought, if we came to ask a favour of another, and he sent us away telling us we were no better than dogs? But she was not at all angry. Why? because she was so very humble: she felt that it was no more than she deserved: and this, my brethren, (mark it well), was the very thing which brought down the blessing she asked. For He did not say only, "great is thy faith," but He added, "for this saying (i.e. about the dogs eating of the crumbs) " for this saying go thy way; the devil is gone out of thy daughter." She prayed, and He seemed not to hear: she persevered, and still He refused, she believed, but even that was not enough, but the moment she took the affront patiently, the Lord's gracious word was spoken.

Would you wish God to hear your prayers, when you say them this very night? Take care to be patient, indulge no bitter thoughts, should any one offend you between this and then. The way to be forgiven and heard is, not merely to call yourself a miserable sinner before God, but knowing yourself to be such, not to be put out when others treat you as such.

It is a great grace: but He will not deny it, if we ask Him in earnest.

SERMON XV.

THE HARD SERVICE OF SIN.

Deut. xxviii. 47, 48.

"*Because thou servedst not the Lord thy God with joyfulness and with gladness of heart for the abundance of all things; therefore thou shalt serve thine enemies which the Lord shall send against thee, in hunger and thirst, and nakedness, and in want of all things.*"

It is no very uncommon notion among men, that if God would change their condition they should serve Him better; the devil takes occasion from some circumstances of their calling or situation in life to put evil thoughts in their hearts, and they commit sin accordingly, and then he, the same watchful enemy, is at hand to suggest an excuse also for their sin. He persuades them, if he can, that the sin is not their fault, but that it is owing to the state in which they find themselves, and could not be helped. E. g. when poor persons are tempted to put their hand to their neighbour's goods, I dare say they very often quiet their consciences more or less, by saying to themselves, it is the fault of their poverty, if they were as well off as such and such others, they would not think of such a thing. Others indulge evil and unclean imaginations, and say, it would not be so with them, if God's Providence did not keep them back from some favourite object of innocent hope and desire. Thus in one form or another, those who have followed Adam in his sin, follow him also in making excuses for his sin. Adam's saying was, "The woman whom Thou gavest to be with me, she gave me of the tree, and I did eat :" as if it were the Almighty's fault, for putting him into such seducing company, so that he could hardly help breaking the commandment.

If any of you my brethren has ever encouraged himself to imitate Adam in laying the blame of his sin upon his Maker, I would ask him just to consider this one thing, how was it with him when in outward matters God seemed most indulgent to him? how was it with us in our prosperous hours, when we had most of our own way? All of us, even the most severely tried, can remember some portion of our life which seemed by comparison bright and comfortable, at any rate, the years of our childhood and our early youth were years of more or less hope and cheerfulness. If we were poor, we had not the care and anxiety of poverty; if some were unkind to us, we had to sustain us, the natural light-heartedness which belongs to the morning of life. Well, how was it with us, in respect of God's service, in those days of hope and prosperity? Alas, too commonly we either forgot Him, we disregarded the Giver in the enjoyment of the gifts, or if we did serve Him after a fashion, having been told of Him by our parents and teachers, and not daring to turn our backs upon Him altogether, the service was in too many ways willfuly imperfect, we did as little for Him as we dared, said as few prayers as we might, without being entirely irreligious; murmured and fretted at the length of holy services, and at being ordered so often to Church, thought it hard whenever we were called upon to give up what we had set our hearts upon, in order to serve Him the better. Is not this too true an account of the childhood and early youth, and generally of the most favoured and prosperous days of many of us? that either we refused to serve God at all, or we refused to serve Him in joyfulness and gladness of heart, what little we did offer, was blemished with our own ill temper and discontent. In this as in many other respects, our fathers who came out of Egypt were too true a type and shadow of us Christians. Not only in the wilderness, encompassed as they were by all manner of special mercies, but still more after they came into Canaan, and were in actual enjoyment of the promises, they either cast aside the Lord's easy yoke, or wore it in continual fretfulness and uneasiness: wishing all the while, that they were free to take the same liberties with the unbelieving nations around them. It came into their hearts, how pleasant it would be if they could be as the heathen, the families of the countries, to serve wood and stone, and enjoy themselves in the feasts of the idols. As their fathers in the desert, even when they durst not make themselves false gods, still went on fretting and murmuring, wished themselves back in Egypt, because they were tired of the manna, and wanted flesh and fruit; so the children and posterity in the land of Canaan were never without some cause of complaint against God; how greatly soever they

The hard service of sin. 153

were blessed with abundance of all things, still they made out for themselves one grievance or another. They wanted to be free to marry wives from among the heathen, they wanted a king to rule over them, they wanted horses and chariots, and silver and gold and all manner of precious things from Egypt and the east; and so they went on making themselves more and more like the heathen, till at last they provoked the Lord to cast them off. The land which flowed with milk and honey, which is the glory of all lands, was their land no more. They would none of God's joyful and contented service there; and so they were cast out, and carried away, some into one land, some into another, to endure hard bondage among the heathen, to serve their enemies which the Lord had sent against them; Assyrians, Babylonians, Romans, and the rest: in hunger and thirst and nakedness and want of all things: as we read in the book of Lamentations, and in the aweful chapters towards the end of Deuteronomy.

Now do not say, this is very aweful, but what is it to us Christians? Oh my brethren, it is every thing to us, in the way of most solemn instruction and warning. For look at our condition as Christians, the privileges granted to every single one of us. Before we could know any thing, our Lord brought us through the river Jordan, i.e. the waters of Holy Baptism, into the land flowing with milk and honey, i.e. into His Church and kingdom, abounding in all spiritual blessings: and the one thing He required of us was, "open thy mouth wide and I shall fill it." Be not slothful, be not fretful: make much of the good things which God hath given thee, and

He will give thee more and more: rejoice and be thankful for what thou hast received, for the grace of Holy Baptism, and He will help thee to rejoice more and more for the grace of Confirmation and Holy Communion. This was His invitation to us all, from the Font even until now: how we have accepted it, each one knows for himself: but one thing is quite certain; that in such measure as we have not accepted it, the fearful word which comes last in our text hath begun already to be fulfilled in us whether we perceive it or no. So far as we have refused to serve the Lord with joyfulness and gladness of heart so far we have already begun to serve our enemies, the world, the flesh and the devil, as the most forlorn and miserable of slaves, in hunger and thirst and nakedness and want of all things. So it is my brethren, the disobedient prodigal child, who has received his portion of goods, only to waste it, we know what he must come to, sooner or later. In the land to which he has wandered, far away from his true home, there is sure before long to arise a mighty famine. The craving, the void in his heart, which nothing but God can fill up, but which he had tried to fill up with base earthly sensual objects, with riotous living and harlots, so speaks our Lord's parable, that aching void will make itself felt, the more miserably for the former vain endeavours to supply it: the soul will turn this way and that, like an evil spirit cast out, wandering through dry places in search of rest, and finding none. And then if the man want courage and dutifulness really to listen to the still small voice which will whisper to him, why not turn and repent? why

The hard service of sin. 155

not seek Him once more, Whom you have found it so evil and bitter to forsake? it is but too likely that he will go on like that same prodigal, to bind the chains of his sins more closely to him: as the prodigal, spent with famine, went and joined himself to a citizen of that evil country, who sent him into his fields to feed swine, so the fallen Christian, remorseful but not yet repenting, will be tempted to cast himself more and more desperately into the captivity of the evil one, and to take any work, however base, which he may set him upon. Have we not seen and known too often, how men disappointed in their worldly ways, fly for comfort to strong drink or gaming, or whatever excites them for the moment? And yet they are not the more comfortable, in all calmer intervals they feel more incurably than ever, the hunger, the thirst, the nakedness of the heart; and so it comes to pass in the case of wicked Christians, far more fearfully than in the case of rebellious Israel, that because they would not serve the Lord their God with joyfulness and with gladness of heart for the abundance of all things, they go on serving their enemies in want of all things: and the longer they give way, the more heavily does the burthen press on them, till it becomes a yoke of iron crushing them by God's just judgement to utter destruction. God forbid that any of us, my brethren should ever come to understand this fully by sad experience: but somewhat of it, more or less, is known to too many of us, to all who at any time have given way to any bad and shameful habit of impure thought, or sensual indulgence; of black sullen, morbid fretfulness in heart and behaviour; of excess in meat, drink, or extravagant selfish expense; of envious feeling towards any of our brethren whatever. In these and in other ways men go on, and become very slaves to sin before they are aware: at times they long to be free, but their vile habits hinder them; again and again they make efforts to disengage themselves, again and again they fail and sink down in despair: they sin and repent, and sin again and hate themselves for it: there is no peace, no rest: from the very deep of their heart they are ready to cry out, with him of whom the Apostle speaks, "O wretched man that I am, who shall deliver me?"

"I thank God, through Jesus Christ our Lord," that is the answer of the Holy Ghost by S. Paul, to the loud and bitter cry of the desponding heart, an answer intended for every one, even the most reckless sinner among us, if he will but listen to it, and believe it and make it his own in good earnest. Yes, depend on it, my brethren, there is freedom even for him, into whose very soul the iron of the chain of his sins has entered: there is deliverance for the worst of habitual sinners, if he will steadfastly look his own condition in the face, and courageously abide by the rules of Him who is come to break the yoke from off his neck. Hear the promise made to backsliding Israel, even when the wrath had come on her to the uttermost. "ᵃIt shall come to pass, when all these things are come upon thee, the blessing and the curse which I have set before thee, and thou shalt call them to mind among all the nations whither the Lord thy God

ᵃ Deut. xxx. 1—4.

The hard service of sin. 157

hath driven thee, and shalt return unto the Lord thy God, and shalt obey His voice according to all that I command thee this day, thou and thy children, with all thine heart and with all thy soul: that then the Lord thy God will turn thy captivity, and have compassion upon thee, and will return and gather thee from all the nations whither the Lord thy God hath scattered thee." Oh, surely, my brethren, these are good and comfortable words, not to the Jewish people only, in regard of their sad dispersion; they are very music in the ears of every sinner among us Christians, who can but have the heart to desire in earnest to be delivered from his sins. Observe, I say, "his sins," for if he only seek to be delivered from the punishment of them, his repentance is no better than that of Esau, which you heard of this morning, no better than that of Judas Iscariot. Esau found no place of penitence, could not be admitted into the number of those who are in a way to be pardoned, because what he sought carefully with tears was not deliverance from sin, but freedom from punishment. Judas' repentance was his ruin instead of his salvation, because instead of causing him to turn away from sin, it drove him into the incurable sin of self-murder. But when people's sorrow is what Scripture calls contrition, it is impossible for God to despise it, for it is His own gracious work. And this is when they mourn, not for the pain they suffer, but with shame and grief to think that they should have behaved so ill to so good a God; have dealt so unkindly with so gracious a Saviour. Whoso has that feeling, and prays to have it more, of him, in Christ's name, the gracious word is spoken to the Church, "If any of thine be driven out unto the utmost parts of heaven," i.e. how far soever any Christian may have wandered into sin "from thence will the Lord thy God gather thee, from thence will He fetch thee." "Him that so cometh unto Him," even from the very husks of the swine, "He will in no wise cast out." Nay the Lord will not only receive him but will give him a chance of the very best of the good blessings which his sins had forfeited. Remember about the prodigal son. Even so it is written, "the Lord thy God will make thee plenteous in every work of thine hand. . . . for the Lord thy God will again rejoice over thee for good, as He rejoiced over thy fathers." Be comforted then, whosoever thou art, that mournest for thy sins, and not for fear of punishment only: deny thyself and order thy doings, in hope: by little and little He will heal and cleanse thee entirely: He hath found thee His lost sheep, and is even now bearing thee on His shoulders: if thou break not away from Him thou art safe. He will never set thee down, until He have brought thee within His own heavenly fold. He is One, Who from the very brink of the pit can and will lift thee, truly repenting, to the very height of Heaven.

SERMON XVI.

GOD'S REFRESHMENTS FOR PENITENTS.

1 KINGS XIX. 7.

" The Angel of the Lord came again the second time, and touched him saying, Arise and eat, because the journey is too great for thee."

IF we begin Lent with holy fear, determined in earnest to deny ourselves in some way or other; if we go on soberly in that mind, and if we are not too impatient for comfort, we shall find before long that comfort comes. It may not come so soon as we had wished or imagined, it may not come in the particular way we should have chosen; for a while it may not seem to come at all; but come it will, sooner or later, to them that in humble obedience resign themselves to the want of it.

Look to those awful times of fasting, which are set before us in Holy Scripture as patterns of Christ's true way of repentance. The Bible tells us of three solemn Lents at least, before our Saviour's Lent in the wilderness: three seasons of forty days, during which God's chosen and faithful ones sought Him in strict abstinence from earthly refreshment. Moses entered into the cloud fearing and trembling, and gat him up into the Mount, and was there forty days and forty nights: he did neither eat bread nor drink water. Once he did this for fear and devotion's sake, that his soul might be more thoroughly awake and alive to contemplate the heavenly things, the pattern to be shewn him in the Mount. Again he did it in fear and anxiety, to obtain God's pardon for his people after their great sin in making the golden calf. He fell down before the Lord forty days and forty nights, like unto the first, he did neither eat bread nor drink water, because he was afraid of the anger and hot displeasure, wherewith the Lord was wroth against His people to consume them. He fasted first for contemplation, and afterwards for repentance; first to obtain the knowledge of God's will, then to obtain pardon from Him for his people's sin. These were Moses' two Lents, kept in Horeb the mount of God. And long after, in the fallen times of Israel, we find both these fasts copied in one, by the great prophet Elijah, in the same mount Horeb, and in a time even of greater distress and anxiety. Elijah was in danger of his life, because he had slain the idolatrous prophets of Baal; he was also utterly downcast and perplexed in heart at the grievous sin and apostasy of his people. The children of Israel had forsaken God's covenant, thrown down His altars and slain His prophets with the sword: and Elijah alone was left, and they sought his life to take it away. He knew not what to do, nor which way to turn. So "he went a day's journey into the wilderness, and came and sat down under a juniper tree: and he requested for himself that he might die: and said, it is enough; now O Lord, take away my life, for I am not better than my fathers."

Moses had put up the same request before him: "ᵃ If thou deal thus with me, kill me, I pray thee, out of hand, and let me not see my wretchedness." Both sayings are to be understood as expressing the deepest agony of mind at the sad corruption of those for whose good they were sent: as well as extreme doubt and perplexity, not knowing what God would have them do, and fearing whatever they tried, to make things worse instead of better.

Elijah then being in this case, a day's journey out in the wilderness, alone, and far from the habitations of men, "as he lay and slept under a juniper tree, behold, then an angel touched him, and said unto him, Arise, and eat. And he looked, and behold, there was a cake baken on the coals, and a cruse of water at his head. And he did eat and drink, and laid him down again. And the angel of the Lord came again a second time, and touched him, and said, Arise and eat, because the journey is too great for thee. And he arose, and did eat and drink, and went in the strength of that meat forty days and forty nights unto Horeb the mount of God:" and there God appeared to him, and told him what to do.

This was Elijah's Lent, the third great type of our Saviour's, and no doubt of ours also. He had to seek God in evil times, and seemed quite forlorn and helpless. He was out in the waste wilderness by himself and thought he was the only one left of God's prophets. But an angel was watching him out of sight: bread and water was miraculously provided for him: strength was given him to bear his fast

ᵃ Num. xi. 15.

and at the end of it he was told what to do, and comforted with the assurance that there were others besides him, even seven thousand in Israel, who had not bowed the knee unto Baal. His body was refreshed with meat brought by an angel, and his soul with the sweet and comfortable knowledge that God had yet a chosen remnant, that there were among His people a few at least, whom His grace had preserved from the general apostasy and idolatry. God was with him, God's faithful ones, though few and undistinguished by the world, were with him too.

As then we might learn from Moses' Lent, with what fear and trembling we should enter on this holy season, so we may take courage from Elijah's Lent to meditate on the gracious refreshments and encouragements which our gracious Master ever provides for those who try to serve Him in true self-denial. "Arise and eat, because the journey is too great for thee" is in truth His message, sent in various ways to various persons, when He sees them really entering on their course of Christian mortification.

Even in those troubles and destitutions, which are not exactly penitential, not of our own choosing to afflict our souls for their good, in the ordinary wants and calamities of life, especially when they are borne patiently, He ever deals with us in that gracious and Fatherly way. "[b]He stayeth His rough wind in the day of the east wind." When things seem most forlorn, yet are there little glimpses and drops of consolation and hope, for those who have

[b] Isa. xvii. 8.

eyes and hearts to attend to them. When all around seems desert, when we look for some to have pity, but there is no man, when we have no place to flee unto, and no man caring for our souls, when people in their weakness have fairly wept themselves to sleep: then the Almighty and merciful One causes them to find an angel at waking, and refreshments ready prepared, bread and water, lest they faint altogether. The water was spent in the bottle, and Hagar had cast the child under one of the shrubs, and she lifted up her voice and wept; and the angel of the Lord called unto her and said, "^c what aileth thee Hagar? arise lift up the lad and hold him in thine arms." Abraham had stretched forth his hand, and taken the knife to slay his son; but the angel of the Lord called unto him from heaven, and said "^d lay not thine hand upon the lad, neither do thou any thing unto him, for now I know that thou fearest God." Jacob was taking his solitary rest in the open air, sent away from his father's house, and in fear of being murdered by his brother: when the Lord shewed him angels ascending and descending to do him good, and promised him to make His covenant with him. So is it throughout the Holy Scripture and so is it, even according to what we can discern, in God's all gracious daily Providences. It is even come to be a sort of proverb, "when things come to the worst they will mend." All that have lived long and thoughtfully in the world must remember instances of it: how they have been cared for, and helped, and consoled, in a thousand ways little and great, which they had no right to look for, just at

^c Gen. xxi. 17. ^d Gen. xxii. 12.

the moments when they most needed it. Events have happened, words have been spoken, sights have come before them, thoughts have arisen in their minds, which to most persons, if they were spoken of, might seem accidental, but the afflicted himself would be afraid so to think of them, rather he feels deeply convinced that it was the Father and God of his whole life graciously interfering and giving him tokens: every such thing was to him as an angel speaking from heaven; as a permission from a compassionate nursing father: "arise and eat," "take this or that little consolation, lest the journey be too great for thee."

But it should be well considered upon what condition these refreshments have been granted to God's people. Examine all the cases which have been now referred to out of the Holy Scriptures and all others like them, and you will perceive that they are ordered by this law: "*Cast thy burden upon the Lord, and He shall nourish thee, commit thy way unto Him, and He shall bring it to pass." When men give themselves up, when they in earnest surrender themselves to Him, then He takes them up. Depend on nothing but Him, seriously give yourself up to His will, hope with trembling that He may relieve you somehow, but dare not to prescribe to Him this or that way of relief: and then you are so far doing right, exercising faith, putting yourself in the way of His mercy. This indeed seems to be the temper of mind which He required in those who came to be healed. "According to your faith be it unto you;" according to your humble and holy confidence in

* Ps. lv. 23. P. B., xxxvii. 4.

Christ the Fountain of all good, and in His doing all for the best.

This is God's rule with regard to comfort in all afflictions temporal and spiritual: and it is especially His rule in that great work of true repentance, the work of this holy season. There is no more common feeling, I suppose, among persons trying in earnest to serve God better than they have done, than a sort of dull heavy dread of the irksomeness and gloom of the penitential life. To acknowledge our faults and have our sins ever before us: to pray without ceasing; to judge, condemn, punish ourselves, that we be not judged of the Lord: to humble ourselves, if need be, before God's servants as well as before Him: to keep our eyes, tongues, appetites in order: to say prayers on our knees often and punctually, and always with real efforts to attend: to deny ourselves pleasures: to be afraid of speaking about others: to be meek and calm in interruption, disappointment, ill-usage: to grudge one's self enjoyment, and watch for ways of self-denial: all these are necessary parts, signs, and tokens of real Christian repentance: and of course, to look forward to a whole life so spent must in itself be a disheartening and dreary thought: somewhat in the same kind of way, as it is disheartening and dreary to a sick person, when the physician tells him he must live by rule, watch himself in his diet and exercise, not take liberties, nor please himself as he used to do. Of course, men had rather have their liberty: yet, if they have faith in the physician, they obey his directions: they put up with some degree of hardness, rather than cast their health away. And mark the consequence: it very generally happens, that the very self-denial, by habit, becomes tolerable and easy to them: besides its benefit to their health, which they do not always feel, it brings with it comforts and advantages which they do feel. So and much more, when penitent Christians try to obey Christ because they have faith in Him, and embrace a life of contrition and self-denial, rather than cast their souls away. It seems indeed dreary beforehand, how should it be otherwise? but that is the trial of their faith. If they truly believe in Christ the Healer of souls, if they truly long for health in their own sick souls, much more if they have any touch of love to Him Who bore all for them, they will not shrink from the remedy because it seems harsh and bitter, they will embrace the cross boldly, and make up their minds both to the heavy burthen of it, and the sharp anguish: and having done so they will find to their amazement a heavenly sweetness mingled in the bitter cup: ten thousand refreshments which they knew not of will help them along the journey which they undertake in faith, knowing it to be too great for them. Refreshment will come, if you do not look for it, if you put away the thought of it from your mind, if you keep saying to yourself, it is not meet for such as I am: I am quite unworthy of it. But if you depend on it, and are vexed at its not coming, that is a bad sign of the truth of your repentance, and looks as if you wanted rather to be comfortable and easy, than to please God. So far as it goes, it is making your own choice not leaving your Lord to choose for you. It is taking the matter out of His hands into your own. A sinner should think it refreshment enough to have a reasonable certainty of his duty for the present, and a reasonable hope of forgiveness and salvation at last.

Any one that will, may bring these truths home to himself by endeavouring to make that use which all saints have ever made of this holy Season of Lent. At the beginning of the forty days, to look forward to spending them strictly, (strictly, I mean, in such measure as health and other duties may allow,) would be to most of us a bleak, dreary kind of thought: it would require faith to make up our minds to do so. A difference in diet day after day: more frequent prayer: keeping ourselves from some customary diversions; doing in short something or other, whatever our conscience, well directed, tells us is best, to mortify our souls and bodies, this is what no one naturally likes: no one of his own pleasure would look forward to it for six or seven weeks together. But those who have in some small measure tried it, tried it conscientiously and in earnest, and not for form's sake, have generally, I believe, found, besides the benefit promised in Scripture to such obedience, a peculiar kind of holy sweetness accompanying their little acts of self-denial. If they really tried to give themselves, for the time entirely to Christ, to rule their tempers as well as their appetites, to be kind to others as well as strict to themselves, to mean what they said in their prayers and confessions, and to do all as secretly as possible, they really have found often-times, a comfort and refreshment in their severities such as they were; a comfort which they neither thought of before, nor can well understand, now they find it. Neither dare they at all depend on it for the future, nor promise it to themselves or others. Their way seems to be, thankfully to take it as it comes, discerning in it an angelic message, much like that which was sent to Elijah "arise and eat because the journey is too great for thee." The Sundays, for example, at this time of Lent, must come, I should apprehend, with a peculiar sort of welcome fragrance to those who have been strict with themselves on the week days. The day of holy joy and thankfulness stands out even higher than usual among so many days of penitential sorrow.

Perhaps too the beautiful spring weather, which always comes in, more or less, with some part or other of the forty days of Lent, may be not untruly regarded by considerate persons as a token of refreshment; an angel touching them and bidding them be of good hope that their prayers and self-denials and alms do indeed go up for a memorial before God, and are graciously received for Jesus Christ's sake, and that their Lent will lead in due time to a happy Easter.

But indeed it is quite in vain, attempting to set down in words, or even distinctly to comprehend in thoughts, the thousand ways and means of consolation and refreshment, which the God of them who repent, has provided, lest the journey be too great for us. With each He deals separately, according to the circumstances and feelings of each: causing words to be spoken, sights to be seen, verses in Scripture and passages from other books to meet our eyes, nay sometimes dreams to be dreamed (there are many such cases in Scripture) which can neither be known nor understood by any but those for whom He means them, but which to them are real hints from Him, hints and whispers on which they act, and do, and were no doubt meant to do, many things for the great good of their souls. But these are His secret messages, to be honoured in secret, seldom if at all to be spoken of to others, nor even to be thought of by ourselves without fear and trembling. Other times and ways of refreshment there are, more regular, and such as may without presumption be looked forward to, when people are encouraging themselves and others to set out on the journey of Christian penitence, otherwise too great for them. Thus, what a blessing it is, when you come to consider it, for those whose time is marked out by regular and very frequent returns of prayer. We know how milestones, or other objects at regular distances shorten a road; so do hours and times of prayer carefully and devoutly kept, shorten the day, and days so spent shorten the week, and weeks the month, and months the year, and years the whole life of the penitent, which when he looked on to it seemed as if it would be a heavy and weary waste, full of strictness for which he was little prepared. Do not think, that what I am now recommending is a thing impossible for poor busy hardworking men. Those at least who know a good deal of the psalms and collects of the Church might easily choose out a short psalm and a short collect, which they might learn by heart and say with the Lord's prayer, every three or four hours, without stopping their work so much as five minutes. If any man were truly touched with a sense of his sins, and wanted to exercise himself in continual penitence, this sort of exercise would be the greatest help to him: and by dividing the time, it would greatly lessen what otherwise might be felt too much of a yoke.

However, the greatest of all refreshments, as well as of all helps, is the Holy Communion of our Lord's Body and Blood, called as it sometimes is, on this very account, the stay of the wayfaring man. Who can tell the greatness of the mercy which invites us so often to arise and eat this Bread, since otherwise our journey would be far too great for us?

Bless God with me, my brethren, for these and all other His untold, unhoped for loving kindnesses, whereby He ever goes out to meet poor returning prodigals, and not only receives them, but clothes and feeds them with His best. Bless Him for these consolations, and use them, when they come, humbly and joyfully, but never forget this one thing, that you are penitents, and therefore should taste but tremblingly of any consolation, even God's. As for such comforts as I have been speaking of, you must neither depend on them beforehand, nor altogether indulge in them, as comforts, when they come, neither may we venture to choose out what sort of refreshment we would prefer, or in what manner, or through whom, God should give it to us. We are but beggars, it becomes us not to have a choice. What God sends, we must take thankfully as it comes. It will seldom be exactly what we should have fixed upon: but it will be enough to stay us and help us on our way home: Elijah had but one meal of bread and water, and it lasted him all through his Lent, till he came to the mount of God. Our refreshments, bodily and spiritual, will be good, if they bring us nearer Christ, and not else.

SERMON XVII.

OUR-EVER PRESENT UNSEEN ENEMY.

THIRD SUNDAY IN LENT.

1 S. JOHN v. 8.

"*He that is begotten of God keepeth himself and that wicked one toucheth him not.*"

LAST Sunday I endeavoured to point out to you certain times, in which our Almighty Father vouchsafes to shew Himself especially near us; such as sudden changes, great afflictions, great deliverances, stirrings of the heart and conscience, and surely my brethren, there is great need to exhort and remind every one of us, how sore and dangerous a burden we lay upon ourselves, when we make light of such warnings, and go on as if nothing had happened.

To-day the Holy Church calls our attention to another set of warnings, the tokens of another presence, very unlike the Presence of God Almighty, but, so far like it in that it is invisible, and that Holy Scripture in many ways and often charges us to take notice of it, as ever we care for our souls. The Collect for this third week in Lent is a prayer put into our mouths by our mother the Church, that God would stretch forth the Right Hand of His Majesty to be our defence against all our enemies. The Gospel tells us what enemies are chiefly meant, the unclean spirits which were driven away from us in Baptism, but are continually watching and longing for a chance to return to the place from which they came out, i. e., to take possession again of our souls and bodies, and have their own way with us. And S. Paul in the Epistle tells us of works of darkness, works which these bad spirits, if they can, will prevail on us to practise in secret. You see then what that other spiritual and invisible presence is, which Christian people must believe and think on, besides the presence of God and His holy angels. It is this, that wherever we go and however we are employed, at all hours of the day and night, we have reason to apprehend that one is very near us, whom we cannot see, nor discern by any bodily sense, because he is not an earthly and a bodily creature, but a spirit, a fallen and corrupt angel; and that he is near us to seek our harm, to make us, if he can, as wicked and miserable as himself, to drag us down with him into that hell which he knows is prepared for him. And he is very strong, very crafty; all the strength and craft of this earth are as nothing compared to his. "*None is so fierce that dare stir him up, upon earth there is not his like; he is a king over all the children of pride." These are God's own words, spoken concerning our adversary the devil. Is it not a fearful thing to know that we have such an enemy ever at hand; untiring, ever awake, without remorse, without pity, ready to spring on us at any moment, sharper and more subtle to beguile and destroy us, than the wisest and most knowing on earth to instruct and save us? Truly I know not how any one of us believing these things, could have a moment's peace

* Job xli. 33, 34.

or quiet, were it not that we believe also that there is One, far nearer to us than he, infinitely wiser, greater and more glorious; infinitely more loving, more desirous to save our souls, than Satan ever could be to ruin them. Greater is He that is in you, Christ abiding by His Spirit in the souls and bodies of dutiful Christians, than he that is in the world. The bad spirit may be ever so *near* us, but the Good Spirit, if we have not driven Him away, is actually and always *within* us. He, not only, "[b] dwelleth with you," but He "shall be in you." It was our Master's assured and gracious promise; and in the faith of it we may live comfortably during the short time appointed for us, although we are not ignorant what an enemy we have at hand.

Still the thought of that enemy is surely enough to make us very serious; knowing as we do that there may be such a thing as our ruining ourselves, throwing ourselves into his net, for all the mighty and loving care of our Saviour. Why does Holy Scripture, why does the Church in her catechism, tell us so much of that wicked one, except it be that we should think much of him, as we go about in that world which is so much in his power?

Is such your mind, my brethren, *do* you often think of your great enemy, how subtle he is, how malicious, how close at hand? and does the fearful thought urge you to cling more and more to the remembrance of your Saviour, that best and only Friend, Who has vanquished Satan for you, and taken you out of his power, and is now holding you by the hand to lead you safe to that home which is *entirely* out of his reach? does the dread of the

[b] S. John xiv. 17.

unseen enemy cause you to press nearer and nearer, like a frightened child to the unseen Comforter and Redeemer? If so, it is well; if not, depend upon it you are in very great danger. It will never do to pass through a country full of bitter adversaries, and never give the danger a thought. It will never do to let go the only Hand which can either keep you in the way, or support you along it. Remember, the nature of our foe is to be then nearest when we think least of him. When a man is living merrily and carelessly, with no thought but that of enjoying the present hour; or when he is wholly taken up with some scheme of his own, when God, and death, and judgement, and eternity, and his soul's danger, are far from his mind; and, if the thought of them should occur, are presently put by as unreasonable and interrupting what he cares more about, *that* is the very time, when, if our eyes could be opened to see what is doing in the spiritual world, we might behold Satan, lurking close at hand, watching with all cruelty and subtlety for an occasion to complete that man's ruin; but when Satan is religiously dreaded, and Christ is loved; when prayers are regularly said, and the heart is kept regularly mindful of the great things out of sight, and conscience is regularly examined as in the sight of God, humbly, truly, and impartially; there is good hope that the evil one, not seeing how he may do harm, may let that man alone; or if he do assault him it will answer no better than with Job; the temptation will only be pain, not corruption, to one of Christ's dutiful servants. For *this* is also carefully to be remembered in all our thoughts and fears concerning the evil one, that he can do us no real harm, but by our own consent. When we are very much afraid of him, and therefore call upon our Lord and keep out of mischief; or when he puts evil thoughts in our minds against our will, to hinder our prayers, or the like: he does us no harm at all, his real power over us lies in his getting us to consent to the bad thoughts, and to do his dreadful work, without any thought of him one way or the other.

But besides this universal warning, Holy Scripture tells us of certain special cases and circumstances, when we are particularly called upon to be on our guard against him. The serpent was more subtle than any beast of the field and he "spake unto the woman;" not unto the man, but unto the woman; and at a time as it seems, when the man was out of sight. Plainly then, when persons are away from those who are bound to look after them, or are otherwise left to themselves, especially for the first time, then is there more than usual cause to apprehend that the evil one may be near at hand, and closely watching them. You are a young person, we will suppose, and you are going to service for the first time, or for some other reason you are going to a distance, and will be out of sight and hearing of those whom you have been used to look up to with love and respect, who have corrected you when you have done amiss, and have guided you with their eye. The very circumstance too of your being in a new place, on a journey perhaps, and among people who know nothing of you, and are not concerned to mind you, sets you at liberty in a way which must prove very dangerous, if you are not religiously on your guard. Be sure the devil is near you at such times; he will not want temptations to put in your way; you had need be strong in prayer, strong in good resolutions, strong in a deep sense of the Presence of Christ within you. The devil will be whispering : "Now you have your liberty, now no one is overlooking you, for once in a way you may do as you please; why should you not enjoy yourself as so many others do? No one here knows you, you will not lose your character." Alas! by these and other like thoughts how many have been deceived to their ruin! how many, who have left their homes in comparison innocent, have become acquainted with works of darkness, of which it is even a shame to speak; and therefore to all who are leaving parents, home, or old friends whom they respected, to all who are going a journey by themselves, or in any way likely to think themselves quite out of sight, I say, be very watchful; remember that you cannot be really alone; never forget the Eye which is evermore fixed upon you; consider what our Lord tells us, that "the unclean spirit walketh through dry places," i. e., he haunts the wilderness, the solitary place, when people think themselves alone; and in this respect the most crowded city is as a wilderness to one who has no acquaintance there; he seems so far left to himself to think, look, speak and act as he pleases; well for him to be aware that there is one who sitteth lurking in the thievish corners of the streets, to get him, if he can, into his net, the net of deadly sin. O! beware of the evil one, use yourself to say in your heart "get thee behind me Satan," as often, as you have the feeling: no eye seeth me.

N

Another time of great danger is when a person is in great need, great and pressing want of any kind, and relief seems temptingly near, but cannot be had without breaking some rule which God has given; as if one who seemed on the point of starving was to be offered how to get his bread in some dishonest and shameful way. Our Lord Himself vouchsafed to undergo this trial, when He refused the suggestion of Satan that He should command the stone to be made bread, and surely we ought to learn from it that times of pressing want, be it either want of bread or of anything else that a man feels he cannot do without, are almost sure to be times of temptation, and ought therefore to be times of special watchfulness and prayer; which are sure, by God's mercy to turn them into times of blessing.

Again, by our Lord's second temptation, when He would not cast Himself down from the pinnacle of the Temple, we seem to be told: beware of the evil one when thou hast any good success, when thou hast been enabled to do more or better than usual, beware; the feeling will come over thee, I have wrought a good work, who knows how much higher I may rise; I feel as if it were in me to do so; and so being lifted up, thou wilt have some grievous fall. This also is a snare of the devil; and the way to avoid it is to be aware of it, and pray and strive in whatsoever God shall prosper thee, that thou mayest not be highminded but fear; for surely it is a ground of deep fear to know that the devil is standing by thee on the pinnacle to which thou hast risen, if haply he may prevail on thee to cast thyself down; that he would fain provoke thee to number and weigh thy own good deeds and good success, and spoil it all, as he once provoked holy David. It is a fearful thought, but it is a good and blessed fear, if it make thee mistrust thyself, renounce thine own doings, and lean more entirely on Him Who only can sustain thee.

In like manner our Saviour's third temptation warns us of another case, in which we may be sure the tempter is coming close to us; and that is, when by sinning once in a way, in something that we might fancy of no great consequence, we may secure to ourselves as we think, some object very precious and valuable indeed; for so the devil invited our Lord to purchase all the kingdoms of the world and the glory of them, by the simple act of once falling down and worshipping him; the prize would seem to a worldly mind out of all proportion to the liberty taken for securing it; it was as when in after times the heathen persecutors invited the Christians to save their lives by sprinkling a few grains of incense on the fire of an idol's altar; a great deal might be said about the sin being small in comparison, and pardonable, considering that it was to win a world, or save one's life; but Jesus Christ and the faith which is by Him said at once, get thee hence Satan; they knew such advice could only come of the devil; and we may learn of them to be quite sure that when we are moved to do evil that good may come, a very small seeming evil to obtain the greatest seeming good, it is, it must be, the devil who is moving us; he is nearer than usual, we ought to be more than usually on our guard.

In to-day's gospel our Lord gives another lesson,

a very distinct one, about a time of special danger. When the unclean spirit is gone out of a man, he goeth up and down restlessly, seeking how he may return unto the place from whence he came out, i. e., may come and take possession of the unhappy soul and body again; not as before, but with seven times as much sin and misery. What is this but a clear warning of the special dangers of new converts? The devil for a long time lingers near them, hoping to find an entrance again. Take notice of this, all ye who by God's mercy have made a good beginning; who have reasonable hope that you are loosed from the chain of your sins. Remember it is *but* a beginning; the enemy may be *outside* the door, and you cannot be too thankful for it; but doubtless he is waiting very *near* the door, and any negligence on your part may let him in again, with seven other spirits more wicked than himself. In the early days of recovery, relapses are more especially to be dreaded.

Satan is very near, again, when a man has been doing wrong, and is found out and reproved; it is a great thing then for the devil's wicked object, if the sinner take the reproof amiss; as for instance in a sullen or scornful way, refusing altogether to be the better for the warning. This was the sad case of Judas Iscariot; we know how it was with him; when our Lord gave him to understand that He knew his wickedness, in the long habits of pilfering, and also his hypocrisy, in pretending to care for the poor, Judas instead of humbling himself under the reproof, resolved to do his Master what mischief he could, and set about contriving how to betray Him to His enemies; and then S. Luke tells us Satan entered into him. Again at the Last Supper our Lord gave Judas the sop, as a token that He knew all that was in his heart, his whole plan and purpose of betraying Him. There could not be a more fearful or a more merciful reproof, but the poor wretch would not be moved; and what do we read next? The second time "Satan entered into him;" and he went away and sealed his own ruin for ever. O my brethren, think on Judas, think on Satan entering into him, whenever you have to undergo reproof for wrong behaviour. You imagine it a slight matter, a matter of course, how you behave at such a time, you think you may with no particular consequence indulge the humour you happen to be in. It is *not* a slight matter, it is *not* a matter of course; it is an affair of very great consequence indeed. He who destroyed Judas is waiting by, to see how you take the reproof, and if you harden yourself, if you take it as Judas did, great indeed is the advantage which you will give to Satan against your own soul.

Two words more. Remember Cain, and believe that the wicked one is not far off when you give way to envy or anger; believe the Apostle telling you that he who doth so, giveth place, maketh room in himself for the devil. Remember Ananias: who it was that filled his heart to tell the lie for which he was struck down dead; and fear exceedingly the next time you seem to yourself to have a good chance to get anything by telling a lie.

Many more instances might be gleaned out of Holy Scripture but these are enough to show how near, how very near, the evil spirit is permitted to come to us: how often, how very often. It is fearful to think of; yet be comforted; Jesus Christ is far more surely, far more intimately near than he: He is with you not *often* but *always*; not at hand, but within your hearts; and you by His grace may keep yourselves that that wicked one touch you not.

I will notice in conclusion one very aweful thought inseparable from what has been said. Those of whom I have spoken, our two invisible companions on the journey through life, Jesus Christ and the evil spirit: we shall meet both of them, face to face in the clear light of the last great day; and Satan will be for accusing us and witnessing against us; but all in vain, if we shall have kept good watch against him and walked dutifully before our Lord. If Christ plead for us, vainly will Satan plead against us; the word will be spoken to him: "get thee hence," once and for ever. He will leave us, departing to his own place, and the good angels will come rejoicing, and minister unto us. Amen.

SERMON XVIII.

THE WILES OF THE DEVIL.

THIRD SUNDAY IN LENT.

2 Cor. ii. 11.

"Lest Satan should get an advantage of us : for we are not ignorant of his devices."

S. PAUL in this verse puts clearly before us all this circumstance in the condition of Christians, that from their Baptism till their lives' end, they are continually being plotted against by Satan; he is daily trying to take them in: he is full of devices, which it greatly concerns them not to be ignorant of. And our Lord in the Gospel for the day, tells us the reason why it is so. Satan is peculiarly desirous to harm Christians, because, as Christians they have been taken out of his hands, and he cannot bear to be so baffled. By nature we were born subject to him, as truly so as the unhappy persons of whom we read so much in the Gospels, who had unclean spirits dwelling in their souls and bodies. But as our Blessed Lord used to come in and cast out those spirits with a word, so the devil was driven away from us, and we withdrawn from his power, by His word spoken to us in Holy baptism, "In the Name of the Father, and of the Son, and of the Holy Ghost." Again, as when our Saviour and His Apostles had dispossessed any devil, that evil one was sure to try to return, and if he could do so, would torment and vex the unhappy person more than ever; so if the Christian permits Satan to return after Baptism, he will by no means return alone, but with seven other spirits more wicked than himself, and they will enter in and dwell there, and the last state of that man is worse than the first. A wicked Christian is more wicked and miserable than any other man, for this reason among others, that he is more under the power of the devil. And a good Christian, as long as he is in this world, has this particular danger to contend with, that the devil has his eye continually upon him, putting mischief into his way and trying to cast him down. In any case it is quite plain, that we entirely misunderstand our own condition, we never can do right or live in safety, except we keep ourselves continually on our guard against Satan, and knowing his devices, take care to give them no advantage.

Nor are there wanting grave reasons, why the Church teaches us this doctrine in Lent particularly. Our Saviour's fasting led in some way to His temptation: when He had gone without food forty days and forty nights, and was afterwards a hungered, then we read in particular the tempter came to Him, and wanted Him to make the stones bread. Somewhat in the like manner we may well believe, that when Satan sees a Christian bent on keeping himself in order, and desirous really of being a good penitent, he will of course lie in wait for him, and earnestly seek occasion to hurt him. If he could, he would have hindered our Saviour from completing His work upon the cross: and if he can, he will hinder us from making the most of our Lent, by daily preparing ourselves to take up our cross in Passion week. Therefore it is quite necessary for a true penitent to watch against Satan and his devices, not to forget that he has such an enemy, full of all malice and subtlety. Nothing, you may be sure, is so desired by him, as that people should forget or make light of him: just as the wolf, if he could reason so far, would be glad for the sheep not to know or think of him at all, for then they will be far more likely to throw themselves in his way. Our Lord in the Gospel makes mention of several sorts of persons, different cases, with which Satan has to deal: and for all sorts it is highly needful that they think very much of Satan. First Christ speaks of our natural state, how men seemed to be left at his mercy. "When a strong man armed keepeth his palace, his goods are in peace:" i.e., while we were in our natural corrupt state, with our weak and fallen flesh such as we had it from Adam, the devil possessed us without hope or help: his goods were in peace: he had it all his own way with us. That wicked one is the strong man armed, and we unhappy, were his palace, i.e., the place where he abode: and if Christ had not mercifully interfered to deliver us from that sad condition, we should have gone on quietly and without remorse in the course which would have been our souls' ruin. But Christ did interfere: "He was made flesh and dwelt among us:" He died and rose again: He went up into Heaven, and sent down from thence His Holy Spirit to unite us to Himself: that good Spirit took possession of our souls and bodies in holy Baptism; thus a stronger than he came upon the strong man armed, and overcame him, and stripped him of his armour. Christ who is stronger than the devil did once for all put him down and his power within us; and now if we will let Him, He will go on dividing his spoils: that is the Spirit of Christ ruling in us will help us gradually to get the better of all the remains of the old Adam, wholly to subdue the flesh to the spirit. This is the best and happiest supposition we can make: it is the case of those in whom grace triumphs, of those who are going on to perfection: God grant it may be your case and mine. But we must not forget that our Lord in the very same discourse gives an account of another case also, a very sad and dismal one: the case of the unclean spirit, returning after he had been driven out, and finally prevailing against the Spirit of God. He warns us that when a Christian falls back into the ways of the heathen, into presumptuous and deadly sin, it is as if the devil, whom Christ had driven out of a man, should find opportunity to return: he would not return singly; he would take to himself seven other spirits more wicked than himself; they would enter in and dwell there; it will be seven sins for one, or one sin multiplied seven fold; and the last state of that man will be worse than the first: very much worse, as sinning more against light, and despising the exceeding riches of God's goodness and forbearance.

These are the two conditions of a Christian man with respect to Satan, which our Lord describes in to-day's Gospel: and for both it is most extremely necessary that we should keep up a serious remembrance of the power, craft, and presence of our unwearied enemy. If men think not at all of him, if they are easy about him, if they account themselves in no particular danger from him, surely so far they are like the heathen, of whom it is said, "his goods are in peace." It is the very thing he desires: you may easily judge of it yourself. If you wanted to do a person mischief craftily, is not this the very thing you would wish, that he should not be at all aware of you: that you might come as near him as you please, as often as you please, without his even having you in his thoughts at all? How fearful then to think, that this should be a true account of the mind of so many Christians towards the great enemy who is lying in wait for their souls! Have you, my friends, each one of you this very morning, seriously thought of that wicked one, as near at hand, of the danger of his touching you this very day, and of the dreadful polluting effect of his touch? Have you heartily committed your soul and body into the keeping of our Lord Jesus Christ, as a child that is aware of a wild beast being near, would run to his father and keep fast hold of his hand? If nothing of this sort has passed through your mind this morning, not even when you said in the Lord's prayer " deliver us from evil; " depend upon it you are in more danger from the devil than you at all imagine. It will be no wonder if some great evil happen before night to your soul or body, and I would anxiously advise you to lose no time in solemnly committing yourself to our Lord for the rest of the day, by saying thoughtfully either His own prayer, or some other good prayer against the snares of the evil one.

But our Saviour's doctrine to-day, sets before us a better state of things than this as between a Christian man and this his great· enemy, and wills us no doubt to have serious thoughts whether it be our state or no. Christ describes Himself as one stronger than the strong man, who has turned him out and is dividing his spoils. If this be so with you, if Jesus Christ has really cast the wicked spirit out of you, as no doubt He did at your Baptism, and if you have not by your grievous sin or carelessness, invited that evil one back again, then ought Christ's work, which is here called dividing Satan's spoils, to be even now going on within you. What is "dividing the spoils?" It is taking what the conquered person had, using it in such a way as the conqueror pleases : as we read that the children of Israel did to their enemies both in their victorious escape from Egypt and in the many wars they had to carry on. Christ then is dividing Satan's spoils, when He so dwells in us, as to use every power of our souls and bodies for good, which Satan had before used for evil : when He takes the tongue which had been accustomed to profane and filthy words, and employs it in speaking His truth, in setting forth His praises, in comforting and instructing His little ones. When He turns away the eyes, which had been used to behold vanity, and opens them to behold wonderous things out of His Law, when He takes the hands which had been stretched out to steal, and uses them in honest labour, or in zealous charity for Christ's sake: in these and in all other ways Jesus Christ may be truly said to divide the spoils of the wicked one. This then is what we have to ask ourselves: is this kind of holy work going on in our souls and bodies? are we growing every day more afraid to let our eyes do the devil's work, by looking where they ought not to dwell; and our ears, by listening after our own praises, and the blaming of others: and all our senses and appetites by taking just what they please? Are we endeavouring by all kinds of watchfulness to lead in captivity every thought to the obedience of Jesus Christ? Is Satan continually being stripped of that armour wherein he trusted to get an advantage of us? That armour is of course the very opposite to the armour of light, the armour of God, the armour of truth, the armour of righteousness, of which we read so much in different parts of the New Testament. The armour of God is truth, Satan's armour therefore is lying; are you becoming more and more careful, more scrupulous to use no sort of deceit? The armour of God is faith; Satan's armour therefore is unbelief: are you every day labouring and praying to have the great invisble things more and more in your mind, and the trifles of this world less and less? The armour of God is holiness; Satan is an unclean spirit: his armour is lust: are you constantly trying to keep under your body, your heart, and your imagination, that no impurity may enter in and defile the soul wherein Christ vouchsafes to dwell by His Spirit? The armour of God is humility: Satan's armour is pride and vainglory : are you schooling yourself diligently in that most difficult virtue; ready to be corrected, glad to take advice, willing to own yourself in the wrong, patient in ill usage ? The armour of God is charity ; Satan's armour is envy: are you in the way of rejoicing more and more to have others preferred before you, and contriving more and more to deny yourself for their good ? The armour of God is watching to do good to all Christians : Satan's armour is temptation and corruption : are you improving in this respect that you try more and more to give no offence, that no soul may be the worse for having come near you ?

A great deal, believe me, a very great deal, will depend upon the kind of answer which your conscience, honestly consulted, gives to such questions as these. For if you cannot truly say, that the evil one is thus gradually losing strength in his warfare against you, then you have reason to fear his getting the dominion over you again: then you have need to watch against the seven other spirits, more wicked than the first, which are ready to enter in and dwell in the heart of the careless, unthinking Christian ; then you have need to cry mightily unto God that your last state be not worse than the first. Then you ought not to lose one hour, nor a moment, but even now to begin asking yourself such questions as these, in addition to what I just now asked you : have I not even now some marks about me of the evil spirits already beginning to return ? what becomes of my good resolutions ? when I promise myself to watch against any particular sin or bad way, am I less able than I was some time since to keep that promise? do I fall more easily? For that is one very bad sign. Again, you may ask yourself, how am I now minded towards my own sins, when they come into my thoughts? do I judge and blame myself as much as I did, or am I rather ready to make excuses, and silently compare myself with others, fancying them worse? Or you may compare your present self with your former, in respect of the kind of thoughts you indulge. Do you praise yourself in your heart more than you did? do you permit yourself to dwell with satisfaction on what you think the good parts of your character? Do you hearken after praise, and cling to it when it comes? I mean, do you find these tendencies growing upon you? for as to being entirely free from them, that is the crown of a whole life of saintly self-denial. I do not therefore expect that you should not have these thoughts to contend with: but what is expected of you is, that you should be in earnest contending with them; and contending by God's merciful grace more and more successfully.

Again how is it in respect of your temper towards your brethren? Have not scornful, morose, peevish thoughts more hold of your mind than they had some time since? If unhappily it be so, you had need look well to yourself, for that sort of disposition is surely a work of the devil: and if you indulge it, you are but inviting him to return.

A delight again in censure and detraction, in reading, hearing, speaking or thinking ill of others, this is a very grievous and subtle snare, by which he too often beguiles imperfect penitents. They seem to themselves zealous against something wrong, while they are indeed giving way to pride and dislike. Watch your heart therefore in this: if you have reason to fear such an evil habit forming within you, fear greatly lest it prove a sign of the devil's returning, and set yourself at once to mortify it with all your might.

I need only just mention, that we should also try ourselves in our devotions. If prayer, whether in Church or at home, if considering our ways in the presence of God, if attending to good books, if fasting and other humiliations, above all, if the Holy Communion, be found to have grown, we hardly know how, more wearisome and less comfortable to us than at some former time, surely we have reason to dread lest Satan be gaining an advantage of us, we have need to rouse ourselves up and shake him off again before it be too late.

Few, if any, are qualified to be their own guides in so great and dangerous a work. But God offers us His holy Church as made known in the Prayer Book, for a guide, and His ministers for friends and helpers: and he that under such directions reads or hears and practises the holy word of our Saviour, he I trust, will be found sufficiently armed, when the evil day comes. Satan with all his seven evil spirits, will draw back from him disappointed: finding always that there is in the house One stronger than he to keep it, and that all his struggles do but end in his losing more of the little power he had left.

SERMON XIX.

DEADLY PEACE OF THE UNAWAKENED CONSCIENCE.

THIRD SUNDAY IN LENT.

S. LUKE xi. 21.

"*When a strong man armed keepeth his palace, his goods are in peace.*"

THAT is, as long as the devil in his full power has possession of the soul of a man, the man is apt to be in a sort of peace and quiet, his conscience not disturbed, but well enough contented with himself.

This was plainly our Lord's meaning, because the words are part of what He said when He was discoursing with the Pharisees about a miracle which He had just wrought in casting an evil spirit out of a man. They in their profaneness and malice said, "He casteth out devils by Beelzebub the chief of the devils:" as if it were a sort of agreement between our Blessed Lord and the evil one, Satan consenting to seem to be cast out, in order that he might in the end have the more power through the people's faith which they should have in his false prophet, for such they blasphemously accounted our Saviour to be. With such a thought they said, "He casteth out devils by Beelzebub." But our Lord shewed them that could not be, because Satan was too wise and crafty to be divided against himself. He, Jesus Christ, as they might plainly see, was altogether against the devil. They might plainly see it, if they would open their eyes and look. They might see that not only did He by His word drive away the unclean spirits, so that they could no longer hurt men's bodies, tear them to pieces, cast them into the fire, or the water, but also that by His holy teaching, if men would but receive and obey it, He would no less free their souls. The devil is an unclean spirit, but Jesus Christ is all for cleanness of heart and life: the devil is all cruelty and malice, but Jesus Christ is love: the devil is the father of lies, but Jesus Christ is the truth: the devil, as a roaring lion, walketh about, seeking whom he may devour, but Jesus Christ went about doing good, seeking whom He might heal and save. Therefore they might plainly see that our Lord was against the devil, not only by His outwardly casting him out, but by the whole course and train of all His ways, and all His sayings.

After our Saviour had shewn them this, and so corrected their error, He goes on to tell them the true state of the case. "When a strong man armed keepeth his palace, his goods are in peace: but when a stronger than he shall come upon him and overcome him, he taketh from him all his armour wherein he trusted, and divideth his spoils." Those who heard our Lord speak, would at once understand that He was describing the warfare between Himself and the evil one : how the devil indeed was mighty, but He, the Son of the Most High, was far mightier, so that when He came upon him, He would at once overcome him: He, the true Seed of the woman, God the Son, made man in the womb of the blessed Virgin Mary, would, in His own good time, bruise the head of the tempting and corrupting serpent. He, the true David, would cast down the true Goliah, would take from him all his armour wherein he trusted, his coat of mail, his sword, his spear and his shield; and would divide his spoils, that is, would deliver out of his hand, the unhappy souls of whom he had made spoil, and would appoint each one of those souls to do some work in the service and kingdom of God. This is called "dividing the spoils," because in war it was usual for the conqueror to take all the armour and precious things of the conquered, and divide them among his soldiers and followers: and so our Lord having overcome the devil, and taken out of his power all the precious things of this world, will employ them all, sooner or later, to His Father's Glory, in one way or another. It is a short way of describing the great victory, of which we read so much in the book of the Revelations: in which the kingdoms of this world were to become the kingdoms of our Lord and of His Christ, and He to reign for ever and ever.

This is the general meaning of the parable; but I wish now to draw your attention to one particular expression in it: viz. the saying that the strong man's goods are *in peace*, so long as he, in his armour, is allowed to keep his palace. We shall find a serious warning in this if we consider it earnestly. For the strong man armed, as I said, is the great enemy. He is strong, for he is a mighty angel, and although for his sin cast down from Heaven, yet he is still permitted to retain a great deal of the strength and subtlety, in which he was at first created. He is therefore a strong one, strong to make war against us: and he is armed, for besides the power and cunning, which as I said was left him at his fall, he is more able to do us harm in consequence of our fall. We have ourselves armed him against us. He has seen, and knows too well, how frail and weak we are, and in what respects—he is like a soldier who has won one victory, and is afterwards called to fight against the same enemy. Something like this has been the case with Satan ever since he won that first victory over our parents, Adam and Eve: he has come to each fresh temptation in more and more hope of prevailing, because of each fresh sin which he has prevailed on us to commit. This is his armour, wherein he trusteth, the wilful sin and wickedness of men: and because this has so abounded in all generations since the fall, therefore the strong one has kept his palace, i. e., Satan has kept in a manner for his own, this fallen and corrupt world. God indeed made it very good, there was no spot of evil, nor poison of sin and death in it: but by man's frailty and Satan's wickedness, sin too quickly entered into it, and it went on from bad to worse, until that became true which S. John writes, "ᵃ The whole world lieth in wickedness," and he was in a certain sense, the prince of this world; the wicked world was his palace and castle, his stronghold, which he held so firmly, that in order to dispossess him it was needful for God the

ᵃ S. John v. 1.

Son to be made man, to suffer and die for us. The world was Satan's palace, and what were his goods, that it was stored with? What, but the lost and fallen souls and corrupt bodies of miserable men, into whom he had entered, as he did into Judas, possessing them for his own, and urging them to commit all kinds of sin, and especially all uncleanness, with greediness? These were the goods, the property of Satan; his stolen goods, his usurped property; he had his will and his way with them from all uncleanness to all idolatry. And so in a manner they were at peace, they had no uneasiness, no misgivings, concerning what might come hereafter, they went on undisturbed in their sins. So it was with the world generally, before our Lord came into the world. So it is now, with the heathen and unconverted world. Satan has dominion over them: they sin on, and sin on, from morning to night, without any misgiving at all: they are in darkness, and have no longing for light. The God Who made them is in the world which He made; He is around them, close to them on every side; but they know Him not, nor have any desire to know Him. This is perfect heathenism, this is what Satan rejoices in; that people should altogether forget God and their souls, and go on quietly pleasing themselves, taking all liberties that come in their way. Thus lived nearly the whole world, before Jesus Christ was born, and thus lives the heathen world now.

But are the heathen, and the men who lived before Christ, the only persons concerned in this saying? are there none among Christians, of whom there is reason to fear that Satan has possession of their souls and bodies too? quiet possession, so that in respect of them also it may be said, "his goods are in peace"? Alas, it is too true as concerning Christians also, that they may, and do, too often fall away from the grace that made them Christians, and give themselves up to the evil spirit, who was driven out of them in Baptism. The holy Church has always believed and taught, that whereas we were born in sin, the children of wrath, and therefore in a manner the property, the slaves of Satan, that chain is broken in Baptism, and the devil commanded to depart, as truly and really as when S. Paul, or any other Apostle, said to any evil spirit, as to that damsel at Philippi, "I command thee in the Name of Jesus Christ to come out of her." Yes, my brethren we are to believe, though with our outward eyes we see it not, that whenever an infant is baptized, that miracle is wrought which our Lord in this Gospel describes. Jesus Christ, being stronger than Satan, drives him away from that child, overcomes him, and divides his spoils, takes that child to be His own. So it is for the time; the child is surely delivered, and if it were to die presently, it is saved. But what if that child growing up, turn aside unto the wrong path? what if its parents live like heathens, and bring it up to live so too? Too well do we know what will happen in such a case. The child, though a Christian, will be like a heathen or worse: he will go on, without remorse or trouble, in sins not fit to be named. His mouth will be full of cursing and bitterness, his heart exercised in covetous and unclean practices:

he will be dishonest, false, envious, self-willed: and in all this he will be in a manner at peace; i. e., he will pass his time without fear about his soul: for why? it will not really come into his mind that he has any soul at all, any eternal being, dependent on his present behaviour. And thus in him, though baptized and living in a Christian land, the strong one, the destroying spirit, will have recovered his palace, and will keep it, and reign in it at will, his goods being at peace.

Why have I made so special mention of this sad, but too common case? why have I tried so particularly to set it before you? Not so much that I think it likely to be the exact case of any of you, my brethren, now here present: when a person is going on in such utter outrageous profaneness as I have now described, this is not the place where I should expect to find him: I trust that how fallen soever any of us may be, there are none here so entirely forgetful of God, and withal so entirely without fear about their own souls: but the special reason why I have now reminded you that there are such persons, is this: I want you to consider how dangerous it is for a man to account himself safe, and in a good way, merely because he is not troubled about his soul. We know there are persons of that way of thinking: they say, they are quiet and comfortable in themselves, they let nothing daunt them, they lie down at night with easy undisturbed consciences: and therefore they take it for granted, all is right. If one tells them of any fault, or still more, if one remind them of any duty left undone, they reply confidently, it does not trouble them, it is not at all upon their conscience, whatever other people may think: and this they take for an answer and go on just as they were. "We are at peace", they say, "our consciences are quiet: what more would you have?" A great deal more, my brethren: for only consider these heathenish Christians, of whom I have now been speaking, who never say any prayers, never come near the Church at all, never speak of God but to blaspheme; are not they too in a kind of peace? are not their consciences quiet? yet surely none of us would say that they were in a good way. So it may be, that although you go on decently and religiously in many things, and persuade yourself that all is well enough; though you have all your life gone on taking this for granted, yet all the while your peace may be the false and deadly peace of the devil's palace, he may be abiding in your soul and body, with all his armour, all the bad ways by which you have helped him to prevail against you, and so you may seem to be at peace, because you have no misgivings, no fear for your soul. It may be so: till you have inquired, you cannot say but it really is so.

Remember the case of those Pharisees, to whom especially our Saviour gave this very warning: they were not troubled about their souls: they thought all was going on well within them. They fasted, no doubt, regularly; they kept to their rules of prayer; they were scrupulous in paying their tithes; many other things there might be in which they were careful to set a good example: and so they were on the whole well pleased with their own doings: they were ready to ask, as one did

Deadly peace of the unawakened conscience. 201

ask in his ignorance, "what lack I yet?" Surely they seemed to have peace: and yet these were the very persons on whom our Lord pronounced such heavy woe, eight times repeating it on one occasion. Though their own consciences troubled them not, they were to His all seeing Eye full of hypocrisy and iniquity. So may any one of us, who at this or any other moment may seem to himself most clear in conscience. We must not trust that all is right merely because nothing troubles us. Rather, if we be wise, we shall very seriously mistrust and suspect ourselves, when we find our souls free from misgiving. When we set to work, as we all ought to do, to examine ourselves before our evening prayers, if we cannot remember anything to reprove ourselves for, instead of making ourselves easy, and being lifted up, let us rather be ashamed that we have not kept stricter account, and let us beg pardon and cleansing for those secret faults, which, if we had been more diligent, we should have been surely aware of. Let us take all the hints which our merciful God may give us, to help us in finding out the plague of our own hearts. Instead of being angry or sullen, let us strive to be really thankful for every thing that at all helps us to know ourselves better. If we thus watch and pray, no doubt He will quickly help us to see enough of evil in ourselves to alarm and make us careful: and so far, our peace of mind may seem in a certain sense to be disturbed: but what of that? it will be but like the noise made in a prison, when he comes who shall deliver the prisoners. O my brethren, joyful and glad in the end will that hour be to you, in which by the light of God's word, you shall come to know of some sin, perhaps some grievous wasting sin, in which you are now living, not aware how bad it is. And let me add, to many of you, blessed will be the hour in which you shall be moved to open your mind concerning your soul, to God's appointed servant, you will bless God by and by for this, and all the ways by which he convinced you concerning your sin, how wretched and how wicked you were becoming unawares. Instead of the false, unreal peace, which you have hitherto seemed to enjoy in your worldly and carnal doings, you will taste the true peace of God, the blessing of them that mourn. Hitherto you have said, we have no sin, no sin that need disturb us; thus you have deceived yourselves and the truth has not been in you; but now if you earnestly search out, and confess your sins, you will find Him here in His Church, faithful and just, to absolve you from your sins, and to cleanse you from all unrighteousness.

SERMON XX.

THE RELAPSED SINNER.

THIRD SUNDAY IN LENT.

S. MAT. xii. 45.

"*The last state of that man is worse than the first.*"

THESE fearful words are our Saviour's conclusion of a parable, which He had just been addressing to the unbelieving Jews. They had said in their spite and malice, that the very miracles our Lord was performing in their sight, were not His own, but the work of an evil spirit. "He casteth out devils" they said, "by Beelzebub, the prince of the devils."

Our Saviour, having first shown them how senseless, as well as how impious this was, went on to warn them of their own extreme danger, in a parable taken from the circumstances of the case. It is likely that if we had lived in that time and country, and had seen with our eyes persons whom we knew to be possessed, as many were then, with evil spirits, we should be so much the better able to understand the particulars of this parable. Thus much, however, we do understand, that God's Providence, for wise purposes permitted the devil to torment men, their minds and bodies, with a kind of madness; which being known to be the evil spirits' work, gave occasion to many wonderful proofs of our Lord's divine power and authority, not only over ordinary diseases, but also over the powers of darkness. And it should seem from this parable of our Lord's, that when a person had been once possessed in this way, and cured, he was yet liable to a return of the mischief, unless he were very careful of himself. So indeed one might suppose, from the restless and malicious temper of the devil and his angels; and so, we are told, it was with them.

Suppose one of them gone out of a man, and wandering, as it were, through dry and desolate places; he would still go on, longing and wishing to be somewhere, where he might practise his power of mischief, to find some one whom he might torment as before. Suppose it occurred to such an evil spirit, to return unto his house from whence he came out: i.e., to go back, and try, if he could possess and torment the same person again. Our Saviour intimates, that if he found the house empty, swept and garnished; i.e. if he found the mind and body of the unhappy patient in a fit state of preparation for him, the relapse would be seven times worse than the original illness; he would take to him "seven other spirits more wicked than himself, and they would enter in and dwell there, and the last state of that mam would be worse than the first." A frightful picture indeed! and one of which the full horror would be understood by those who heard Him speak, much better than we can understand it, because they had seen such cases; indeed they had just that hour been present, while He cured a very malignant one; and they knew, most likely, among other things, how apt the evil spirit was to return, and how dreadful and hopeless the affliction then became. So much the more must they have been alarmed, as many as had any serious thought, when they heard Him, in conclusion, apply this dreadful parable to themselves; "So shall it be also to this evil generation;" i. e., "you Jews, who have rejected My Gospel, will find before long that it is with you, as if an evil spirit had been cast out, and had returned with seven worse spirits, and gotten entire hold of a man. Your last state will be worse than your first."

To understand this, we may consider what was the state and temper of the Jewish people, at the time of our Lord's appearance among them. Having gone on for some hundred years without any kind of idolatry, they reckoned themselves especial favourites of Almighty God; considered themselves chosen, above all the nations of the earth, to be His people, in such a sense, that they need not fear His ever rejecting them. On this, as on other occasions, our Saviour took pains to correct this great and deadly mistake of theirs. It is as if He had said to them, "Your nation was once of old, like this man before he was cured, in the power of an evil and unclean spirit. You were, as your own Scriptures tell you, wholly given to the worst idolatry, and to those deadly sins, which idolatry brings with it. For this, you were carried away captive to Babylon, and other miseries came upon you, which, by God's grace, succeeded at last in driving out the unclean spirit; you have now lived in your own land more than four hundred years, free from what, in former days, was your great sin, the worshipping of idols. But do not therefore lift yourselves up, nor imagine yourselves safe in God's favour. The evil spirit, once cast out, may return, may find a place prepared for him, may enter in and dwell there; and your last state may be worse than your first. Nay, it is sure to be thus with you, if you go on as you have now begun. For although you have not worshipped false gods, you have not set up images to kneel to, yet you have rejected the true God by rejecting His Son, and ascribing His miracles to the devil. Beware how you go on to reject His Holy Spirit too. Your last chance will be then gone; He will give you over to a reprobate mind; the evil spirits will work their own way with you, and bring you to destruction both of body and soul."

Such, in substance, was our Lord's warning to the scorners and unbelievers of His time. And in a few years they found it as true, as all unbelievers, before long, will find the terrors they now scoff at. Having crucified Christ and blasphemed the Holy Ghost, as if many devils had entered into them, they plunged into such sins, and underwent such a grievous punishment, as have made the very name of Jew (according to the prophecy) "[a] an astonishment, and a proverb, and a by-word to all nations under Heaven."

But our Lord did not utter the warning for those impenitent Jews alone. It holds just as good of all who have been in any sense, by His mercy, delivered from their old sins, from those perverse and evil habits which possessed them like unclean spirits. It

[a] Deut. xxviii. 37.

is true of every one of them, that as long as they are is this world, they are in danger, more or less, of relapsing into their bad ways, and that if they do so relapse, their last state will be worse than their first.

As Christians, baptized into Christ's Church, taught to pray to the Father in His Name, favoured with the promise of His Holy Spirit, we all are like persons delivered from an evil spirit, i. e., we are put in such a condition, we have such help placed within our reach, that we may shake off the chains of darkness, we may love and serve our Redeemer, if we will. But our enemy is not finally put down, nor are we quite beyond his reach. There is not a Christian soul in the world, but has great reason to fear continually, lest the devil return and undo that good work which was begun at Baptism, and which the Church is daily labouring to complete, by instruction, warning, prayers, and sacraments. He is always restless and uneasy, like a person turned out of his home, and wandering in dry and desert regions, till he can lay hold again of those souls, which the grace of God and the care of the Church, bringing them to early baptism, has taken away from him and put in the arms of our Saviour. For this purpose he loses no time, but, from the very moment they are able to think, carefully throws temptations in their way; persuades them that prayer, the service of God, obedience to parents, and respect for their betters, are dull, unpleasant, wearisome things, for which there will be time enough by and by; for the present, they need only to enjoy themselves.

These lessons of the evil spirit we are but too willing to practise: they fall in with our corrupt nature, and suit us so perfectly well, that it is surprising how thoroughly we contrive to learn them, often before we are out of our childhood: and as long as men refuse the means of grace, every hour of their trial on earth, which was meant to prepare them for eternal life, will only make them more and more the children of hell and of lost spirits.

Thus it happens, that Christian countries are full of persons of all ages and stations, leading the lives and practising the tempers of heathens; persons of whom we may reasonably say, that it had been better for them had they never been baptized, better had they never seen a church, nor ever heard the names of God and of Christ. Their present state (let us hope, by God's grace, that it may not prove their last state,) is surely much worse than their first: as much so, as impenitent wicked Christians are worse than mere ignorant heathens.

There is however among Christians one kind of wickedness, more particularly answering to our Saviour's description in the text; the wickedness of those who relapse into any sin, after they appear to be cured of it, when, by the grace of God's good Spirit, the habit of ill-doing appears to be broken, and they seem to be able to keep themselves in order. Concerning such as these, I suppose, the Apostle S. Peter gives us warning: "[b] If after they have escaped the pollutions of the world by the knowledge of the Lord and Saviour Jesus Christ, they are again entangled therein and overcome, the latter end is worse with them than the beginning. For it had been better for them not to have known

[b] 2 S. Pet. ii. 20, 21.

the way of righteousness, than after they had known it, to turn from the holy commandment delivered unto them. But it is happened unto them according to the true proverb, The dog is turned to his own vomit again, and the sow that was washed to her wallowing in the mire."

It seems that the Apostle is speaking, more especially, of such sins as the word "pollution" would lead us to think of; such sins as are not fit to be named, much less practised, among Christians. Into these "sinful lusts of the flesh," he seems to say, a relapse after penitence is especially to be dreaded; and sad experience shows us the reason. It very rarely indeed happens, that persons who have once, by God's special grace, been recovered from sins of that kind, if they again fall into the same evil habit, finish by an effectual repentance at last. Their hearts become cold, and hard, and dead; after one or two relapses, they scarcely think it worth while to repent, knowing as they do by fatal experience, how likely they are to sin again; and thus, in mind and desire at least, they do not leave off sinning till they die.

Consider again the case of the drunkard. Suppose a man, touched with remorse, beholding the misery his wicked selfishness causes to those who are nearest, and ought to be dearest to him; and, moved to remorse by the good Spirit of God, suppose such a man to leave off his dangerous habit; suppose him to resist so many temptations as to be reckoned a sober man. If he is not a religious man too; if he has not used himself every day to beg pardon at the foot of the Cross, and to implore the grace of the Holy Spirit;

P

it is but too likely that in some unguarded hour the old temptation will prevail against him : he will be again entangled therein, and overcome; and having once given way, the devil will find no great difficulty in persuading him that he may as well give way twice, then three times, and so on, as often as may happen to be pleasant or convenient. Whenever his conscience begins to smite him, whenever God's Providence sends a warning, or calls him by the motions of His good Spirit, the chilling thought will arise at the same time, "I have tried all this before, and it ended in nothing; it will be but trouble lost. I may just as well enjoy myself as other people do, and think no more of it." Thus the wretched drunkard goes on, plunging into sin deeper and deeper, till his conscience is seared with a hot iron, and he quite loses all wish to repent.

By these two examples of sensuality and intemperance (and it is much the same in all others sins,) you see that a man's condition is *naturally* worse after relapsing, than before repentance : to which the Scripture teaches us to add, that he is in a spiritual sense far worse off, because he has done so much more towards grieving God's Holy Spirit. It is somewhat in the same way, as when any person in worldly matters fall into error and imprudence, after having been repeatedly checked in it by the warnings of a kind and good friend. The friend, vexed and offended, departs, and checks and warns him no more. So when people wilfully relapse, after they had found by their own experience that the Heavenly Comforter was willing to help them, that they might be good if they would use the means of grace; this is just provoking Him to do as He did to the Jews in His anger; to give them up to their own hearts' lusts, and let them follow their own imaginations. And if they have not God's Holy Spirit to help them, how can they go right for a single moment?

What then is to be done, seeing relapses are so very dangerous, and human nature so very weak? Some, perhaps, may try to flatter themselves, that they may as well continue in their first sin, and spare themselves the trouble of all kinds of repentance. That is, having a sickness on them, which is sure to be mortal, left to itself, they will not take the only medicine which can cure them, lest they should fail to take it properly, and relapse and die after all. I trust there are some at least here, who are more grateful to their Saviour, and more careful of their souls, than to deal so madly, so unkindly, with them. They will consider, what our Lord had pointed out as the true reason of these sad and frequent relapses. The evil spirit in the parable, returning to his house whence he came out, found it empty, swept, and garnished; and therefore it was no hard matter for him to enter in and dwell there, and seven worse spirits with him. So when any man's darling bosom sin had appeared to be cast out by the grace of God, it is but too common for that man to be found, when next the same temptation returns, with a mind empty, swept, and garnished to entertain it. That is, though men leave off their transgression for a while, they do not in earnest turn their hearts towards other and better things; they do not fill up the void in their desires, with thoughts of Him, Who is their only hope, Christ crucified for their sins;

they do not humbly and constantly seek that grace and strength from above, without which they can do nothing against God's enemies and their own. They imagine they have done great things in turning for awhile from some one evil habit; quite forgetting that God would have them not only obey Him but love Him; would have them love Him in Christ Jesus, with all their heart, and all their soul, and all their mind, and all their strength. That is the only preparation of heart which will enable you to resist your spiritual enemy, when having been once repulsed, he returns to the charge, in the hope of taking you unawares. An earnest wish to please Him who laid down His life for you, cherished and maintained by fervent prayer for the help of His Almighty Spirit, and by humble communion with Him in all the ways which He has ordained; this will keep you armed at all points. But without this true Christian piety, your partial amendments for the world's sake will not secure you from grievous relapses; will not free you from the sentence of those, who shall be found at the last day to have received the grace of God in vain.

SERMON XXI.

PERIL OF HALF-HEARTEDNESS.

THIRD SUNDAY IN LENT.

S. LUKE xi. 23.

"*He that is not with Me is against Me, and he that gathereth not with Me, scattereth.*"

OUR Lord in to-day's Gospel gives us an account of the kind of warfare which is continually going on between Him and the great enemy. It is not so much like regular fighting in the open field, with large armies on the one side and the other, coming to one large conflict, which decides the matter once for all. But it is a never ending course of severe and dangerous conflicts, in which one side disputes with the other the possession of every nation, every parish, every family, every individual person. Thus in one of the parables which you just now heard, the devil is compared to a strong man, a great warrior, in full armour, keeping his palace. We seem as we read, to have before our eyes one of the great lords of the Philistines, or one of those who in our own country, when times were unsettled, seized upon castles, and made them a kind of strongholds of robbery; so the prince of darkness and author of all evil, having once gained a footing in the world by the fall of our first parents, has never ceased to occupy, one after another, the houses and hearts, the souls and bodies of men. Born in sin as we are, and children of wrath, each one of us is by nature a palace or castle of the evil one, a place where he abides, to do all the mischief he can, both to us and to all who come within reach of us. And as long as the Almighty permits this, his goods, the possessions of the evil one, are in peace, he has his own way with the unhappy sinners who are possessed by him, there is no struggle, no distress, no misgiving of conscience: people come to be past feeling, they give themselves over to lasciviousness, to commit all uncleanness with greediness: they go contentedly down the broad way. This is the full power of Satan of which S. Paul speaks, the condition of those who are without God in the world: a condition the more fearful, by how much those who are in it are less aware of it. Out of this our natural heathenish condition, God delivers men when He converts them and brings them by holy Baptism to be members of Christ: as it is written, "[a] He hath delivered us from the power of darkness, and translated us into the kingdom of His dear Son:" and again to S. Paul He saith, "[b] I send thee to open their eyes and turn them from darkness to light, and from the power of Satan unto God." And accordingly it has been very common in the Church of Christ, and still is practised in some countries, to use in the Baptism service a regular form of exorcism, the priest in the Name of Jesus Christ commanding the unclean spirit to depart from the child or person

[a] Col. i. 13.   [b] Acts xxvi. 18.

to be baptized: and we may understand in much the same sense our own short prayer which we offer up just before the blessing of the water: "grant that he may have power and strength to have victory and to triumph against the devil, the world and the flesh." Jesus Christ thus coming to us in Baptism, or if we have sinned afterwards, by true repentance and Absolution, is that Warrior stronger than Satan, Who will not let him possess his goods, his ill gotten goods, our souls and bodies, in peace. He cometh upon the old serpent as that Seed of the woman, promised of old time, to bruise his head, not without a severe combat, viz., His Death and Passion: that bruising of His Heel, His lower nature as man, by which from the very first He undertook to save us. The Son of God coming thus upon the evil spirit to whom we were in bondage, overcame him, took from him all his armour wherein he trusted, his power, craft, command of the world, the honour in which he is held by poor deceived mortals; all this Christ taketh from Satan, when He getteth the victory over him, and divideth it as lawful spoil by the rules of war among His own servants, the enemies of Satan. How is that? how may it be said that the spoils of Satan are divided among Christ's soldiers? Partly perhaps because from that time forward whatever portion any of us may have in the good things of this world, riches, power, pleasure, skill, wisdom, knowledge, &c., it is all given up to Jesus Christ and His service: partly again because redeemed man is intended in some sort to fill up the place in God's world which the fallen angels have left vacant: as it is written, "we shall judge angels," and "we shall be made like unto the angels." And so the spoils which Christ takes from Satan are the souls and bodies before lost, but now redeemed, regenerated, saved, and so far "divided," in that each of them is employed by God's grace and Providence in such particular work as the Great King knows to be most for His glory and the good of souls, and will each have assigned his own special reward, his own mansion in the Father's house.

In short, our Saviour here teaches that not only those unhappy ones who were actually possessed by unclean spirits in the way the Gospel describes, but each one of us, every child of Adam, has by nature a spirit of an unclean devil, which can only be cast out by the Holy and Good Spirit entering into each one separately, and uniting him to the second Adam as by birth he was united to the first. Every such case, every Baptism, every effectual repentance and Absolution, is a victory won over the strong man armed, by one stronger than he. It is a warfare which goes on continually, and will go on, from Pentecost to the end of the world.

But now observe the next thing, as concerning this warfare, which the great Captain of our Salvation most expressly warns us of. It is a warfare in which it is utterly impossible for any one to stand by and be neutral. In all wars and quarrels here we know there are many who take no part at all, but only just look on. But in this war between Christ and the devil, that cannot be the case with any one. We must all take a part in it, whether we will or no. "He that is not with Me is against Me, and he that gathereth not with Me, scattereth." Even as in another place He says, "he that is not against us is on our part." Do you hear this, my brethren? it is a fearful sound, surely, for us all: more fearful than if a trumpet sounded from Heaven, for a signal which we must obey, to range ourselves on the right hand or on the left, on the side of Christ's enemies or of His friends. For such a trumpet would only be an angel's voice, but these are the very words of the Judge, spoken to the very inmost conscience of every one of us. Some of us may find it hard to receive them, just as it is hard, very hard, to bring it home to ourselves that we must all without exception, every single one of us, either go away at last into everlasting punishment with the wicked, or with the righteous into life eternal. O! if we could indeed realize this, if we could keep it steadily before our mind's eye, how would it help us in the right way! what power would it give us against temptation! and in like measure, if we could really settle it in our hearts to feel that we are, even now, in one or other of two great armies, if we could by faith constantly discern our King on the one side, and our enemy on the other, and ourselves ranged under this banner or that, would it not make us very serious? would it be possible for us to go on as if our conduct signified little?

One thing at any rate is clear, if we will take our Lord really at His word, that such as feel quite easy in their minds, such as have no anxiety concerning their duty and their souls, can hardly be on Christ's side, and in the way of salvation. For as on the one hand we read, "^c happy is the man that feareth

^c Prov. xxviii. 14.

always," so on the other hand when the strong man armed keepeth his palace, our Lord tells us his goods are at peace: i. e., when the devil has his own way with us most entirely, then we are quite entirely free from spiritual anxiety and misgiving of mind. We say to ourselves, peace, peace, most confidently when there is no peace. I have heard people boast that they let nothing daunt them, that they always kept up a good heart, and I have had reason to fear that their hope was little better than an ignorant deadness to spiritual things; that they were going on at the very time in plain, open, grievous sin. Therefore, I beseech you, let us greatly beware of indulging easy views of our condition: I mean our condition towards God: let us shrink from the thought that all is safe, let us say often in our hearts, What if after all I should be lost? Whatever else is right or wrong, this we are quite sure must be wrong, for a soldier in the midst of the battle to go on as if there was no enemy, no danger at all, for a Christian in the wicked world to feel entirely at ease about his soul and his behaviour, as if all would go right of itself. Such an one is surely against Christ, if he did but know it.

So, too is he (no uncommon sort of person I fear,) who thinks he may stand off for a while, and take no part in this warfare, until he is older, or differently circumstanced: then he fully means to be religious, but he thinks he may be otherwise as yet; not irreligious, from such a thought he unfeignedly shrinks; but still not disposed to serve God entirely and always. What shall we say to such a man? that he is like a soldier in sight of the enemy, refusing to put on his armour, and declaring the hour of the battle to be not yet come: as if, when the order was given to charge, some should stand still, and say to themselves and to another, it will be time enough by and by to take up our arms. Nay, who told you that you should be here to take them up? who told you that they should still be within your reach? who told you that you shall not by that time be in the other world?

Bear with me, my brethren and sons in the Lord, if I say distinctly that this way of putting off your duties is far too common among you. I will just mention one instance: and many of you will guess beforehand what I am going to say. You all know in your hearts, you have been taught it from your childhood, and you have no doubt of it, that to be a good and thorough soldier of Christ, to be really and truly with Him and against His enemy, you must be one with Christ and Christ with you, and you know also that this is promised to those only, who eat His Flesh and drink His Blood, as He bade them, in remembrance of Him. How can you put this duty away from you, and yet hope to be counted on our Saviour's side? Good intentions I dare say you have. I daresay you think you shall begin to prepare yourselves, and come by and by. But remember that a wise and good man used to say, "hell is paved with good intentions." The greater number of those who go down that miserable road mean to repent at some time: only the time never quite comes. Our Lord did not say, he that does not purpose at some time or other to be with Me, but He said distinctly, he that is not with Me, not with Me now, not fighting now on My side, now at this very time, he, be he who he may, is against Me. He needs a great change, he is still in the snare of the devil.

But some might say, surely we are on Christ's side, the other day we resisted such a temptation, yesterday we performed such and such a good work, and though we have perhaps to-day fallen under the same temptation, and failed to do the same kind of good work, yet will not one tell against another? are we not on the whole with Him and not against Him? I would ask you, my brethren one question. Suppose in battle you saw a soldier striking a blow or aiming a shot or a dart now against his own comrades, now against the enemy: on which side should you imagine him really to be, in the purpose and intention of his heart? Should you not judge this of him, that his secret purpose was rather on the side of the enemy, and that what blows he struck at them were rather to save appearances, or for some other selfish reason, than for any loyalty or duty which he had in his heart? In like manner you may be quite sure that as long as you allow yourself in any known wilful sin, you cannot be quite sincere in any part of your duty, you are not a faithful soldier and servant, you do not love your King and Master. He Who sees into your heart cannot reckon you to be with Him.

Besides, what is the real consequence, even outwardly and before men, when Christians thus allow themselves to be half on the devil's side? Much the same as it would be in an army, when the soldiers should now and then turn against their own leader, in the very moment of action. There would be no confidence, no one would know on whom he could depend: the end would be confusion and flight, as our Lord goes on to say, "He that gathereth not with Me, scattereth." We see and hear and feel daily, the like sad effect of our many backslidings and inconsistencies. The unlearned and unbelievers say, behold how these Christians, these men professing godliness, do in their hearts and works deny it. Why then need we care for it? And they are bold to break off from God more and more. O! depend on it, it will never do, it is what neither God nor man will endure, for Christ's soldiers wilfully to go on striking one blow for Satan and another for Christ. They will find in the end that they have been against their Lord altogether.

Neither again will it answer in this warfare if any man think to be passively on Christ's side, i.e., to lie still and merely do nothing against Him. We cannot do so, my brethren if we would. Even if the hands could be idle, the mind, the will, the heart, must be employed, the whole soul must be tending this way or that, upwards or downwards, towards hell or towards Heaven. I suppose there are not a few, who looking on the sad falls and strange inconsistencies of such as have appeared earnest in religion, are inclined to shrink from being earnest themselves, as though there were some deceit in it: and so they are contented to go on, not only cold and indifferent in their devotions, but careless too, and loose in their rules of life, to their own and others' great danger and harm. I wish they and all of us considered more what the Great Shepherd here assures us, he that is not actively engaged gathering the flock with Me, is really scattering it. It is vain to think of being on Christ's side, and not being earnest and active in His cause. Remember the wicked and slothful servant: what cast him into the outer darkness? not his ill using his talent, but his not using it at all. Look round you, my brethren, and see, see what comes of lukewarmness, and ordinary ways, of being or seeming indifferent to the cause of God and His Church. The bad example speaks: one after another says, my neighbour is not particular, why should I be? my friend, my father, my master does not communicate, why should I? my mother, my mistress, my elder sister bears with unwomanly discreditable conduct, why may not I keep company with whom I will? Look into your own hearts, consider how much you are losing of God's grace and blessing. You might be fervent in prayer, you might be full of all good thoughts, holy seasons and communions might be a joy and crown to you: what a pity to lose all this for want of courage and exactness in your doings! Look again towards the enemy, see how you encourage him. Depend upon it, he rejoices in every moment you lose, every opportunity you neglect. Look, above all, to that which you know, or may know, to be written in God's book, as concerning your daily falls and backslidings: the positive sins, of will and temper at least, into which you are continually betrayed, for want of a courageous purpose of being entirely and zealously on God's side. O! if we will but turn our minds towards it, we shall see that Heaven and earth all around us, are full of tokens how blessed a thing it is to serve Christ with our whole heart, how fatal to serve Him with half a heart.

SERMON XXII.

THE DUMB AND DEAF SPIRIT.

THIRD SUNDAY IN LENT.

S. LUKE xi. 14.

"*He was casting out a devil, and it was dumb, and it came to pass that when the devil was gone out, the dumb spake.*"

As the holy time of Lent begins with the remembrance of our Lord overcoming Satan, so during the course of it we are warned by the Church, again and again, of our warfare with the same evil spirit. Last Sunday we heard of an unclean devil being cast out of the daughter of a Canaanitish woman; and by and by, as the week of Christ's Passion comes on, we shall hear more and more of Satan entering into Judas, and continuing to do Christ all the mischief he could. And on the third Sunday again we are told of a very remarkable case, a very signal blow struck in the warfare betwixt our Saviour and our enemy.

Jesus was casting out a devil, and it was dumb; the evil and malicious one delights in undoing God's work in every way, and in spoiling God's gracious gifts. Speech is one of the best of His outward gifts. It is one chief mark by which mankind are distinguished from the beasts that perish. No wonder then if Satan take pleasure in tying men's tongues, and taking away the use of them; and no wonder if our merciful Redeemer, Who came to undo Satan's work in all things, was ever ready to restore speech to the unhappy creatures whom He found so afflicted.

But this was not all the meaning of the miracle. As every one of Christ's mighty works, wrought on men's bodies, was a token of good done to their souls, so we may be sure was this, of giving speech to the dumb. Neither is it hard to see what particular spiritual good it signifies. The devil, though he be not often allowed to take away our natural gift of speech, is yet evermore busy in making us dumb towards God.

First and chiefly, he will if he can make the hearts of Christians so stupid and dull as concerning heavenly things, that they shall never readily move their tongues in prayer; they shall be most unwilling to learn the good lessons which the holy Church would teach them, and if they have been taught they will make all haste to forget them. Alas, there are I fear but few of us who do not know too much of this sad kind of dumbness; few who have not too often felt a strange backwardness, even when there was a real call to say something of God and Christ and Eternity. I know indeed that very often it is far better to keep silence on holy things; we feel, it may be, that we are not the persons to speak, or that our speaking would very likely do more harm than good. There is a natural shyness and modesty, tying the tongue, and hindering it from saying anything, even on those matters of which the heart is most full. All this is very well; it is fear and reverence, not carelessness and dulness of heart; it is to be improved and encouraged, not to be blamed. But when we have made the best of it, surely we must needs own, that our silence is often of a very irreligious kind. We say no good words because we have no good thoughts to express. We neglect to join in good prayers because we are not trying to pray in heart. We give no good advice because we do not really care how people are going on. When good advice is given to us we make no answer, because we had rather not hear it. All such cases are but too plain tokens of the power which the evil spirit has still over us. There is need of Jesus to come near and cast him out. We must try and pray better than we do at present; we must make the most of all the good thoughts and notions, which He at any time may graciously put into our minds; and we must put ourselves in the way of being helped by the prayers of the Church, and of all our good friends and acquaintance.

Oftentimes such a deadness as this towards God is joined with a kind of sullenness towards one another. Sullen, peevish silence, the kind of behaviour which grown people so often complain of in children, is unhappily no rare thing among grown people themselves. We feel how provoking it is, when children or servants, or any whom we have to correct, know perfectly well that certain words ought to be spoken, the truth to be told, a fault to be confessed, pardon to be asked, kind things said instead of unkind ones, and they cannot find in their hearts to say those words. If they would but do so, they would set all right in a moment, but they will not do so, they will rather go on for half hours, and hours, and sometimes for days, feeding and cherishing bitter thoughts, which make both themselves and all around them unhappy. I wish it were only young children that do so; but who has not felt to his cost, that Christian men and women, long after Confirmation and Communion, too often allow themselves in the same dark and miserable tempers; and if we are provoked with children for doing so, how much more provoking, think you, must it be to Almighty God, the God of love, and to all the blessed and loving spirits in Heaven, to behold us so practising the lessons of the evil and sullen spirit? Perhaps something has happened to vex us, and we know in our hearts that one grave and gentle word would very likely set all to rights; but we have not the heart to speak that word; we rather go on for days, perhaps for weeks, brooding over the thing in silence, disquieting every one by our gloomy looks and ways. What is this, but a dumb spirit? the evil one unseen at our side, whispering that to be, or seem, good natured just then, would be a poor unmanly thing, and so for our pride's sake he prevails on us to go on in that wretched mind, instead of going at once to Jesus, Who we know would cast him out with a word, and enable the dumb to speak, and make all peaceful and contented again.

Again, it is an evil and dangerous silence, a dumbness which comes of the bad spirit, when persons have done wrong, and ought to confess it, and refuse to do so. You know, my brethren, what merciful promises are given in many places of Holy Scripture to those who come before God in penitent confession. "ᵃWhoso covereth his sins shall not prosper, but he that confesseth and forsaketh them shall find mercy." "ᵇI said, I will confess my sins unto the Lord, and so Thou forgavest the iniquity of my sin." "ᶜDavid said unto Nathan, I have sinned against the Lord; and Nathan said unto David, the Lord also hath put away thy sin; thou shalt not die." And accordingly the Church instructs us all to come daily to Christ's footstool, owning our sins as humbly and as truly as we can. And so we all do in words, when we use the general confession, which begins, "Almighty and most Merciful Father;" or when we say the fifty first Psalm, or any other prayer of the like penitential meaning. But it is very plain that we may use those humble words without being humbled in heart. The rest of the congregation saying them with us, they put us to no particular shame. It is therefore a very great help to our contrition, and a very good sign of its truth, when God by His Providence calls us to a more exact and particular confession, a confession to man also, and we dutifully obey the call. And this happens not seldom; among other ways it happens as often as people are suspected of somewhat wrong, and are called to account for it, and put by excuses, and frankly own themselves in the wrong. As long as they refuse to do so, they are plainly guilty of two great sins, stubbornness and falsehood; of course then they are in the power of an evil spirit; a devil has the mastery of them and makes them dumb; but when our Lord comes to them, and touches their hearts by His grace, and

ᵃ Prov. xxviii. 13.   ᵇ Ps. xxxii. 6.   ᶜ 2 Sam. xii. 13.

they happily attend to His call, and are ready to acknowledge their fault, not to Him only, but to those also who call them to account here on earth, this is like Jesus casting out the dumb and deaf spirit; their honest and humble confession is a sure token of a great blessing which God intends for them. My brethren, I wish we thought more of this; it is so very seldom that we take courage manfully to own the transgressions we have committed, without unduly hiding or softening things; we are so very ready and sharp with our excuses, so quick in perceiving how we may hide some portion at least of our guilt, so little scrupulous in laying the blame on others. What are our confessions towards God better than a mockery of Him, if we prove so false and hypocritical and cowardly, when it is our duty to confess to man? We never think our servants or children truly penitent for any fault they have been guilty of, if we find their confessions in any sense untrue. How then dare we think of satisfying God by untrue confessions? O that we would open our hearts frankly to the gracious influence of that Saviour, Who alone can say with power, "thou dumb and deaf spirit, I charge thee, come out of him, and enter no more into him." None of us can say how much good it might do him, how great a blessing it might win him from the Almighty, if he would simply force himself to be quite honest when he has a fault to acknowledge.

Other kinds of evil silence might be mentioned, as when persons out of cowardice or sloth, neglect to reprove or instruct those committed to their charge: or when, out of envy, they refuse to join in praise or approbation of any one. But let us now consider the happy change when the Lord of spirits comes with authority and power, and commands even the dumb spirit, and he departs. Presently the mouth which had been closed in cold indevout silence, is opened, and the tongue loosed, and the man speaks and praises God. Before, he might go to Church Sunday after Sunday, and never take any part in the devotions of Christ's people; now he devoutly prays with them when they pray, joyfully sings with them when they sing, reverently repeats with them the articles of the Christian Faith. Before, when cheerful discourse was going on, good and merry hearts were overflowing with a grateful sense of God's mercies, the man took no part in it; for why? he was full of dissatisfied, discontented thoughts; nothing pleased him, because he had not made up his mind to submit his own will to the Will of God. Now God's grace has taught him better; he has learned to be pleased with what pleases his Maker; he no longer sits like Nabal, churlish and moody in the midst of comfort and refreshment; he is not too proud to acknowledge the overflowing bounty and goodness of his Saviour. Whereas before he hardened himself against all acknowledgement of sin, now he humbly confesses it; confesses that when he went wrong it really was his own fault, his own grievous fault, and takes reproof and hard usage as things which he must expect, because he has too richly deserved them. Before, being as it were tongue-tied by the bad spirit of sloth, he cared not what serious duties he left undone, in the way of warning, instructing, comforting his brethren; persons all around him were left to take their chance, because he felt as if he could not bring himself to utter in season one grave and charitable word. Now he is ever on the watch to do good, and to speak a word in season; using all the while deep reverence and godly fear. In all these ways, and more, the Presence of the great Healer, makes itself manifest; the tongue, the best member that man has, being delivered from the enemy, and put to the best use. The change perhaps is more striking, and more talked of, when one who had been used to bad words, to swearing, or filthy talking, or ill-natured slander, visibly and openly repents and turns from that sin. The change in that case may be more striking, but it is not surely at all more wonderful. A peevish sullen silence is often harder to be cured, than any custom of bad words; and when it is cured, is too apt to return, if people do not earnestly watch and pray against it.

Finally, inasmuch as these faults of the tongue, and their respective amendments, are more within other people's knowledge than many other parts of a man's character, it concerns us much to have the right thoughts concerning them, when we see others either the worse for them, or the better. And on this again our Lord, in this day's Gospel, gives us ample instruction. Observe how differently the people behaved who were present when He healed the dumb man possessed with a devil. First, it is said, the people wondered. They were astonished at what they saw, and there was an end. Let us beware of such barren, useless astonishment, when we are standing by and seeing Christ's works. At one time or another, we have often the comfort of seeing, how much better such and such persons are going on than they formerly did; and we are very apt to remark upon it; but never let such a thing pass, I beseech you, without our saying seriously to ourselves, we too have our faults, many and great; and the same grace which cured these, will cure our's also, if we ask for it in earnest.

Again, when our Lord cast out the dumb spirit, the multitude not only marvelled at it, but they added as the truth was, "Is not this the Son of David?" That is, they became sensible of the immediate Presence of an infinitely holy and heavenly Being, their Saviour, and it filled them with deep awe, with adoring love. Let us make the same use of every amendment we notice in others. Let it be a sign and token to us that Christ is really in all our conversations and companies, waiting to do us good, to hallow our words, to make our tongues really the best members that we have. He is always walking and discoursing in a spiritual inward way with us as He was with the two disciples, though as yet our eyes, like their's, are holden that we cannot know him. But we may know Him, as really present, by faith, and knowing Him, how can we help watching our words, as in His hearing, continually?

Again, some were so recklessly obstinate, as even to attribute Christ's miracles to the help of a bad spirit; as if Satan should cast out Satan. This, to be sure, was the extreme of folly and spite; but be assured my brethren, that we go some way towards it, as often as we put cold, uncharitable interpretations on any seeming improvement in our neighbour's conduct. You shall hear people sometimes say scornfully, How good such a person is grown! Take you care of such words, such tones, lest perchance you be mocking and trifling with God's grace. Alas! how shall we answer for it in the last day, if our Lord's healing our brother, in our sight, made us worse instead of better?

SERMON XXIII.

OBEDIENCE, NOT PRIVILEGE, THE MEASURE OF BLESSEDNESS.

THIRD SUNDAY IN LENT.

S. LUKE xi. 27, 28.

"And it came to pass, as He spake these things, a certain woman of the company lifted up her voice, and said unto Him, Blessed is the womb that bare Thee, and the paps which Thou hast sucked. But He said, Yea rather, blessed are they that hear the word of God, and keep it."

THAT is, it is a blessed thing to have great spiritual privileges, to be brought especially near to God; but it is a more blessed thing to make the best use you can, of the privileges you have, be they little or great, many or few. This is a lesson which our Lord was continually teaching, especially to His own disciples and apostles whom He had brought so very near Him. Of course when God shewed Himself on the earth as Man, and conversed with men, and when He began to call us, Adam's children, one by one to be members of Himself, partakers of a Divine Nature, there was fear lest being carried away by the sense of such exceeding favour, we should neglect to walk worthy of it: as the Jews, because they had Abraham to their father, flattered themselves that there was no need for them to do the works of Abraham. Therefore our Lord, over and over kept warning them, as in that last parable just before He went away, I mean the parable of the talents. It was well, He signified, to have five talents; a great honour and favour to be so trusted by the King: but it was far, far better to have one, and make the best of it, than five, or five hundred, and hide them, or throw them away.

This lesson God had taught from the very beginning of the world, in a peculiarly awful way. Think of Satan, my brethren, as he was at his first creation, a bright and glorious Angel, son of the morning; shining out among the other Angels, as the morning star among the stars: and compare him, in that his first estate, with the very least and lowest of God's reasonable creatures, the least and lowest of mankind, truly trying to serve his Maker. Which of the two would you rather call blessed? your own heart will answer, and your Saviour Himself has taught you. "ᵃWhen the seventy-returned again with joy saying, Lord even the devils are subject to us through Thy name, He said unto them, I beheld Satan as lightning fall from Heaven." He says, "I was by, and saw with Mine own eyes, when Satan as lightning fell from Heaven. Rejoice not so much if the spirits are subject to you: take My word" (God's own word) "for it, it. is better to be the poorest, the simplest little infant, dying when it is just baptized, and so having its name surely written in Heaven, than to be such as

ᵃ S. Luke x. 17, 18.

Satan was, having power over hosts of Angels, and priding himself on it."

Again, it pleased our gracious Lord, so to order the course of His Passion, as that in it there should be two wonderful examples, one for warning, one for encouragement: one of the nearest to Him, cast away; one of the farthest, brought near and saved. The castaway, I need not tell you, was Judas: the forgiven one, the thief on the cross. How very unlike were these two in their opportunities of knowing Christ! the one, chosen out by Him, as one of the twelve, who should constantly attend on Him during the whole remaining part of His ministry, witnessing all His mighty works, hearing all His gracious words, as they proceeded out of His mouth; going in and out with Him, seeing how not only diseases, but even the winds and the waves, and the very spirits of hell obeyed Him. All this Judas had seen with his own eyes, and heard with his own ears, and had become familiar with it all, as much so as S. Peter or S. John, or any other of His beloved and favoured ones. He had also been especially trusted by our Lord; entrusted with the power of working miracles, and with the authority of an Apostle: to Judas, as to all the rest it had been said, "He that heareth you, heareth Me, and he that despiseth you, despiseth Me." Besides that our Lord had given to him the sole charge of His own and His Apostles' common purse; the little stock that they had to live upon in their poor way, so that in respect of being near to Christ and knowing Him after the flesh, few indeed have ever been so highly privileged as that wicked traitor.

On the other hand who was further from Him, or less likely in appearance to be His for ever, than that robber and malefactor, down to the very time of his crucifixion and beyond it? for he went on reviling with his fellow malefactor, even when they were hanging on their crosses by Jesus' side, and after the sun had begun to be darkened. Then, when all things seemed to be against Jesus of Nazareth, and He hung on the tree, the accursed tree, forsaken, so it seemed of Heaven and earth, then, in spite of all these appearances, this one person found grace to believe and own Him: and our Lord, beginning to lead captivity captive, took him, as His companion into Paradise; the first fruits, so to speak, of His victory. So the last was first, and the first last: the blessing of Abraham came on him that was afar off; and a curse very like that of Satan, on him that was nigh. Privilege was nothing, hearing and believing was all in all.

Wonderful indeed is the way in which Scripture leads us to compare Judas Iscariot with the penitent thief; yet there is another comparison still more wonderful: it is that which our Lord Himself made, when He compared His own Mother's blessing with that which any ordinary Christian may by God's grace secure to himself. He had been speaking of the great danger of the evil spirit returning when he had once been cast out: i. e., what a fearful thing it would be for Christians to relapse into sin after Baptism: their last state would be worse than the first. And it was providentially so ordered, that then, as once before, attention should be drawn to the high privileges of His Mother, and so He took occasion to assure us that, great as her privileges were, if you could fancy them apart from such holy obedience as any ordinary Christian might practise, they would prove in the end, nothing worth. For as the devil cast out, and allowed to return, has power to do more harm than ever, so a person brought very near to God, but not partaking of God's holiness, would find a curse instead of a blessing.

Certainly if any outward privileges could, of themselves, make a soul happy for ever, our Lord's own Mother would be an instance. For her's were indeed the very crown and height of all privileges, an honour inconceivable, had not God Himself told us of it: too high, one should have thought, for any created being. For it is nothing else my brethren, than to be the Mother of Jesus Christ; Mother of Him Who is the Most High God: i. e., Mary, when she conceived Jesus Christ in her womb, the memory of which great thing we shall soon have to keep, became in very deed the Mother of Him Who is the Most High God. You cannot deny or doubt this, without denying or doubting that Jesus is God.

Try to think of this only for a moment: God over all, blessed for ever, the Most High God, Creator of Heaven and earth, Creator of her His own Mother, among the rest, did not abhor the Virgin's womb; He vouchsafed to be enfolded in her arms, to be fed from her bosom, to be clothed, laid to rest, carried about, waited on in every way, by this poor woman, the carpenter's betrothed wife of Nazareth, to be subject to her, to call her Mother, to obey her as His Mother, all the days of His life. I say it was the Most High and Holy God Who thus made

Himself her true and perfect Son, and having once made Himself her Son, He continues her Son for ever, as surely as He continues to be true Man and our true Mediator, presenting Himself before the Father, in never-ceasing intercession for us. As surely as Jesus is God, so surely is Mary, for ever, the Mother of God.

The good woman who uttered that cry, in admiration of our Lord's teaching, "blessed is the womb that bare Thee, and the paps which Thou hast sucked," had no notion at the time, how great a word she was uttering. She spake as an earthly mother of an earthly child; as any mother in Israel might call Hannah blessed, because she was the mother of Samuel. But we know much more of the hidden meaning of that word "blessed", when it is spoken of the Mother of Christ. It is the same which she herself uttered, when she broke forth in her hymn of thanksgiving, which we call the Magnificat. "Behold from henceforth all generations shall call me blessed." But even she herself, it is likely, was not fully aware of the deep meaning of the words which the Holy Ghost had put into her mouth. She seems to have been only coming by degrees to the knowledge that the Holy One which was born of her was indeed the great Almighty God. When the shepherds, sent by the Angels, came and worshipped Him, she kept all those things and pondered them in her heart, as persons do, when something has happened which means more than they can yet explain. When having lost Him, she found Him in the temple, and He said "Wist ye not that I must be about My Father's business?" she understood not the saying, and kept it afterwards in her heart, musing no doubt, what it might be. That which took place at the marriage in Cana, and again when she came with His brethren desiring to see Him, He being in the act of teaching the people, looks very much as if she were still imperfect in her knowledge, and perhaps like the holy Apostles, she might so continue, until the Holy Ghost came down upon her and them together.

The blessedness then of our Lord's Mother, was more than she herself knew of: indeed it is one of His mysteries: it is more than we can imagine: but we are bound reverently to think of it, as of the very highest privilege, as far as we are told, to which any mere creature ever did or could attain. Honour her we must: how can we help it? but we may not worship her; God never commanded us to do so, and it would be too much like making a graven image to worship.

Now then, observe it well: even of His own blessed Mother, and of her exceeding privileges, our Lord will not have us think so much, as of that which we may all attain to, by simply trying our best to be good Christians. Our Lord does not of course mean us to understand, that His own Mother's privileges are no greater than those of any ordinary believer. But thus it was: the good woman who addressed Him, was herself perhaps a mother, or at any rate, had a mother's heart. Like many more, she was carried away, as it were, and beside herself with loving wonder, at His mighty works of healing, at His teaching with such Divine authority, and at the gracious words which proceeded out of His mouth.

So not able to contain herself, she lifts up her voice in the hearing of all, and exclaims, how blessed must be the mother of such a child. Our Lord checks her as He afterwards checked the young man, who came running unto Him and calling Him "Good Master," "Why callest thou Me good? there is none good but One, that is God;" as much as to say, take care how you speak at random of such holy and awful things; there is but one Being that is really good, good in Himself; good with such a goodness as is entirely His own, not at all borrowed from another; do not use the word lightly, according to your own fancy and feeling at the moment, and account this or that man good, and that it will be enough if you try to be like him; but take God's account of goodness, of such goodness as will prepare you for Heaven. "If thou wilt enter into life, keep the commandments." He did not in that answer deny Himself to be good, neither in our text did He deny His mother to be blessed. But as always in His teaching, so in both these instances, He would have us, one and all, to understand, that feelings, however earnest for the moment, and privileges, however high and glorious, will not save a man without dutiful obedience. When we might be inclined to cry out, "blessed is the womb that bare Thee!" He says to us, yea rather, think in your hearts, "blessed are they that hear the word of God, and keep it."

Are they not most awful as well as most comfortable words? most comfortable, in that they assure us, that we, even the simplest of us all, may be, in our measure, blessed as she was, blessed with a blessing like hers, if we will only hear His word and

the measure of blessedness. 241

keep it. At the same time it is, I repeat, very awful to be told that our privileges are so great, since we are sure that the more is committed to us, the more He will ask of us. As it would have been a fearful thing, even in our eyes, too shocking almost to be imagined, for our Lord's own Mother to have proved unholy and untrue, and to have gone the wrong way at last; so is it most fearful, and as it were unaccountable, in the sight of the holy Angels, for any Christian to refuse to hear God's word, or having heard it, not to keep it.

Concerning the woman to whom our Lord thus spake, we are not told how she received His warning. But we have read of some, yea a whole town, and that His own town, where He had been brought up, and dwelt for thirty years, who hearing Him, could not choose but bear witness, and wonder at the gracious words which proceeded out of His mouth, and yet when He began to tell them of their faults, they were filled with wrath, and ready to cast Him down headlong. Do you think it impossible for any thing like this to take place among Christians? Do not make too sure of it brethren. Can you not imagine a person carefully and lovingly brought up, abundant means of grace around him, churches open, Communions frequent, good examples and good books thrown in his way: can you not imagine such an one, giving way secretly or openly to one or more of the devil's many enticements, and going on till he comes to hate his own privileges, and wish he had never known them, that he might be more at ease in his sin? disgusted and angry when he is told the truth, and altogether realizing the Prophet's fearful

R

description, "ᵇThou saidst, there is no hope:—no: for I have loved strangers, and after them will I go." If you have ever known such an one, if you have ever, but for a short time, indulged the profane obstinate temper in your heart, then you can understand but too well the behaviour of those wicked Nazarenes to our Lord; and you have need, indeed you have special need, to repent and watch, watch and repent, all the days of your pilgrimage here.

And if by the blessing of God, you have been preserved from such sad backsliding, if He has given you grace to find pleasure in waiting on Him here in His own house, in the hearing and study of His word, in His blessed Sacraments, it is a great favour, and you cannot be thankful enough; but do not rest in that, nor flatter yourself that of course all is well. The sure token is if you go on serving Him, when you do not find pleasure in it; in irksome and costly duties, in doing good to the unthankful and the evil, in prayer that seems not to bring comfort. Not to those only who find and feel most sensible consolation in waiting on Him, but to every one, in comfort or in dreariness, who is stedfastly minded to do His Father's will, is the word of promise spoken, "the same is My brother, and sister, and mother."

ᵇ Jer. ii. 25.

SERMON XXIV.

TO BE WITHOUT GOD, UTTER DARKNESS.

AMOS v. 18.

"Woe unto you that desire the day of the Lord; to what end is it for you? the day of the Lord is darkness and not light."

I MUST again put you in mind of the terrors and awefulness of the Last Day, as the Gospel sets them before us, especially in the early weeks of Lent; that so being moved by a holy fear, what may come of our sins, we may set about the work of Lent, which is repentance, and approach nearer and nearer to the end of Lent, i. e., a happy Communion at Easter. As therefore the Church put you in mind, a fortnight ago, of the *suddenness* of that great Day, by the history of Sodom; and last Sunday, by the history of Esau, how it will be a day of *separation*, the Judge dividing the sheep from the goats; so it may be well to set before you to-day, how that Holy Scripture plainly declares that to the wicked it will be a day of *darkness*. So the prophet Joel, blowing the trumpet in Zion, and sounding the alarm in God's holy mountain, which is His Church, bids all the inhabitants of the land, i. e., all Christians, to tremble; [a] for the Day of the Lord cometh, for it is nigh at hand. And why should they tremble? because, as he goes on to say, it is "[b] a day of dark-

[a] Joel ii. 1.   [b] Joel ii. 2.

ness and of gloominess, a day of clouds and of thick darkness." And another prophet, Zephaniah, almost in the same words; "ᶜThe great Day of the Lord is near ; it is near and hasteth greatly, even the voice of the Day of the Lord: that day is a Day of wrath, a day of trouble and distress, a day of wasteness and desolation, a day of darkness and gloominess, a day of clouds and thick darkness." And in the New Testament, S. Peter taking up an old prophecy, made proclamation in the very first Christian congregation that was ever gathered, "ᵈThe sun shall be turned into darkness... before the great and terrible Day of the Lord come." And the Lord and Judge Himself, sealing and making good all that His servants had said : "ᵉafter the tribulation of those days, shall the sun be darkened, and the moon shall not give her light, and the stars shall fall from heaven." All these and other like places make good the saying in the text, "the Day of the Lord is darkness and not light," and it is repeated presently after: "Shall not the Day of the Lord be darkness and not light? even very dark and no brightness in it?" Of course when Holy Scripture says thus plainly that the Day of the Lord will be darkness, it means that it will be so to the wicked and unprepared. To them it will be darkness indeed, but the children of the true Israel will have light in their dwellings. As it was when the Lord smote Pharaoh and Egypt with the plague of darkness. "ᶠThey saw not one another, neither did any rise up from his place for three days; but the children of Israel had light in their dwellings."

ᶜ Zeph. i. 14, 15.   ᵈ Acts ii. 20.
ᵉ S. Matt. xxiv. 29.   ᶠ Exod. x. 23.

That was the outward darkness of the body; but the darkness threatened at the Last Day is far worse than that, it is the inward darkness of the soul. What is the darkness of the soul? We may understand by considering what is the light of the soul? "God is light and in Him is no darkness at all." As the light of the body is the eye, so the light of the soul is God. And the Godhead becomes the light of our souls through the Second Person of the Blessed Trinity, God the Son, Jesus Christ. For "[g]in Him is Life, and the Life is the light of men." "That is the True Light which lighteth every man that cometh into the world." When Christ comes to our souls, and lends us, as it were, His eyes, that we may see things in some measure as He sees them, then we see them as they truly are, not before; just as the natural light of the day shews us the things of the world, but in the darkness of night we do not see them. God in Christ then, being our light, our darkness is to be without God and Christ. The heathen nations were so, "without God in the world," and therefore they are spoken of, as "sitting in darkness and the shadow of death." As "[h]he that walketh in darkness knoweth not whither he goeth," so the heathen, and they who through their wickedness are without God in the world, know not what their doings will end in. They are on their way along the broad road, down towards the bottomless pit, and have no notion of it themselves. And again, as in the night no man can work, so those who are without God and Christ cannot really work for God. "They that are in the

[g] S. John i. 4, 9.   [h] 1 S. John ii. 11.

flesh" says the Apostle, "cannot please God." Thus you see how the heathen and those Christians, whose wickedness has made them like heathens, are altogether in spiritual darkness. But those who shall be lost and condemned at the Great Day will be in far worse darkness. They will be separated from God and Christ for ever. The "horror of great darkness," which will then fall upon them, will never be relieved by the least glimmering of light. The Saviour of the world will be no Saviour, God will be no Father, to them. Consider how dismal it is to be entirely in the dark, even in respect of this earthly light, and you may the better understand the misery, when our Lord shall turn away His Face for ever.

One thing for example, which goes along with darkness, is more or less of fear and dread. Everybody knows, most know by their own experience, how natural it is for children to be afraid in the dark. God has ordered it so by His wise Providence, in order that being afraid, though of what we are afraid we do not well know, we may be kept from venturing into places which the want of light would make dangerous to us. This most likely is the reason why darkness is made naturally frightful, but whatever the reason be, such undoubtedly is the fact; to almost all children it is a trial to be left alone any while in the dark. Let those who can remember anything of this in themselves, or who have had occasion to see much of it in others, think what it must be, to be left alone in that outer darkness, the door of Heaven shut for good and all, against the miserable lost spirit, no gleam, not the faintest, reaching it at all, in any way. Who can imagine the strange intolerable fear which must at that moment take entire possession of the soul, not knowing what may come next, only knowing that it will be far worse than anything we have ever imagined?

Again, as what people do in the dark is generally all confused and wrong, so there will be no doing, nor thinking, nor speaking, anything at all right; no beauty, no truth, no order, no regularity; all will be confusion, disorder, unseemliness; and this perhaps may be signified by the strange uncouth shapes and frightful imaginations, which have been common in all ages among Christians, concerning hell and its wretched inhabitants?

Again, if people lose their way, or get wrong, in the dark, they commonly go on from bad to worse; and this is a most fearful circumstance of that day of darkness, that those who shall have gone astray in it, will have no chance of ever finding the right road again. It is a bottomless pit, so the Holy Ghost in the Book of Revelation repeatedly calls it; a gulph in which they who shall be plunged will keep on sinking lower and lower.

Again, in all darkness there is a lonely feeling; you cannot see your friends near you, nor any token of them; therefore it is, so far, as if they were at a distance; and so, when the Lamb in His wrath shall finally hide His Face from any, that miserable person will find himself utterly forsaken, quite alone, it will be a day of entire desolation. Or rather, I should say, he will not be altogether alone, but alone in regard of friends and helpers, left alone in the midst of cruel and scornful enemies. What our Lord standing in the place of us sinners speaks concerning His own sufferings, will in that day, we may suppose, be fulfilled in those who shall have forfeited the benefit of His Passion: "¹Many oxen are come about me; fat bulls of Bashan close me in on every side. They gape upon me with their mouths, as it were a ramping and a roaring lion. Dogs have compassed me, the assembly of the wicked hath inclosed me." Our Lord was soon delivered from this; He delivered Himself for He could not be holden of it. But those on whom it will come in that day, will not be able to do anything for themselves; they will not be able to pray; the Holy Spirit will not be there to help them, nor the Lord Jesus Christ at His Father's Right Hand to intercede for them. They will be left in the dark, to contend with the powers of darkness.

Thus you see how "the Day of the Lord will be darkness and not light; even very dark, and no brightness," not a glimmering of light, "in it," to those who shall die in a heathenish impenitent state. Only think then brethren, what a thing it must be, for any person in sport or rashness to desire that day, to pray that it may come, for the ruin either of others, or one's self, and yet this is what they continually do, who have used themselves to utter words of cursing and swearing, they are for ever, with their own lips devoting themselves, and their brethren, to that utter darkness. And it is something of the same kind of folly, when people in long distress and disappointment grow altogether impatient and pray that God would take them; how do we know that such a petition in the lips of such as we are, is not

¹ Ps. xxii. 12, 13.

praying for our own ruin? How can we be sure that the prophet, if he could speak to us also, would not say, as to the people of Israel, "why desire the Day of the Lord? It will come too soon for you; to you it will be darkness and not light." Alas! is there not chance enough of a man's going wrong in that day, among the many and grievous temptations which are around us, but we must as it were bring the temptation home to ourselves, invite it and pray for it by presumptuous and profane cursing, or as some others do, in a sort of unbelieving, sportive way, challenging God as it were to do His worst with us; saying, "[k]Let Him make speed, and hasten His work, that we may see it, and let the counsel of the Holy One of Israel draw nigh and come, that we may know it?" What will such unbelievers do, when they shall find God taking them at their word? when His dreadful work of judgement shall indeed come hastening on, and they, looking on to Eternity, shall behold nothing but darkness and sorrow, and shall feel themselves driven to darkness, forced onward to that never-ending darkness, which God had told them of, and they would not believe.

And yet had they chosen, they might have perceived even in this present world the beginnings of that miserable state. For even in this world, as Scripture warns us, and as is very plain to be seen by the lives of wicked men, even in this world, if men give themselves over to sin, the very light which is in them becomes darkness, " and how great is that darkness!" That very reason and understanding, which God gave to be a "lantern to their ways"

[k] Isa. v. 19.

shines, so far as it does shine, with a false light; it is worse than darkness to them. As for example, dishonest persons employ all their wit and cleverness in contriving how to cheat and steal, and unchaste persons in inventing ways to come to the satisfaction of their sinful lusts. And again; many turn even the mercy, which God has shewn them for the salvation of their souls, into an occasion for eternally ruining their souls; they make themselves easy in some of the worst sins, saying to themselves, "These sins will not be laid to my charge; Christ has died for me and borne the punishment of them; and so why need I trouble and grieve about them?" Thus they go on, and die without serious repentance: and what is this, but practising beforehand the dark stumblings to which they will be brought, who will lose their way in the other world? It is our Lord's own description of such: "[1] He that walketh in darkness knoweth not whither he goeth:" and "If a man walk in the night he stumbleth, because there is no light in him:" and "He that doeth evil hateth the light, neither cometh to the light, lest his deeds should be reproved," and S. John says, "[m] He that hateth his brother is in darkness, and walketh in darkness, and knoweth not whither he goeth, because that darkness hath blinded his eyes." Thus the Bible plainly tells us, that when we walk blindly in any sin, we are not only *earning* our own damnation, but are already *entering* on it, practising beforehand the miserable blindness which will itself be a great part of the pains of hell.

Yes, it is indeed a sort of hell upon earth, when

[1] S. John xii. 35. xi. 10. iii. 20.   [m] 1 S. John ii. 11.

Christian people, quenching the light that is in them, blind their own eyes, turning them away from God's truth, in order that they may go on more at their ease in some darling sin. So it is continually in regard of sins of impurity. They do in an especial manner, (as Solomon says) take away the heart; they destroy the very power of discerning right from wrong; people become past feeling when they give themselves over to lasciviousness, and they "love to have it so," they love to put out their own eyes, to silence the misgivings of their own better minds, that they may "commit all uncleanness with greediness." And it is much the same with the spiritual sins, such as malice, pride, covetousness. In such measure as a Christian indulges himself in any of these, he blinds his own heart, he plunges himself beforehand into the same dark condition, in which, if he do not repent here, he will be left for ever at the Last Day.

These are all works of darkness, doings and imaginations of which men are naturally ashamed, and they who give themselves to such things, of course love and court the darkness; and by the Lord's most righteous decree, they shall have the darkness which they desire; the darkness of evil habit and wilful ignorance in this world, in the other world the darkness incurable and intolerable, of being for ever without Christ, Who is the true Light.

Do you, my brethren, earnestly desire to be freed from this horrible sentence? We may be freed from it, we may have secured to us a place in the heavenly light for ever; if we do but desire that blessing, steadily and in earnest. For then we shall endeavour to "ⁿwalk in the Light, even as He is in the Light;" "ºto walk honestly as in the day;" to be true, real, frank, open, unfeigned, in all our behaviour to God and man. We shall be true and real in our thoughts; not hiding our eyes from truths which are uncomfortable to believe, but accepting them with all their discomfort, because they are truths; looking our past sins boldly in the face, when we are about examining ourselves; and also facing boldly the tasks whatever they are, pleasant or unpleasant, which our Master may set us to do. We shall be true and real in our words, especially in confession of sins, and in all sayings uttered to any one relating in any way to ourselves. We shall·be true andreal in our actions, "*doing* the truth," as S. John says, i. e., really behaving as if the great things we profess were true. Thus, and thus only, shall we be found walking in the light, as He is in the light; and the Blood of Jesus Christ shall cleanse us from all sin.

ⁿ 1 S. John i. 7.   º Rom. xiii. 13.

SERMON XXV.

SELF EXAMINATION; ITS SHARP BUT HEALING PAIN.

Psalm cxxxix. 23, 24.

" Try me O God, and seek the ground of my heart; prove me and examine my thoughts. Look well if there be any way of wickedness in me, and lead me in the way everlasting."

If we really seek to please God we must make up our minds to more or less of suffering. The Cross must be in some way taken up; something unpleasant must be endured for Christ's sake. We are not to think to enjoy ourselves altogether, while He is in the wilderness; to have none but pleasant company while He is with the wild beasts. And I have told you of one sort of suffering likely to try many of us; viz., the rude remarks, the jeers, the dislike, the scorn of those, who think it strange that we run not with them to the same excesses as before. This will be found trying, to those especially, who have to make visible outward changes in their conduct.

But there is another sort of suffering inseparable from Lent exercises (i. e., from the practise of real repentance) on which I shall now speak; an inward invisible penance, yet not the less real. I mean the pain and horror of searching out our own sins, of looking back and seeing wherein we have done amiss. This is quite needful for us all: we cannot be saved without it, and yet there are a good many who seem to think we can, and who seem to be vexed more or less, when themselves, or others are told to weigh and number their own sins, as exactly as they can. I will explain the sort of case I mean. Many a man when he is sick, or finds himself growing old, or when anything has happened to alarm him, will seem to himself to have good feelings, to make good resolutions for the future, and so will satisfy himself that all is right; and when he comes upon such directions as those in the Prayer book, or in the approved books of preparation for Holy Communion, he will start back from them, or pass them lightly over; he will say in his heart, "God I trust, will take me as I am. I have left off these sins now; why should I trouble myself with mourning over them any more?" This I fear is a very common feeling, and so people after an ill spent life, take things easily, in their latter end.

But what saith the Scripture? It says distinctly, that our sins are to be confessed, not our sin, nor our sinfulness, but our sins, so "[a] He that covereth his sins, shall not prosper; but whoso confesseth and forsaketh them shall have mercy." "[b] And they were baptised, confessing their sins." "[c] And many that believed came and confessed, and shewed their deeds." And if the Church, for good reasons, dispenses with our making such confession to men, which yet she recommends in some instances, she is only the more earnest in directing us to make it to

[a] Prov. xxviii. 13.   [b] S. Matt. iii. 6.   [c] Acts xix. 18.

God. For she will have none come to Holy Communion without going through the following process of self accusation. "The way and means," to prepare yourself, she says is, "To examine your lives and conversations by the rule of God's commandments; and wherein soever ye shall perceive yourselves to have offended, either by will, word or deed, there to bewail your own sinfulness, and to confess yourselves to Almighty God, with full purpose of amendment of life," and this to be done " not lightly, and after the manner of dissemblers with God;" but in earnest, as honestly desiring not to leave out anything of consequence. For this is how a person would deal with his physician; he would tell him all his case, or else be very foolish in expecting to be cured. You will say, why tell it over to God? He knows it beforehand far more perfectly than we remember it. To be sure He does: and so He knows all our wants before we pray to Him, and yet He has appointed us to pray, e. g., for our daily bread: and so He has appointed us to confess. And one reason of this we may partly understand, that we shall never be sorry as we ought, we shall be far from a right notion of the amount of our sins, and so we shall not be half humble enough, unless we are as particular as we can be, in going over them; just as in debts, it is very common for those who keep no exact account, to fancy themselves much less behind hand than they really are. And of this false reckoning with regard to sins of omission particularly, we may a little judge, by the case of those who set themselves no special rule in coming to Church, or to Holy Communion. I am sure they often have no idea themselves how long it is since they came; and if the same forgetfulness extends through a whole life, only think what the consequence may be. I myself have known very deadly sins indeed, entirely forgotten, and passed away from the person's memory, until something occurred, which caused him to remember, and humble himself for them: had he not done so, I suppose they would have met him again, in some way or other; if he had not judged himself, surely he would have been judged of the Lord. Therefore you see, if we would be humble, if we would see and feel the real truth, about ourselves, we must get into a way of going over our sins one by one, and confessing them one by one to God.

And this is what the Psalmist in the text asks for grace to do. "Try me O God, and seek the ground of my heart." He asks the Lord to do it for him, for it was too hard a work for himself: too hard, and too powerful; much like asking the surgeon to probe, and search your grievous, festering wound, with some of his very sharp instruments. People do so, because they wish in earnest to get well, and when we wish in earnest for our souls to be well, then we shall do so in respect of them. But it will and must be very painful; for it is asking Christ Who is the Living Word of God, to deal with us and with our distempered hearts, in the way which the Apostle describes. "[d] For the Word of God is quick, and powerful, and sharper than any two-edged sword, piercing even to the dividing asunder of soul and spirit, and of the joints and marrow, and is a Discerner of the thoughts and intents of the heart.

[d] Heb. iv. 12.

Self-examination; its sharp but healing pain. 257

Neither is there any creature that is not manifest in His sight, but all things are naked and opened unto the eyes of Him with Whom we have to do." Are not these fearful words? And yet this is neither more nor less than a description of a Christian seriously examining himself. Such an one, like S. John in the Revelation, prostrates himself in heart before the aweful vision of the Son of Man, and before the sharp sword that goeth out of His mouth, the power of His written or spoken commandments, which is indeed sharper than any two-edged sword, keener than the finest and subtlest surgical instruments, used in the most delicate operations. A Christian on his knees examining himself before his evening prayers is in fact beseeching Christ to apply His sharp sword to him, not to spare him,—but to probe, and search the very tenderest corners of his secret soul,—not to leave him, nor let him alone, until the whole mischief be searched out, and cut away; and how can this be, without pain and agony proportioned to the evil and corruption which has to be got rid of? No, my brethren, I must not deceive you, when I call you, when I invite and press you to repentance, I must not tell you that it is an easy task, a task without trouble or anguish, to which I am calling you. So far otherwise, that if there be any person who seems to himself to have repented sufficiently, and to have as it were a right to be comfortable, without any such feelings as the Scripture describes, without having trembled at the presence of the quick and powerful Word, without having shrunk from the sharp two-edged sword, the commandment of the old and new Law, going out of His mouth, I should advise that man to

s

go over his repentance again,—again to consider and recollect his whole life, from the moment he first knew right and wrong, and to compare it with the rule of God's commandments, praying earnestly and always for grace to know himself, and to judge himself here in time; that he may not be judged of the Lord in eternity.

Do not draw back from this endeavour, I beseech you; it is quite necessary for us all: it is what we must all do, if we would receive Christ's Sacrament worthily, or go to Christ when we die: painful it is, and must be, but it is healing pain; it is the kind Physician hurting that He may cure. That one thought, my brethren, if you will steadily consider it, will be more than enough to reconcile you to all the pain you will have to put yourselves to. I mean the thought not only of our healing at last, but of our being all the while in His Hands, Who prepared Himself to be our Physician by Himself enduring our pains. Do we not know when any sharp trial is to be gone through, how it supports the weak soul and body to know that some one is present who is as one's self, who can tell, as the Psalmist says, "all our flittings?" It is a great thing at such a time, to have a parent or dear friend to cling to: but for penitent souls it is a far greater thing to know that Christ is with them in the agony of their penitence: it is His Hand which guides the sharp two-edged sword, which is dividing even their very soul and spirit. He gives the pain, Who died, that that pain might be healing. O let us thankfully accept it at His Hands, let us by His help patiently endure the inward shame and confusion of heart which must needs go along with all true self-examination. For He, the Lord our God is with us all the while holding us by our right hand, He knows how much we can bear, and He will not suffer us to be tried beyond our strength, if only we will trust Him and open our inmost heart to Him.

SERMON XXVI.

BLESSEDNESS OF THE SOUL CONFESSING ITS SIN AND FORGIVEN.

Ps. xxxii. 1.

"*Blessed is he whose unrighteousness is forgiven and whose sin is covered.*"

THE thirty second Psalm, the second of those called Penitential, has a special mark put upon it by the Finger of God in the New Testament, in that the Holy Ghost by S. Paul has declared that it contains the Christian doctrine of justification: which is, that we are pardoned and accepted by the Most High God, not in virtue of our own works and sufferings, our own repentance, faith, hope, or charity, but entirely because of God's free grace, for the merits of our Lord and Saviour Jesus Christ.

This doctrine in the Epistle to the Romans, S. Paul teaches by the history of Abraham; and in the fourth chapter, he points out, by the way, that it is taught in the Psalms also. "Even as David also describeth the blessedness of the man unto whom God imputeth righteousness without works, saying, 'Blessed are they whose iniquities are forgiven and whose sins are covered.'"

Now of course we all acknowledge this in words. Every one of us, if he was so asked as to be made to

Blessedness of the soul confessing its sin and forgiven. 261

attend and know the meaning of the question, would say that "we are accounted righteous before God, only for the merit of our Lord and Saviour Jesus Christ, by faith, and not for our own works or deservings." We all own it in words, and we think, I suppose, that we own it in heart. But how is it with us in fact? May we not all the while be deceiving ourselves in thinking that we lean on Jesus Christ and on nothing else for our salvation? This Lent and every Lent is intended to help us in judging and trying ourselves on this great point. For Lent is a time of confession. It calls on us to "lament our sins and acknowledge our wretchedness," because that is the way to obtain of Him Who is "the God of all mercy, perfect remission and forgiveness."

This confession, this deep constant feeling of our own sin and misery, is in a manner one half of that faith, that true conversion, on which our All entirely depends. For faith and true conversion is turning to God; and he who turns to God, must turn away from the world. There is no middle way. He must choose between one and the other; he can no more serve two masters, God and Mammon, at the same time, than he can turn his face two ways at once, than he can look to the east and the west at the same moment. Therefore in Holy Baptism we renounce the world the flesh and the devil, in the very same act whereby we receive God's Truth to believe in, and His Commandments to obey. We cannot do one without the other; we cannot at once turn our back and our face to our Saviour. Now that exact and religious confession, which the Church calls on us to practise in Lent, is just this: it is going over our past sins as distinctly and earnestly as we well can, in the bitterness of our soul; and at every sin feeling, owning to our Saviour, Whom we know to be present all the while, how bad and inexcusable it was; and with purpose of heart promising to Him to watch against that sin for the time to come, and to practise by His grace all the contrary virtues. This is true confession; and is it not the working in the heart of those two precious gifts, justifying faith, and true conversion? Surely it is: the confessions which the time of Lent calls on us to practise are a sure way of knowing, whether we be sound in the faith, and whether our hearts are truly converted to Christ.

As this is true concerning the whole of the Lent services, so I should say that it specially holds good in our use of this second penitential Psalm, the thirty second. For this is eminently a Psalm of confession. As the sixth Psalm [a] teaches us how to think of that first and chiefest misery of sin, that it makes God angry with us, and keeps us in the power of our enemies; so this Psalm more particularly reminds us of that other grievous misery, the burden of concealment, the uneasy sense of shame, which sooner or later must come upon all persons for every thing which they do amiss. It may set us on thinking of the misery which Adam and Eve endured, as soon as ever they had sinned, from the shame of their nakedness; as the former Psalm might, of that other and worse misery that they could not bear to be with God; they were fain

[a] [Which we considered last week.]

to hide themselves from His Presence. And as in the end of that former Psalm the poor lost soul cries out for joy on finding that God still heard her prayer, that He did not pass by, but called, as to Adam, "where art thou?" and gave hope of the perfect overthrow of all her enemies by and by: so in this Psalm, the soul cannot be thankful enough for the relief afforded by true and full confession to God. Let us go through the Psalm verse by verse, let us consider it very thoughtfully; and we shall see, by God's blessing, how this Psalm may both help us to repentance, and also confirm us in the true doctrine of justification.

The Psalm supposes one admitted to penance, as sinners used to be at the beginning of Lent. For all those who then came to the Church door came there after confession of sins, humbly praying to be admitted to penance; i. e., to be allowed to do certain penitential exercises in the way of fasting, prayer, watching, public confession, and other severe ways of discipline, for a certain time appointed by the Church, more or less according to their sins : at the end of which time, showing themselves truly penitent, they would be absolved, and admitted anew to Holy Communion. Very severe and sharp was that godly discipline : very hard for persons in these days to think of enduring it with any kind of patience. But true penitents in those days endured it all with joy and thankfulness, because they knew it was the regular way for them to put off themselves, and come back to Jesus Christ; it was the way to recover that justifying grace, which they cast away from them by their sins. Such an one, calmly and deeply considering in his heart the unspeakable mercy set before him, might take up this thirty second Psalm, as a Psalm of unutterable joy and gladness, however sharp, however disgusting, the penance he had to bear in the mean time. The Holy Spirit would teach and help him to say with all his heart and soul, " Blessed is he whose unrighteousness is forgiven and whose sin is covered." Observe the very words: each one has a deep meaning. Blessed is he, and only he, among men;—for that is the meaning of the word "blessed" very often in the Psalms; it does not generally signify that there are several ways to go right, but this way is the best of all; rather it means, there is no other way but this. As in Ps. ii., "If (Christ's) wrath be kindled, yea but a little, blessed are all they that put their trust in Him ;" i. e., well will it be for them and for them only; the rest will find nothing but ruin. So in this Psalm, "Blessed is he," not "who is without spot of sin," who has no iniquity, no unrighteousness at all, but "whose iniquity is forgiven, and whose sin is covered." As much as to say, that for all mankind, except Him Who was alone without sin, pardon, free gracious pardon, is the only way to God's true blessing. It cannot be of works: it must be entirely and always of grace.

And now observe the word "blessed" once more; for it is a very remarkable word. In the original language, as David wrote it, it is said to mean "blessings," and in this place is as much as to cry out, " O the blessings of the man whose unrighteousness is forgiven !" he is not merely blessed, but he is all blessings ; his whole being in Heaven and in earth is made up of them. If this seems strange (considering the trials of this world), I would just ask you to consider one case, the case of a little infant, baptised and dying before it commit any actual sin. Who will say that the death of that child, or the pain, whatever it be, that goes before death, is any thing at all to be compared with the greatness of that child's blessing? Surely it may be said of him, he is all blessings, forgiven and sanctified and saved freely; taken at once to his Saviour's bosom; nothing at all to interfere with his bliss.

But if you judge thus without any question as concerning that little child, think again, and you will surely find that the same thing holds just as true of any person, dying with his unrighteousness forgiven, and his sin covered. Any temporal punishment, which it may please God to lay upon him, is nothing, nothing at all in comparison with the blessings sealed to him of eternal pardon and grace. He is all blessings and shall be so for ever.

"His unrighteousness is forgiven and his sin is covered," i. e., his sins, even the worst, which before his conversion made such a sore burden, too heavy for him to bear, are untied and loosed from him, and laid upon One Who hath vouchsafed to come down from Heaven on purpose to bear both him and his sins: his sins on the Cross: him, as the lost sheep, on His shoulders. So it is, I say, even with the worst sins, the worst transgressions of God's holy law, truly repented of, they shall be entirely pardoned : only observe, that the two words " truly repented " are very great words, and no man must hastily apply them to himself. Yet, thank God, it is true : the most horrible of crimes are pardonable when a man comes truly to Christ; for His loving word is plain, "Come unto me, *all* ye that travail and are heavy laden." He would not have said "all," if there were any beyond reach of His healing.

The worst transgressions and disobediences He will bear for us, and the worst follies and errors He will forgive. "Blessed is he whose sin is covered:" over whom Christ's skirt is spread: on whom He hath put the wedding garment, hiding all the spots and stains, which by reason of his frail and corrupt nature have gathered on him since his first cleansing. Blessings, nothing but blessings shall that contrite and forgiven one find, when he shall rise and stand yet trembling, for ought we know, before the Judgement seat, and the Judge shall say unto him, " Enter thou into My joy, I have cast all thy sins behind My back." Thus the merciful Redeemer hath promised finally to take off the shame of sin, as well as the burden.

But once again : sin is an immense debt, as we know by the parable of the unmerciful servant, who owed his Lord ten thousand talents; and behold here again our Lord's third blessing on those who are finally justified: "blessed is the man unto whom the Lord imputeth no sin." He does not say, who never was in debt, but whose debts are not imputed to him: the entries that stood against him are all blotted out of the account. Who does not know in a small way the relief of such a circumstance as that? But no man, not the greatest and wisest of saints, can know the relief, when the Judge shall say at the last moment, "thy sins are forgiven: thy name is in the book of life, not now for a time, but for ever."

But take notice, particularly, my brethren, what the Judge tells us at the end of this second verse, " Blessed is the man unto whom the Lord imputeth no sin, and in whose spirit there is no guile." The necessary condition of this perfect and most blessed justification is this, "in his spirit there is no guile." It answers very nearly to that aweful third commandment, "thou shalt not take the Name of the Lord thy God in vain;" for what is taking God's Name in vain, but putting it to a lie? as every Christian does, who, professing to trust in Him for pardon, still takes part with His enemies. Believe it, dear brethren ; think of it very deeply, let it never go out of your mind : no fraud, no hypocrisy, must be used in our dealings with our Lord Jesus; else we destroy the virtue of that Holy Name, in which only we can be saved. So also we find in the book of Revelation, when the holy beloved disciple was permitted to see the blessed company of those who stood on Mount Sion before the throne and the Lamb. It is very particularly set down that "[b]in their mouth was no guile."

Now do you not see how exactly this agrees with what comes after about confession ? How truth is that very duty which requires most to be borne in mind, when people are confessing their sins to God, either directly, or through any of His servants the priests ?

But now let us see what this great penitent tells us about penitential confession. First he says, "while I held my tongue," i.e., as long as I could not

[b] Rev. xiv. 5.

make up my mind to confess, "my bones consumed away through my daily complaining." It is a very distressing bitter feeling, which sinners who will not confess have to endure. Not that they are all alike: these words of the Psalmist might be taken up by two very different sorts of persons. Some hold their tongue in sullen silence, because they will not believe Christ; they do not really care to be forgiven through Him. They will not say a word in the way of faith and confession, but are they therefore in peace? Far from it: their bones consume away, i. e., their whole life is a weariness and a waste and a disturbed time because of their worldly passions and discontent.

But there are others, in better dispositions, who wish to believe and repent and be forgiven through Jesus Christ, but for one reason or another, they are a long time before they can make up their minds to do it thoroughly; I mean to do it to God in secret; I am not here speaking of those cases, in which the Church recommends our confessing to the priest. I say there are a great many who shrink from confessing their sins one by one, and from thinking deeply on them, as they appear before Him. They have never been used to it, they have never been taught it, they do not know how to set about it. Whatever the cause be, it is a wearing, wasting thought to them, that they are not fully nor truly confessing their sins unto the Lord; and so their bones, the very strength and sinews of the Christian character, become weakened: and too often, the Evil One, who rejoices most especially to make men false and hypocritical in their Confessions, gains more or less advantage of them.

And so in their better moments these imperfect believers and penitents are fain to cry out in agony, "Thy hand is heavy upon me day and night, and my moisture is like the drought in summer." God's Hand, His Power and Providence weighs heavily upon them, and His grace dries up, or they feel as if by degrees it was doing so. This is sad enough if it happen through timidity or ignorance: if in unbelief or hypocrisy, far, far worse.

And there is but one remedy, but that a most perfect and effectual one. "I said, I will confess my sins unto the Lord, and so Thou forgavest the wickedness of my sin." Confession to Christ is the one true unfailing cure for those who have been worn out with the sense either of sin or misery. How perfect, how blessed it is, the rest of the Psalm goes on to tell you: but we must not hurry it over; by God's mercy we shall consider it on Friday [c].

And since in the meantime, we shall each one of us, have at least two solemn confessions to make, the sins of this day, to-night; and to-morrow, to-morrow night; let us at least secure the blessing for those two nights, by making our evening self-examination and confession as complete, as sorrowful and as true as we can.

[c] The sequel of this sermon could no where be found, nor any more of the series of sermons on the Penitential Psalms, to which this sermon manifestly belongs.

SERMON XXVII.

THE REPENTANCE OF MANASSEH.

2 CHRON. xxxiii. 12.

" When he was in affliction, he besought the Lord his God."

THE history which I am about to speak of is that of Manasseh king of Judah: and the lesson to be learned from it by us sinners, wishing to be penitent, is always to fear, but never to despair.

Manasseh was the son of Hezekiah. He had therefore one of the best of fathers, one who no doubt took pains to have him brought up in the fear of God. But Hezekiah, to his great loss, died while Manasseh was very young; for he was only twelve years old when he succeeded to the kingdom. And such bad counsellors had he, and so wildly and wickedly did he give himself up to the temptations which were around him, that he soon became as great a pattern of impiety as his father Hezekiah had been of faith and devotion. "He did that which was evil in the sight of the Lord, like unto the abominations of the heathen, whom the Lord cast out before the children of Israel." It seems as though he lost no time, as though he fell away almost immediately, and made haste to be as wicked as he could be.

Great indeed and fearful were his sins, yet not greater nor more fearful than those of too many among ourselves.

For what if Manasseh fell away immediately, as soon (so it seems) as he was left to be his own master? Too plainly do we also, a great many of us, make the wrong choice, as soon as ever we are left to choose for ourselves. As soon as ever we know God, it is our bounden duty to turn ourselves heartily toward Him, and give ourselves up to His service, come what will: choosing rather to die than to displease or disobey Him. But how few are there, who in their childish years do anything at all like this! How much more common to get into a way, even as children, of pleasing ourselves, without caring whether God is pleased or no: and so even before we have come to Manasseh's twelve years, to have gone a great way back from the way of our Baptism, into the ways of the heathen, of the evil spirits whom the Lord by His grace had cast out when He made us members of Himself.

Hear how Manasseh went on. He built again the high places which Hezekiah his father had broken down, and he reared up altars for Baalim, and made groves, and worshipped all the host of heaven, and served them. He took a perverse pleasure in bringing back the very mischiefs which his father had done away. I dare say he thought it a fine, manly, noble thing; and I dare say also that flatterers were not wanting, false friends, devilish advisers, ready to praise him for all that he said and did thus boldly in the way of the heathen; telling him it was true courage to sin thus with a high hand; even as bad men and boys encourage and cheer up one another in all sorts of daring and desperate wickedness, calling it brave and manly and spirited, to swear without flinching, to drink without shame or measure, to corrupt one's self and others without blushing or trembling. One idol was not enough for Manasseh: he seems to have even searched around for all the false gods he could find, to honour each in his own way: and so you may be sure the wicked Christian will not be content with one sin, nor with one course and way of sinning. Encourage one wicked spirit, and you will find him everywhere at hand, intruding where one might least expect: and not him alone, but seven others as bad as himself: where there is drinking, there will generally be swearing, and where there is cheating there will be lying, and where there is uncleanness there will be a miserable falseness of heart.

Again Manasseh made his idol altars in the very courts of the Lord's house, where the Lord had sworn His Name should be for ever: and do not wicked Christians bring their sins with them here? their profane, unkind, lewd, rebellious thoughts, their plans and notions of mischief, their ungoverned looks and fancies? and what is this, but setting up altars to so many devils in the very temple of the Lord? and if they come in such sin to the Communion, this is bringing the idol into the Holy of Holies.

Again, Manasseh caused his children to pass through the fire to his gods: and the worldly wicked heart cares not how it corrupts wife, children, friends, brethren or sisters, how it tempts them away from innocency, and so causes them in the end to pass into the unquenchable fire. Manasseh observed times, enchantments, and witchcraft: and fallen Christians often pride themselves on their knowledge and wisdom in the ways of the world: which, except they be ordered by the fear of God, are no better than the way of evil spirits. Manasseh made Judah and Jerusalem to err: and who knows not how infectious deadly sin is among Christians? so that one bad example, especially in a person who has had many helps and privileges, is like a little leaven, leavening a whole Parish or Kingdom. Manasseh's sins and the sins which he encouraged were worse than the heathen: and so surely are the wilful, deadly sins of us Christians: seeing that we not only know better, but have so great a treasure and gift of grace to keep us from sin, all which we are wasting; nay, we have God the Holy Ghost residing personally in our souls and bodies; there is not a sin of ours, but it vexes and grieves Him. The Lord spake to Manasseh and to his people, but they would not hearken. And does not the Lord speak to us, both in Church and out of Church? and are we always willing to hear? Manasseh was so unwilling, that he persecuted the prophets who warned him; and for one, as there is good reason to believe, he slew the great prophet Isaiah. He, it is said, was sawn asunder by order of this wicked king, for telling him truths which he did not love to hear. It is not the way of our times, openly to persecute God's messengers out of their lives: but I fear we can too many of us understand, how the unbridled love of sin will cause us in time to hate

T

the good men who reprove us; and if we hate them, and had been in Manasseh's place, I much fear we should not have minded killing them.

Thus on the whole a person may see, that miserable as this history is of good Hezekiah's wicked son, it is not one jot more miserable and shameful than the daily history of too many thousands of Christians, who go on resisting warnings, and carrying with them deadly and notorious sin into the very holiest places. Children as they are by Baptism of the great and good Father, they seem now to have sold themselves, body and soul to the Evil One. It seems as if, at the Last Day, their privileges, more especially the Blessed Sacraments of Christ, which they are abusing, would only sink them into a lower deep. How vain then is all trust in privileges, without earnest and continual prayers and endeavours to improve them!

But, God be thanked, this is not the only instruction which a thoughtful heart may gather from the history of Manasseh. As those who have privileges may learn to fear, so those who have abused them, yea grossly, yea even by deadly sin, may learn not to despair. And there are persons, to whom such teaching is very necessary. For observe, my brethren, how it is with men if they unhappily permit themselves to forget God and fall away, when they have been made partakers of His blessed and saving grace. The devil will do all he can, as long as he can, to keep them quiet in their sins. He will suggest all manner of subtle excuses, and will be very skilful in preaching peace where there is no peace. But when their eyes come to be opened, and they begin to discern something of their own miserable condition, and can no longer be at rest in their wickedness, on the edge, as it were, of hell, then he will try the opposite kind of temptation: he will say, "you cannot get back, you may just as well cast yourself down. You have sinned past repentance and past forgiveness: you had better dismiss all thought of it, and enjoy yourself while you can, a little longer." Thus he tempts men to desperation: but God's merciful Providence has given us, even in this very same history, effectual help against him in this temptation also, if we will take it. Who would not have thought Manasseh's case a desperate one? Such great privileges abused, such mountains of deadly sin, so many souls corrupted, such merciful warnings slighted! Yet behold, the next thing we learn of him is, that God chastened him and brought him to repentance. Hear the most gracious and loving history. "ᵃThe Lord spake to Manasseh and to his people, but they would not hearken: wherefore the Lord brought upon them the captains of the host of the king of Assyria, which took Manasseh among the thorns, and bound him with fetters, and carried him to Babylon." O unwearied and persevering mercy! The sinner will not be taught, he will not be warned; words, good books, sermons, even Scriptures, are to all appearance wasted upon him but God will not so give him up. God has yet another way in store: His afflictions come down upon us like the captains of the king of Assyria; they overtake us among the thorns, in the rough, crooked, unmanageable ways into which our sins

ᵃ 2 Chron. xxxiii. 12.

have brought us: troubles, I say, from the Lord come upon us; we are as persons taken, bound, carried away captives: we are at last convinced that the world cannot help us, and we cannot help ourselves. Then, as I said, the Evil One will beset you, if he can, with the temptation to despair: but do not you listen to him: think of Manasseh, the wicked, idolatrous, murderous Manasseh, in his fetters in the Babylonish prison, and see how he employs himself. The good seed, which no doubt his father Hezekiah had sown, now begins to shoot out, having been stifled for so many years, since he was twelve years old, by his sins. Manasseh is come to himself; he thinks, like the young man in our Saviour's parable, "were I but in my Father's house, I should have bread enough and to spare: but now I perish with hunger." He listens not to the devil, tempting him to despond, as unhappy Judas listened: but being in affliction, he beseeches the Lord his God, and humbles himself greatly before the God of his fathers, and prays unto Him: prays heartily, prays so, that God is intreated of him, and hears his supplication, and brings him again to Jerusalem into his kingdom: so that he is settled in heart to believe that the Lord, He alone is God, and the idols after which he had gone are nothing in the world. This is the repentance and conversion of king Manasseh: and, blessed be God, like unto it has been the repentance and conversion of thousands, who in our Christian times, alas! have abused greater privileges to worse sin. Like to it, by His grace, may our repentance and conversion be, in whatever respect and degree we have gone after the world and the flesh. Only let us not trifle with God. He who warned and afflicted Manasseh, is even now warning us: let us not wait till He afflicts us; till age, or sickness, or poverty, or trouble take away our taste for our sins; let us not stay till we are taken among the thorns, and in prison at Babylon, but let us put away our idols, break off our bad ways, at once. It was well that Manasseh repented in Babylon; but have you any doubt that, if you could ask him, he would say he could wish to have repented long before? But even his repentance, late as it was, was not too late to bring forth fruit. "When he was come back to Jerusalem, he took away the strange gods and the idols out of the house of the Lord, and all the altars that he had built in the mount of the house of the Lord and in Jerusalem, and cast them out of the city: and he repaired the altar of the Lord and sacrificed thereon peace-offerings and thank-offerings, and commanded Judah to serve the Lord God of Israel." That is, having truly repented, he did all he could to undo his former sins. He did not only humble himself for them, but worked against them with all his might: and laboured to reform the people whom he had before corrupted. Christian penitents, learn we of Manasseh, that ours must be a watchful and active repentance. We must not give way to any kind of sloth. We must not sit at home merely regretting the past, but we must go out and fight the battles of the Lord, as He shall call and enable us. Little enough, alas! can we do, to repair the sad effects, secret or open, of our past sins. Manasseh's penitence, earnest as it was, could not undo the results of his transgression. The people whom he had so much helped to corrupt, continued corrupt when he was changed. The sentence which God had passed on Judah and Jerusalem for the sins into which Manasseh had led them, continued in force even after Manasseh's repentance. This is a sad and fearful thought. The penitent, when he has done his best, will find that he can but very imperfectly cure the mischief he has occasioned. Too often, much of it will abide for ever. Consider it well; and while you thank God that in one sense true contrition can never come too late, be sure that every moment of delay must be paid for one day, with loss and bitter regret.

SERMON XXVIII.

THE REPENTANCE OF NINEVEH.

Jonah iii. 2.

"God saw their works, that they turned from their evil way, and God repented of the evil that He had said He would do unto them, and He did it not."

Our Lord God is exceedingly merciful in forgiving all sin. We saw it last Friday in the case of the wicked king Manasseh: whose true confession was, "I have sinned more in number than the sands of the sea, and I am not worthy to look up and behold the height of Heaven;" and yet he was forgiven, when in his captivity he turned to his God in earnest; and so will even the worst sinners among Christians be forgiven, if they turn in good time and lay hold of the Cross, with a repentance which sincerely tries and longs to be in some measure proportionate to the sin. The Prodigal child may have wandered into a very far country, he may have wasted all his substance over and over with riotous living, he may have been fain to fill his belly with the husks, to give himself up to the basest and most swinish pleasures; and yet, if he not only wish to arise, but really *do* arise and go to his Father, not minding the pain, the shame, the self-denial, the perplexity; doubt not but his Father, Who watches him a great way off, Who indeed is, all the while, with him in secret, putting the penitent thoughts into his heart, He will before very long come out, and fall on the mourning sinner's neck and kiss him, and will admit him, as he shall be found worthy, to all the graces and comforts of his home.

God is very merciful, and will forgive all sorts and all measures of sin: but then the sinner must really and practically repent, must repent in deed, not in word and imagination only. All, even the very worst who have not quite lost all sense of the difference between right and wrong, must at times wish to repent, wish that they had the heart to do so. It may for the time be a very earnest wish: it may move the heart, and draw tears from the eyes. But if that be all, it is not repentance; it is but a wish to repent. Then it is repentance indeed, when in addition to these inward feelings it begins to make a difference in their conduct: when being still within reach of temptation, they refrain from the sin which had before been too mighty for them: when they do what in them lies to keep themselves out of temptation, or strengthen themselves against it; and also when, in humble sense of past sin, they vex and punish themselves for having been guilty of it: judging themselves, as S. Paul says, and as the Church recommends in the Communion Service, that they may not be judged of the Lord. I will try to make my meaning plainer. It will many times happen, that by the time a person begins truly to repent of his sins for God's sake, the very temptation to commit it may have almost or quite passed away: so that he has now no difficulty in quite refraining from it. He seems to himself to loathe and abhor it, but how can he be reasonably sure that he does so, seeing that he is no longer tried? As for example, if a poor man tempted to steal were to become suddenly rich, it is no trouble to him then, and no thanks, to keep from stealing: but how is he to know that he really repents of past dishonesty? Mere inward sorrow is a sign, a good sign: but he will wish and long, that if God pleases, he might do more than mourn inwardly; and it will naturally come into his mind, "As I have sinned by taking what does not belong to me, so will it not help my repentance, if I give away for God's sake a good deal of what *does* belong to me, even to my own inconvenience and hindrance?" Again, if a man have sinned by fleshly desire, will he not naturally think of punishing his body by some kind of wholesome self-denial, in the hope of *that* also doing him good in God's sight? Penitent persons, very commonly, have had such thoughts as these: and you may be sure that there is something good in such thoughts; for there is great encouragement for them in Holy Scripture, both in the Old Testament and in the New. From Adam downwards, there has been great encouragement to sinners coming before God not only with contrition in their hearts, but with the outward signs of it in their bodies and behaviour: such as fasting, weeping, and mourning, sackcloth and ashes; abstaining from pleasures which they might have enjoyed, and patiently enduring all manner of pains and affronts, as sent on them for their sins.

Consider with this view the short history set before us in the Book of Jonah: how God threatened the great city Nineveh, and how, on the king's and people's repentance, He mercifully spared them. Go back in your minds to that time, and draw in your imaginations two opposite pictures. First, imagine to yourselves Nineveh, as it was in the morning of the day when the prophet Jonah came to it. Nineveh was a great city of three days' journey: that is, as it should seem, it took three days to march through it, so many and so large were the palaces and temples with the gardens and grounds belonging to them, besides the many long streets of ordinary houses. The ruins, a very little of them, have lately been searched out and brought to light, after being for thousands of years hid as it were in the sand, and very wonderful are the buildings and carved works, both for size, beauty and number, giving the surest proof what a rich city it was, how great, mighty and populous. Such was Nineveh on that morning, quite dazzling to the outward eye: the people and nobles enjoying themselves, and working at this world's tasks with all their might. Such was Nineveh in the morning: but come to it again in the evening, and what will you see? The king has arisen from his throne, he has put his royal robe off from him, he has covered himself with sackcloth, and is sitting in ashes. The whole people also have put on sackcloth, and are fasting: rich and poor, young and old, from the greatest of them, even unto the least of them. The very beasts do in a manner fast, the care of them is neglected for the present, that the men may give themselves up more entirely to penitence, and they are clothed with sackcloth, they wear mourning as well as their masters. The one employment of the whole city is, crying mightily unto God, and turning every one from his evil way, and from the violence that was in their hands.

Now what has happened to make this marvellous change in the chief city of the whole earth? Why such a difference in Nineveh between the morning and evening? A solitary man from a far country has come into the place with a message from God: he has travelled one third of the way through it, i.e. about one day's journey: and as he goes along through the streets, he proclaims aloud, and says, "Yet forty days, and Nineveh shall be overthrown." This person is the prophet Jonah, and his message is direct from the Lord. The Ninevites believe him, most likely because they have heard the wonderful doings of God towards him, in delivering him from the whale's belly. He is a true sign to them; God has put it into their hearts to repent at his preaching, and this is one immediate way of shewing and practising their repentance. They cannot undo the past, but they may punish themselves for it. They cannot bring to life those whom they have murdered, nor restore to purity the souls and bodies which they have corrupted, be they their own or others': but they may be very sorry, very much humbled, for having done such things: they may vex and punish themselves in their diet and dress and behaviour, not minding the pain, the shame, nor the inconvenience. They wish and try to do all this: and now mark what comes of it. God had said in plain words: "Yet forty days, and Nineveh shall be overthrown." They knew that He was merciful; but they had no express notice, that we read of, how that on truly repenting they might even now be forgiven and spared. However they resolved to do what little they could, and they actually set about doing it with all their might: "for," said they, "who can tell if God will turn and repent, and turn away from His fierce anger, that we perish not?" This was their thought, and their way was, punishing themselves: and observe what came of it. The forty days passed away and yet the city stood undestroyed. "God saw their works, that they turned from their evil way, and God repented of the evil that He had said that He would do unto them, and He did it not." God, Who cannot lie nor repent, did yet make as if He repented: so great with Him was the power of true, self-denying penitence, even in that heathen people.

So it was with the great city Nineveh more than two thousand years ago. Is there nothing like it in the world now: even now, so long after Christ and His Apostles have come, and have preached the full Gospel of repentance? Surely we all know of a city and a country, too like Nineveh, both in her greatness and in her sin. Who knows not of London, that great city, to compass which on foot would now, I suppose, be a good three days' journey? Who knows not of England, that powerful and populous island? too like Nineveh both in her glory and in her sin: only that her sin is so far worse, as she is Christian, Nineveh was only heathen. Yes, here we are with our pomps, our pleasures, our gains, making the most we can of this world, as did the Ninevites in Jonah's time: and behold the Prophet too is here: the Church, which is Christ's Prophet on earth, has long ago entered into our country, not a day's journey only, but from one end to another, saying, Yet a short time, and I do not say Nineveh or London, but the whole world shall be overthrown. There will be an end of the world, and He shall come to judge the quick and the dead. Word has been brought to us all of this: if not to every one in London or in England, yet at least to every one of us here. God is angry, and the world will soon perish, and those who are yet in their sins must perish with it. All our lives long the Prophet has been in our streets, crying this message aloud, and sparing not. And this time of year especially is the time of repentance; the time when, by common consent of good Christians, all should be busy in humbling themselves, and turning from their sin. Look round you then; look at London, or at England, or at any portion of England, as it is. Which of the two is it more like, Nineveh in the morning, when Jonah came to it, or Nineveh in the evening, sitting in sackcloth and ashes? By the grace of God, I trust that there is in the country a great deal of true fasting, a great deal of humiliation and self-denial, real, if not outward and visible. And it cannot be said that it is not enjoined by authority, for in the whole Prayer book nothing is plainer than the directions to observe Fasting days. I dare say they are observed, more or less, by a great many: still I suppose it is as I just now said, that London or England even at this time of Lent, is more like Nineveh in its glory and gaiety, than like

Nineveh in its repentance. Now I think it may do us all good, if we try a little to bear this in mind. Let us not too rashly conclude that all is well enough with us, that we are repenting deeply enough of our past sins, especially if they were at all of a serious and deadly character, merely because we think we have left them off; or because, when we think of them, we feel that we had rather not have committed them. Perhaps it may be that, instead of our leaving them, they have rather left us. Perhaps our dislike of them may not be such as would stand if the temptation could return. But let us humbly and discreetly take all the ways which the Bible and Prayer book recommend, as helping to perfect our repentance, and so appease our Maker through Jesus Christ. Let us endeavour, for what little remains of this Lent, to be more earnest in prayer than we have been: as penitent Nineveh cried mightily unto God during her forty days. Let us humble and deny ourselves in secret, as the Ninevites wore sackcloth. Let us fast, truly and really, in one way or another, as our health and duty may permit. Let us watch night and day against the least and subtlest remnants of the sins we seem to have been delivered from. Who knows how great a blessing such obedient ways may obtain for us in a very short time? Before the end of that forty days, Nineveh had so far turned from its evil way, that God repented of the evil, and turned it away. How do you know but the sword of judgement may even now be drawn out over you, and this Lent may be the appointed time for you effectually to repent in? If you knew for certain that it was so, what would you do? Do just the same now; it will be your wisdom. The Ninevites in their penance had no positive certainty. All they could say was, "Who can tell if God will turn and repent?" But it was enough, because they dealt with it sincerely and truly. Do you the same: try in earnest what you can do in watching, praying, overcoming ill ways and ill tempers. If you think you have won a victory, and put your enemies to flight, yet turn not again till you have destroyed them. Do not so much look toward other people, to see what they do. You have not perhaps their difficulties, nor they your helps. If you are at a loss, come to the Priest: it will be your own fault, if you fail for want of asking advice. Try: for if all London or England, nay if all the world besides go wrong, yet the way of the Bible and the Church will surely save him who tries in earnest. All Nineveh indeed repented at the preaching of Jonah, but in Sodom, we know, there was but one who repented, and he with his house was saved alone out of the burning.

SERMON XXIX.

JOSEPH A TYPE OF CHRIST AND A PATTERN TO CHRISTIANS.

FOURTH SUNDAY IN LENT.

HEBREWS ii. 11.

" He is not ashamed to call them brethren."

THE Holy time of Lent was intended for the mortification of all our sins, spiritual as well as carnal, our anger as well as our lust. For although sins against chastity and temperance are more especially meant when we speak of "fleshly lusts," yet the Apostle in reckoning up "the works of the flesh" makes mention also of "ᵃ hatred, variance, emulations, wrath, strife, seditions, heresies, envyings, murders." All these, though not sins of the body, are sins of the flesh, because they follow upon improper indulgence of desires and fancies, as natural to us as our own bodies. They belong to that fallen and corrupt nature, which we have, as offspring of Adam, conveyed to us, we know not how, through our bodily descent from him.

Since therefore Lent is appointed to help us in subduing the flesh to the spirit, we are to use that holy season in fighting against our pride, as well as

ᵃ Gal. v. 20, 21.

against our evil desires. We are to deny ourselves, our whole selves, so far as they make it hard for us to take up our cross, and follow Christ. Our angry passions must be kept in order, as entirely as our unclean ones. We must exercise ourselves in charity and humility as well as in purity.

And this so much the more, in that whoever keeps Lent well, must be all the time looking to the end of Lent, which is Easter. These forty days of retirement and self-denial ought to be days of self-examination and amendment, in preparation for the feast of our Lord's Resurrection. It is a time for the purifying the soul's garments, soiled too sadly by the dust and refuse of the world, and still more sadly by our own inbred corruption. Our business during these weeks is to search and examine very diligently where our baptismal robes are stained, and by prayer and confession and true repentance and humble use of the Church's Absolution to wash out those stains in Christ's Blood as well as we may, before we go in to the marriage of the King's Son, to which at Easter we are specially invited. A very bad thing it would be, a deep grief to all good Angels, an intolerable burden to our own souls, were we, after all this, to come to our Lord without forgiving. We might as well, when we draw nigh to Him, have our bodies defiled with lust, as our souls with uncharitableness. Many of us indeed know this, we have our Lord's express warning for it. "[b] If thou bring thy gift to the altar, and there rememberest that thy brother hath ought against thee, leave there thy gift before the altar, and go thy way; first be reconciled to thy

[b] S. Matt. v. 23, 24.

brother, and then come and offer thy gift." So dangerous is it to draw near without forgiving, that even if you seemed to find yourself in all other respects well-prepared, but were conscious of bearing malice, indulging unkindness towards any one, the Lord of the feast commands you to withdraw for the present, and not to come again till you are in a better mind. He will not accept your gift, if you bring it with malice in your heart towards any one of His and your brethren.

The example then of the holy Joseph, which the Church sets before us to-day, is very especially a history suited for Lent, an example to encourage and to warn us in our hard fighting on both sides, on the one hand against fleshly lusts and impurities, on the other, against all unforgiving, unbrotherly ways. We may learn of him both to bear and to forbear, to bear the ill usage of others, to forbear from indulging ourselves improperly. In Potiphar's house, as you heard this morning, he was a pattern of purity under very sore temptation; in his dealings with his brethren afterwards, as we shall hear this evening, and next Sunday, he is no less admirable a pattern of forgiveness towards most inexcusable wrong-doers. Both ways, if we will, we may find in Joseph's history the greatest help towards cleansing and quieting our souls, worthily to receive our Lord at Easter.

And no wonder; when we come to reflect, of Whom Joseph was an appointed type and shadow. He, the beloved and injured son, forgiving his brethren who had done him so grievous wrong, and after all saving their lives, comforting their hearts, and making them feel that he accounted them still his brethren! Who, as they read of him, can help thinking of that only and Well-beloved Son, Who, when we had sinned against Him and used Him as ill as we could, stooped to be one of us, came into the world to save us, humbled Himself to the death of the Cross, to the lowest pit, and that a place of darkness, and even now, after all our backslidings, is not ashamed to call us brethren? Christ the Son of God humbling Himself to be one of Adam's family, and vouchsafing to make of Adam's sinful children, brethren and sisters to Himself, sons and daughters to His Father in Heaven. This is the great truth of which Joseph is an appointed shadow. Consider the two histories together, Joseph's and our Lord's, and see how they answer to each other, and what reasons may be found in each for brotherly love, forgiving love, love that yearns to do good to its worst enemies, love that grudges nothing, and can never at all wear out.

First, as we read that Israel loved Joseph more than all his children, so Christ is the Only-begotten Son, Who is in the bosom of the Father, and was twice pronounced by the Father's own Voice from Heaven to be His own, His Well-beloved. The coat of many colours which the fond father made for his child may well represent the manifold glory, wherewith the God and Father of all is said to have invested the Son, when by His Incarnation He became one of us. So speaks a holy bishop of the early times of the Christian Church: even as S. Peter says concerning Christ, "[c] He received of God the Father honour and glory, when there came such a

[c] 2 Pet. i. 17.

voice to Him from the excellent glory, This is My beloved Son in Whom I am well pleased."

Again, as Joseph's future glory was foreshewn by those marvellous dreams, so was our Lord's by the prophecies of the Old Testament, and by His own miracles and parables. As Joseph's brethren envied him their father's favour, and the exaltation which his dreams foretold, so did the Jews, our Lord's brethren after the flesh. "He came unto His own, and His own received Him not." And yet He was sent to find them; as Jacob ordered Joseph out into the field, to see whether it was well with his brethren, and well with the flocks, so our Lord came down from Heaven, sent from the Father to seek us, His lost sheep. When Joseph came to his brethren, we know how they used him, much as the wicked husbandmen in our Lord's parable treated the householder's son who was sent last unto them: they seize him, they strip him of his beautiful robe, the pledge of his father's love, they sell him to heathens who knew not God, he is cast as a malefactor into prison, and then by God's wonderful Providence he meets with deliverance, and is lifted up to be next to the throne of Pharaoh king of Egypt, at a time when Egypt was the mightiest kingdom of the earth. Who does not see in this the image and likeness of our Lord's humiliation and glory? Sold for money, seized and bound by His enemies, taking on Himself more and more the form of a servant, given up to the heathen Romans, falsely accused, cast into the dungeon of the grave, and that between two, one of whom remained in condemnation, the other was taken the same day to meet our Lord in Paradise. Thus far Joseph's troubles answer to the Passion of Christ: and when the king sends and delivers Joseph, and the prince of the people lets him go free, when Pharaoh makes him lord of his house, and ruler of all his substance, to inform his princes after his will, and teach his senators wisdom, who that knows the Creed can help thinking of the Angel sent, the stone rolled away, the Lord first rising, then ascending and taking His place at the Right Hand of God, and from thence sending down the Comforter to inform and teach His Church? When we read that they cried before Joseph, "bow the knee," what is it but S. Paul declaring the divine decree, "That at the Name of Jesus every knee should bow?"

But the point, with which we are most especially concerned to-day, is the holy Joseph's forgiveness of those who had used him ill: his not being ashamed or unwilling to call them brethren, after their acting so unbrotherly a part towards him. Mark his whole behaviour towards them; how, when they come to buy corn, he makes himself indeed strange unto them, but it is to prove them, not out of any unkind feeling: how his heart yearns towards them at the very first token of repentance. "They said one to another, we are verily guilty concerning our brother, when we saw the anguish of his soul, when he besought us, and we would not hear, therefore is this distress come upon us. And he turned himself about from them, and wept." Still he did not give way to his feelings, but for their good restrained himself, until he had throughly tried them, first by making them bring Benjamin, concerning whom he feared that they might have used him as they had done himself: afterwards by contriving that Benjamin might seem to be in great danger, whereby it became manifest that they had really and deeply repented, since they shewed themselves ready to suffer in Benjamin's stead. Then at last he received them openly as his brethren: he was not afraid nor ashamed to shew how entirely he forgave, how he loved them with all his heart. He bade them, "Come near to me, I pray you: and they came near; and he said unto them, I am Joseph your brother, whom ye sold into Egypt: now therefore be not grieved nor angry with yourselves that ye sold me hither: for God did send me before you to preserve life." And again after their father Jacob's death, when they feared what Joseph might do, he wept when they spoke unto him, and said: "[a]Fear not.... ye thought evil against me, but God meant it unto good, to bring it to pass, as it is this day, to save much people alive. Fear ye not, I will nourish you and your little ones. And he comforted them, and spake kindly unto them." Surely he was in all this the true token, so many years beforehand, of that gracious Elder Brother of ours, Whom we have so many times crucified afresh by our sins; yet He ceases not to say unto us, as by His servant S. Peter He did to those who actually put Him to death, "[e] I wot that through ignorance ye did it, as did also your rulers: but those things which God before had shewed by the mouth of all His prophets that Christ should suffer, He hath so fulfilled." Surely Joseph's kind words to his

[a] Gen. l. 19, 20, 21.   [e] Acts iii. 17.

brethren are spoken out of the abundance of the same charity, which invited the very crucifiers of Christ to repent and be baptized in His Name, to receive for themselves and their children the promise, "I will feed you and your little ones." Forgiveness, true brotherly forgiveness, the owning them as brethren who had behaved most unbrotherly, this is that good and holy and most needful lesson, which the Holy Church teaches us to-day, by the example first of Joseph, and then much more of Him Who is the true Joseph. All of us have need to learn this lesson. If we live any time in the world, one way or another we shall all have enough to forgive, though not so much, perhaps, as we may imagine ourselves. We must expect from time to time to be ill-used, or to fancy ourselves so; sometimes, may be, by our brethren and the house of our father: some of us, it is likely, have the feeling even now in our hearts, more or less, towards some one or another: though not in any degree like Joseph, much less like our Blessed Lord.

However, be our wrongs little or great, we all of us, when we are asked, profess that we forgive them. At least it is a rare thing to hear any one say he cannot forgive. And in about a month's time a certain number of us will come together, testifying this our forgiveness in the most solemn way: we shall, if it please God, take the holy Sacrament upon it. We could wish, I am sure, every one of us, not to be deceiving ourselves; to be quite in earnest in doing such a thing as that. Well here is the example of holy Joseph, forgiving his brethren, set before us: let us try our own forgiveness by comparison with him. Perhaps you bear no malice at present: but did you forgive, did you try in earnest to forgive as soon as ever you were stung with a sense of wrong done to you? Joseph had forgiven his brethren long before he declared his forgiveness of them; and our Lord's prayer, "Father, forgive," went up at the very moment that His murderers were nailing Him to the Cross. And the rule of Christian forgiveness is, "'Let not the sun go down upon your wrath,'" tread out the spark of anger as soon as you perceive it. Remember, my brethren, that however entirely we may have forgiven by this time, we have need to humble ourselves before God for every moment that we ever put off our forgiving. Again, in *forgiving* we should try at least to *forget*. I do not say we always sin in not forgetting any wrong that may have been done to us: sometimes we cannot, sometimes we ought not, even for the offender's sake. We must watch him, perhaps, that he do not repeat the offence: but never let us permit ourselves to dwell on any wrong thing that may have been done, *as* a wrong or an affront to ourselves; let us not feed an illnatured fancy with dwelling on other men's bad behaviour, and keeping ourselves in anger because of it: it is just giving place to the devil, making room for it in our hearts. Joseph, when he suddenly saw his brethren, looked upon them *as* his brethren, not as those who betrayed and all but murdered him. Again, you *say* you have forgiven: but are you in all brotherly kindness watching to do good, as God may enable you, to those whom you had to forgive? If not, your forgiveness is unlike Joseph's: for he,

f Eph. iv. 26.

when his brethren were once again brought within his reach, never tired of doing them good, and making them as happy as he could. And this, not only by substantial gifts, but by his extreme and most touching sweetness in his *manner* of dealing with them. " Be not grieved nor angry with yourselves." " Fear not, I will nourish you and your little ones." It highly concerns us to remember this: for, as a wise man says, "Is not a word better than a gift?" Sweetness and good temper towards those who may seem to have affronted you is often a sure sign of loving and forgiving charity, when greater things are not needed, or are beyond our reach. Finally, if we would really follow the blessed example set before us in Joseph, we must accustom ourselves, as often as we are, or seem to be ill-used, to call up in our minds the remembrance of the Presence of God, of Him to Whom alone vengeance belongeth: as Joseph when he first saw his brethren after their selling him for a slave, remembered his dreams, remembered it was all God's doing. We should say to ourselves, when revenge and anger are tempting, when unkind thoughts are swelling in our hearts, and unkind words are rushing to our lips, "Am I in the place of God?" Above all we should remember our own Elder Brother, Him Who made Himself such, that our wrongs done to Him might be pardoned. Did we really and in earnest think of Him, and pray in His Name, our saying "we bear no malice" would not be a mere word of course. We should truly forgive, and truly try to love, in hope of His love and forgiveness.

SERMON XXX.

ISHMAEL'S MOCKING A TYPE OF THE WORLD'S TREATMENT OF CHRIST AND HIS PEOPLE.

FOURTH SUNDAY IN LENT.

GAL. iv. 29.

" As then he that was born after the flesh persecuted him that was born after the Spirit, even so it is now."

THE Church sets before us to-day a parable from the history of Abraham: and wonderful it is to see how in the good Providence of God the things which happened so many years ago among the men of the East so many thousand miles off, are made to signify the greatest counsels of the Almighty, and to help us and all Christians in our daily duties to God and to one another. Abraham had two sons, the one by a bondmaid and the other by a freewoman, the Law of God at that time allowing, as you know, of more than one wife. Ishmael, the son of the bondwoman Hagar, was born in a natural way, without any thing strange or miraculous. After him was born Isaac, the son of the freewoman Sarah, in a wonderful manner, by miracle, his father being a hundred years old, and his mother past age : and this in fulfilment of a special covenant which God had made with Abraham a great many years before, during all which time he had been waiting for it in faith. This difference between the two sons the Apostle explains by saying, "Ishmael, the son of the bondwoman, was born after the flesh, but Isaac the son of the freewoman was by promise." And then he goes on to explain that this whole matter was an allegory or parable. Abraham represents Almighty God, the Father of us all; Ishmael represents mankind in general, who are the children of God born after the natural way; Isaac represents the Christian people, God's children by adoption and grace; God's children, because by a heavenly and spiritual union they are made members of His Only Begotten Son; born again of God, born of water and of the Spirit. The elder son is in bondage, because until people are mystically united to Jesus Christ they are in slavery under sin, death, and the devil; they are not free to obey God's holy commandments; even if they have misgivings, and some sense of what is right, they must confess as one did of old, " The good that I would, I do not, and the evil that I would not, that I do." But the younger son Isaac, is free, because the children of Christ and of His Church have power given them by His Holy Spirit to keep His commandments if they will. Those then, who choose to go on as if they could not help sinning, are in fact making themselves slaves, when God has made them free: those only are free indeed, who stand fast in the liberty wherewith Christ "hath made them free," and do not suffer themselves to be again entangled with the yoke of the world, the flesh and the devil. The children of the bondwoman, like the heathens who know not God, are content to be in slavery to their sins; the children of the freewoman are free to serve God, and try with all their might to do so. With one sort or the other you and I and all of us must take our place. Which shall it be, my brethren? On which side shall we be found? It is no small matter: it is for our life. And we have but a short time to choose in. Very quickly the time is passing, at the end of which it will be too late for us to think of having any choice at all. And if any man say, "Well, I do not wish to choose; I had rather not have any thought about the matter; I will take my chance, as so many others have done:" the Word of God tells that man loudly and plainly, "it cannot be so with you: you must make your choice; if you go on thinking to have no care about your soul, know that there is one close at hand who is all the while busy in destroying that soul, winding his net about it, that it cannot escape. To say, you will not care for your soul, comes to just the same as if you said, I will give my soul up to the hands of the devil."

Look to it well therefore, my brethren, that you are really behaving as children of the freewoman. Why should you of your own accord invite the Evil One to put his chains on you again? And Holy Scripture gives you many signs, whereby you may know on which side you are at present. One of these signs is, whether or no you are going on in a way to hurt and distress the people of God. You heard just now what the Apostle says of persecution, "As then he that was born after the flesh persecuted him that was born after the Spirit, even so it is now." He that was born after the flesh, in Abraham's family, was Ishmael: he that was born after the Spirit is

Isaac. How did Ishmael persecute Isaac? The history tells us: it was by scorning and mockery. On the day that Isaac was weaned, Abraham made a great feast to his household: and in the course of the festival hours it came to pass that Sarah, Isaac's mother, saw Ishmael mocking. Ishmael was then a lad of fourteen or fifteen years old, likely enough to have high spirits and rough ways: and when Sarah saw him inclined to be so disrespectful to his father and herself, so unbrotherly towards Isaac, she spoke to Abraham of casting him out, and the Lord confirmed his word.

Now, this mockery of Ishmael's was a type and token of the Jewish people, the children of the bondwoman, the Synagogue, rejecting, mocking, persecuting, murdering first the Lord Jesus, and then His members, for which also the Jewish people were cast out of the Lord's house, as Hagar and Ishmael from Abraham's. Even so it is now, saith S. Paul: the children of the bondwoman stood round the judgement seat and cried out, "crucify Him;" they stood round the Cross deriding and saying, "Let the Lord deliver Him now, if He will have Him." Thus they sported themselves, they made a wide mouth and drew out the tongue, against the Holy One of Israel, against their Lord and Redeemer enduring the worst of torments for them. Was not this the very depth of malice, the very extreme of unpitying persecution? not being themselves carried away with the heat of false zeal, to have pleasure in seeing how cruelly others treated Him, Him the very God of pity, the most meek and merciful Saviour!

And as it was with our Lord, so it was with His

Apostles and His Church: according to His own prophecy, "ᵃIf they have persecuted Me, they will also persecute you." The Jews and the heathens too, being both children of the bondwoman, both in slavery to their sins, did from the beginning persecute in all ways the members of Christ, the children of the freewoman. And so the noble army of Martyrs grew, as you know, to a great number, and their blood was the seed of the Church, it bare fruit an hundred fold: as was said of the Israelites in Egypt, the more they were afflicted, the more they multiplied and grew. You might think that upon this the persecutions would at length be worn out, that Christians would no longer have to suffer for their religion, that the son of the bondwoman, being effectually put down, would cease to disturb the son of the freewoman. But it is not so: the same Apostle informs us, that "ᵇall who will live godly in Christ Jesus, must suffer persecution." Somehow or another it must be so, in our time and in all times as well as in the beginning of the Gospel: in our country and in all countries, as well as in Judea and ancient Rome. There are the same Church and the same world as ever: and these are contrary the one to the other; there can be no peace nor truce, nor mutual agreement. The one sort cannot bear the other any more now, than in our Lord's own life time. The Pharisees (for instance,) who were covetous, and derided Him then, would no doubt deride in our days those who tried to walk in His steps. The children of those Pharisees, proud and unbelieving, yet outwardly decent and calling themselves respectable, are in general violently set

ᵃ S. John xv. 20.   ᵇ 2 Tim. iii. 11.

against all, whom they see generous and devoted in the service of Christ. The passionate, haughty man cannot bear the humble and meek; he frets against him, he is glad to get out of sight of him. The mere lover of pleasure cannot bear the lover of God: it is a trouble and a vexation to him; very irksome and uncomfortable to an irreligious person, when he is thrown into company with one who tries to be thoroughly and consistently religious. This is the spirit of persecution : and however its outward violence be restrained by a good Providence, it is sure to break out more or less one way or another. Whoever comes in earnest to serve the Lord must prepare in good earnest to suffer persecution from men.

You will say, "How is it then that any Christians live in peace? How is it that if we look round, in this or any other place, we appear to see so many living quietly, with no trouble, no ill usage to endure for religion's sake? Do not people in this country go in and out, to Church or elsewhere, as often as they please, and no one interferes to hinder them? Are there not many who are accounted more or less in earnest in their Christian duties, and instead of losing their lives and properties, they appear to be all the better thought of, and many are anxious to help them in one way or another? How can it be said that all these suffer persecution? and yet the word of God plainly says they must do so, if they really wish to live godly in Christ Jesus. How can these things be?"

Holy men of old explain, that ridicule and contempt and evil report is one sort of persecution, and to many, most terrible. Ishmael, as you heard just now, did but mock at his brother Isaac, and it was judged such direct persecution, that the two could not dwell together in the house. Here is something for us to think of, when we see persons stricter than others, or supposed to be so, brought into reproach or contempt: a bad name given them, every thing said and done to put them out of countenance, and make men ashamed of belonging to them. Some years ago, if any one was at all more serious than his companions liked him to be, he was presently called, as you know, a Methodist, now it may be some other name: but the spirit which gives men such names is just the same, and you may depend upon it they are a part of real persecution, though they touch neither a person's body nor his estate: yet they give many a real pang, and cause many a sad disappointment. To be mocked and scorned is to many (as to holy Job himself) the bitterest of pains: and it proves a sad hindrance in the way of our being useful: and this in itself, to a good and charitable mind, is a sore trial. They seek to make others better and happier, but they cannot, because in some way those others have been taught not to respect or trust them. Again and again they try, and again and again Satan hinders them. It is really as bad, in the way of disappointment, as if they were banished or imprisoned.

But further; holy men teach us that the very suffering which the servants of Christ endure when they see others, especially those belonging to them, wicked and setting themselves against Christ, those very sufferings are really and truly a persecution. Righteous Lot in Sodom, how sorely was he vexed with the filthy conversation of the wicked, how did he from day to day by seeing and hearing, vex his righteous soul with their ungodly deeds! Very loud and rude were the people of Sodom in their wickedness, they made no secret of it, they prided themselves on shewing and practising it in the open streets: and this all the more, when they saw how it shocked and distressed the righteous man. They were as truly persecutors as if they had sought to throw him to the wild beasts or to cast him down headlong. Our blessed Lord as His Passion drew on vouchsafed to endure more and more of this kind of persecution as well as of all other outward and inward suffering. When he saw Judas giving way to covetousness first, then to black-hearted malice and treachery; was it not, think you, a sorer pang by far to the heart of that Blessed One, than all the torment of the thorns, and stripes, and nails? Imagine my brethren, as well as you can, what it must have been to Him to look down day after day and hour after hour for many months into that wicked and corrupt bosom of His false disciple, and to see the evil brood of sins one after another coming into being, and growing into strength within him! according to that saying of the Prophet, "ᶜThey hatch cockatrice's eggs, and weave the spider's web." Even to a mortal man who has any real love of goodness, to be aware of certain grievous sins committed very near him, is absolutely loathsome: who can understand that deep suffering Judas' fall must have occasioned to our Lord Christ? the Scripture teaches us to call the like of it, "crucifying afresh:" is not this the worst of persecution?

ᶜ Isa. lix. 5.

And as Jesus Christ was, so are they that belong to Him, in this world. If it was unspeakably bitter to Him to see the wickedness of those whom He came to save, be sure it is bitter, in its degree, to His people also; the more bitter, the more truly and entirely they are His. Not bitter in the sense of making them angry, as if they were better than the rest, and it were an affront and indignity to have any thing so foul brought near them; that is the Pharisaical feeling, not the Christian; but he who is beginning to love Christ will love all souls because Christ died for them, and loving them, it will break his heart to see them ruining themselves and affronting Christ. Now to bring upon a person that which will break his heart is surely very like persecution. You see then brethren, what you were doing, if ever any of you through wicked wantonness, and braving as it were all consequences, has been tempted to make a shew of any sin, and bring it on purpose before the eyes of persons who would be most shocked at it, not caring how you annoyed and vexed them. Is it so very uncommon a thing, for a person to swear, or utter other bad words, or go on with other wickedness, all the more recklessly and impudently because there is some one near whom such things shock and distress, and who feels it his duty to speak a word of warning against them? Alas, when young persons or persons of any age are gathered together not in the fear of God, when they are set to have their own way, to please themselves with all greediness, too certainly they will be guilty of this sin of persecution too: him who is unwilling to sin with them they will persecute by mockery and ridicule, and when, being helped by God's grace, he shews himself unmoved by their scorn, they will often still go on to persecute him, as the men of Sodom did Lot, by the very sight of their sins. "He will needs be a judge," they say: "now will we behave ourselves more fearlessly than ever, to shew that we do not care for him." This is direct persecution: but it is also quite real, though less direct, when people suffer from beholding the general wickedness and unbelief, uttered and practised, without any thought of them. A man writes and publishes, we will say, a scornful sentence against something holy in a book or a newspaper: that man is a persecutor: he sets himself to vex and punish all who are pained, when holy things are set at nought. Or it may be a profane word spoken: the pain and persecution to a believing hearer, is just the same. By this one instance you may judge what a common sin this of persecution is: and it will no longer sound strange to you to be told, "[d] Even so it is now, all that will live godly in Christ Jesus must suffer persecution."

Fearful indeed must it be to take part with the persecutors, i.e., to take part with the Jews and Judas against our Lord: but one word of caution may be not amiss, for those also on the other side, who wish to do right, and are therefore in danger of suffering persecution. Our Lord encourages them not only to be patient but joyful: "theirs," he says, "is the kingdom of Heaven:" well may they rejoice and leap for joy, for they are beginning to enter into the portion of the Saints and Prophets. But let them be very careful that their suffering is really for right-

[d] 2 Tim. iii. 12.

eousness' sake, that they do not bring it on by any conceit, any inconsiderate selfish ways of their own: if the Ishmaels, the children of the bondwoman, seem to persecute them, let them see to it that they are themselves not in bondage to any sin: let them make good their title to be free by forgiving and loving and doing their best to help others to be free also: in fear and pity earnestly praying for all who are now on the persecutor's side, and if they may, tenderly warning them of the peril they are in, in so taking part with Christ's enemies.

SERMON XXXI.

GOD'S WAYS OF PROVIDING FOR OUR BODIES AND OUR SOULS.

FOURTH SUNDAY IN LENT.

S. JOHN vi. 5.

" Whence shall we buy bread that these may eat?"

THINK for a moment, my brethren, Who asked this question. It was the Creator of Heaven and earth, the Maker and Provider both of all food that is eaten, and of all who are nourished by food. He gave His blessing in the first place to the earth, that it should have power and virtue to bring forth what might nourish and sustain life. Every hour He continues that blessing, not only to the great world altogether, but to each little insect and blade of grass; He cares and provides for each one as perfectly as if there were only that one to be cared and provided for. He it was and no other; it was the great Almighty Creator Himself, Who as He stood that day on the grassy mountain near the sea of Tiberias, and saw a great company come unto Him, now after many hours of attendance, had pity upon them, knowing that they were faint and weary, and the provisions with which they had left their home, if any, had been exhausted, and He, the All-knowing and All-merciful, Who had taken our nature upon Him, in order that among our other infirmities, He might know the pangs of hunger, and Who to that end had once fasted forty days and forty nights, He had pity on them, and decreed in His own mind to relieve them. And how does He proceed? He seems to consult His disciples. "Whence shall we buy bread that these may eat?" He, the Maker and Preserver of all, seems in a manner at a loss how to provide for that hungry multitude, and He makes as though He were asking aid and counsel of His servants, as any Teacher or Master might among men.

And we need not wonder at this; for, when we come to consider it, it is just what He is doing every day by His Providence, as Governor of the world. He does not in general supply us at once, without any trouble or pains; on the contrary, we know too well how much labour, how many difficulties, how many various contrivances come into most people's minds, when we talk of "getting one's bread." It was, as we know, a part of the sentence on Adam, "In the sweat of thy face thou shalt eat bread;" not without much labour, not without manifold ways and devices, as if God were asking His creatures, where shall we find bread, that these who are My family may eat? Thus our Lord on the mountain, referring to His Apostles about the refreshment of the people, was but doing the same kind of thing which He does continually in His Providence, governing and keeping us all alive upon the earth. He knows well what He will do, how bountifully He will provide for us; yet it pleases Him to ask us from time to time, and to set us on asking ourselves, where are we to find food for so many? how shall we ever be able to get on? And when we are most at a loss, even then, if we trust and obey Him, He wonderfully helps us.

And so He does in respect of His grace also. He helps our souls as He helps our bodies, through the aid of ordained means; and sometimes He may cause those means to fall short, and then may supply them as suddenly and abundantly as He multiplied those loaves and fishes. A person may have but little learning, he may be quite unable to read, and may seem to himself as if he did not well understand what he hears, and yet if he have the fear of God in his heart, and try to live accordingly, he shall eat and be filled with spiritual meat and drink. One good lesson, one verse, one prayer, may be a treasure to him, which he shall never lose. He may be a good way from Church, he may have few helps at home, but if he really try to make the most of what little he has, God can and will make a great deal of it, *to him.* Half a prayer remembered as having been learned in childhood, an old torn Bible or Testament on a shelf, the remembrance of some good Christian formerly known, his sayings, his tone of voice, his manner of coming in and going out, all these and other such things are as the scanty fare of that multitude, the five barley loaves and two small fishes, which became abundant under His creative Hand, enough to feed and to fill many thousands.

We in our poor way cannot understand His wonderful ways. We are apt to be like one or other of the Apostles to whom our Lord spake. When He saw the multitude draw near, He turned to S. Philip first, with the question, "Whence shall we buy bread that these may eat"? and S. Philip after his simplicity, answered, "Two hundred pennyworth of bread would not be sufficient for them, that every one of them may take a little." He was scared by the greatness of the want, as he saw them come crowding on, one after another. How shall we ever get enough for them all? was his thought, a thought but too familiar, my brethren, to many of you. He did not consider that it was all one to Him Who made and preserves all alike, to save the many or the few. He can maintain a large family as easily as He can a small one.

Again, we in our distress naturally look on our scanty supplies, and say to ourselves, what am I to do? I have only just so much. This again is not unlike what passed between our Lord and S. Andrew; for when S. Philip in that desponding way had spoken of the number of persons to be fed, Andrew remarked, "There is a lad here which hath five barley loaves and two small fishes, but what are they among so many?" So might some of you my brethren, say to one another at the week's end, when prices perhaps are high, and wages are low, "our family is very large, we have such and such allowance or earnings, so many shillings a week, but what are they among so many?" How often do such thoughts occur? but in a good and believing heart they are presently followed by another thought, "God is here, God will provide, God will make a little go a great way;" His word is, "Seek ye first My kingdom and righteousness, and all these things shall be added unto you." My brethren, I am sure there must be some of you who know something of the happiness of this thought, the thought of clinging to God only, and living under the shadow of His wing; the thought of reposing on Him, relying on His Fatherly care, lying down and sleeping soundly at night, however bad the times may be, because you know that He is watching over you, and will be near you to take care of you in the morning, to take care not of yourselves only, but of those whom He has trusted with you and commanded you to love. May you know more and more of this comfortable trust, this "peace of God which passeth all understanding," this only refuge against the fretting cares of the world: and that you may know more and more of it, I advise you to acquaint yourself more and more with the ways of His spiritual Providence. Think not only of the meat that perisheth, but of that meat which endureth unto everlasting life, which the Son of Man giveth unto you. We know by this miracle and by the conversations which followed upon it, between our Lord, the Jews and His disciples, that bodily meat is but a type of the true Spiritual meat, the Body of the Son of Man, the Living Bread which cometh down from Heaven. This is the Bread which He provides for our souls. There in respect of our souls, He mercifully answers His own question, " whence shall we buy bread, that these may eat?" as if He should say to men and angels, "Here is all this great multitude, these lost children of Adam, I have compassion on them, for they have naturally nothing to eat, nothing to do their souls any good, they have lost the fruit of the Tree of Life, to which at first I permitted them to approach, and the Tree of

Knowledge has proved only poison to them ; and now what can they do ? they will surely faint on their way to Eternity : but I will take pity on them ; I know where to buy bread, which shall be enough for them and to spare." Thus may we understand our Lord to speak ; and if you ask Him " what bread ?" He will answer " My own blessed Body, spiritually, but most really and truly received, by faith, in the Holy Communion." If you ask Him further, "what is the cost of that Bread ? for how much was it bought? this is the reply, the most wonderful and gracious reply, " It cost every drop of the Blood of Him Who is both God and Man, it cost all that pain and misery which He bore on the tormenting Cross. That we might feast on this Bread, and live for ever, He poured out His Soul unto death. That is our Bread and thus He bought it for us to eat. You think much, all of you, of course you think much, of those ways of God's Providence whereby He helps you to your ordinary, bodily food. O ! that you would think more, a great deal more than you do, of His heavenly and supernatural ways in His holy Church. You labour hard for the meat that perisheth ; O ! that you would do something, something real, something earnest, for the meat that endureth unto everlasting life.

For in this point again the two kinds of good, the bodily and the spiritual, resemble one another, that in both He expects us to do our own part, though both, truly speaking, are free and undeserved gifts from Him. We do not expect to reap without ploughing and sowing; we do not come into the garden and expect to find plenty of fruit, if we know it has been neglected : no more must we expect to obtain or keep the grace of Christ's Sacraments, if we neglect what is required on our part. See how it was in this miraculous feast on the mountain; Christ could have cured the people's hunger at once, without any loaves or fishes at all, if He had pleased; and so if it pleased Him, He could give us grace without Sacraments. But as He then employed the meat which was ready to His Hand, so it commonly pleases Him to give us His grace by the outward forms, first water, then bread and wine. He could have commanded the people to help themselves, as in Moses' time they helped themselves to the Manna, but it pleased Him that they should sit down and wait to have it given them. He might have given it with His own Hands, but He chose to do it by the hands of His disciples. So it is with His Sacraments now; we are brought to His ministers for Holy Baptism, we come to them for Holy Communion; the grace is given in each case through His ministers. When our Lord said to His disciples "make the men sit down," it was as if He should say, "You, the Apostles and Elders of My Church, and you, Bishops and Priests who are to come after, see that you do your best to bring all to My Holy Table, and to make all come decently and in order. Shew them the way, help them to prepare themselves; warn them how dangerous it is either to forsake Communion or to receive unworthily." And whereas S. Mark says, "they sat down in ranks, by hundreds and by fifties;" this seems to tell us something of the admirable order of Christ's Sacraments; and also how it depends upon us whether that order be observed or no; as those men had they chosen, might have refused to sit down, or might have sat down irregularly; and then, I suppose, they would have missed their portion of the feast. See too how careful our Blessed Lord was to order His doings in such a way as the disciples would be sure to remember, when about a year after He should appoint the Holy Sacrament itself. He took the bread, and blessed and brake it, and gave to His disciples to set before the multitude. The very act of Consecration, as some here know, was represented bodily by our Lord on that occasion. You cannot read the miracle without thinking of the Sacrament. And as you read, you feel more and more that our Lord meant us to think on It. It becomes plainer and plainer to us, that even as those men, had they churlishly refused to wait and be prepared for the meal, must have gone without any refreshment; so, if men neglect the Lord's Supper, if they will not join in offering to God the appointed memorial of His Death;—there is no help for it, you must do without His Intercession.

But I am persuaded better things of you, beloved brethren, I know there are some among you who have serious thoughts about their own past neglect of Holy Communion. I would say to them, "take care of these your good thoughts: value them highly; do not let them waste in mere thoughts. Take your thoughts about Communion with you when you kneel down to say your prayers; remember it when you come to speak of "our daily bread." That you may come worthily and in order, come to those whom our Lord has appointed to marshal His guests at this His wedding banquet; report yourselves to the Priest, let him judge of your fitness to come.

Do this before Easter; let not the holy time find you still negligent. Lastly, take especial care, having come once, to come again, and that often; not for the loaves' sake, but for the miracles; not for what you can get in this world, as comfort, credit, inward satisfaction; but for Christ's sake and His Blessed Body's sake, because you know that your souls cannot live without Him. Come to Him, not for earthly but for heavenly reasons; so will you come prepared, and depart with a blessing.

SERMON XXXII.

TIMES OF PENANCE, TIMES OF REFRESHING.

FOURTH SUNDAY IN LENT.

Acts iii. 19, 20, 21.

"Times of refreshing shall come from the Presence of the Lord, and He shall send Jesus Christ, which before was preached unto you, Whom the Heaven must receive until the times of restitution of all things."

HITHERTO we have had to consider the dark and awful side of the Great Day, for which our self-examination in Lent, and all God's discipline over us, were intended to prepare us. We have regarded it as coming suddenly as a day of separation, a day of darkness. And it is well for us ever to remember that we have such a serious time, such a time of dread and amazement before us. We must come to it: we are daily and hourly drawing near it: our turning away our minds and refusing to think of it does not in the least keep it back from us; it only keeps us unprepared and unready to meet it. Therefore it is well on every account that we should think of that Day continually with fear and trembling; that we should look our true condition, as it were, in the face. But at the same time God would not have us altogether taken up with these dismal and overwhelming thoughts. The Day has a bright aspect as well as a dark one; unutterably inconceivably bright, as on the other side it will prove dark beyond all words and thoughts of ours. In one sense it will be a day of darkness and gloominess, a day of wrath, a day of vengeance. But no less certainly will it be also a day of Redemption, a day of Salvation, a day of Restitution of all things. And now, as we come nearer Easter, the Holy Church instructs us to think of the more hopeful and merciful sayings which we find in the Bible concerning our Lord's second Coming. For Easter is the time of love; Easter Day coming after Good Friday is love sealed by unspeakable suffering: and however unworthy we know ourselves to be, and how fearful soever the Day may appear to us when we look on to it, yet when we really think of Christ crucified and risen again for us, we must feel that all is not lost: by God's mercy we have yet a chance: in our bitterest humiliation He invites us to thank Him and take courage.

So, this very day, this Mid-Lent Sunday, as it is called, we are invited as it were to keep a time of refreshing, one of those times which the Apostle in the text speaks of. "Times of refreshing shall come from the Presence of the Lord, and He shall send Jesus Christ, which before was preached unto you, Whom the Heaven must receive until the times of restitution of all things." You see here are two sorts of times mentioned: times of refreshing and times of restitution: the one occurring, when it pleases God, for the support and refreshment of His Church and people in their hard trial here on earth; the other, sure to come at last, but kept back for an uncertain time. And the refreshing, which comes and goes, is given us for a pledge, and earnest, and sample, of the complete restitution and redemption, which when it comes will never again go away. And I say, that the Sunday services this week lead us to think of such refreshing, and to feel how much we owe to our good God for it. For first the Collect, while it acknowledges that we, even the best of us all, "do for our evil deeds worthily deserve to be punished," yet goes on to pray that "by the comfort of God's grace we may mercifully be relieved." "Relieved," it says; it does not say in the prayer, "redeemed," "delivered," "thoroughly and eternally restored," but only "relieved" for the time. That is, that God would give us lightening and seasons of refreshment, breathing times in our hard work, glimpses in our cloudy and dark days, cheering messages and tokens from Himself in our many misgivings and vexing thoughts. This is our petition in the Collect, and the Gospel as so often happens, may be taken as an answer to that petition, God's own gracious answer. For the Gospel as you will recollect, is the account of that wonderful feast, in which our Lord fed five thousand and more with five loaves and two fishes. They were hungry and weary, and thirsty, and faint in the wilderness, and He would not send them away empty, lest they should faint in the way: and so by His Almighty Power, He provided for them a feast in the desolate place. And we know what this is to us: it is a sure token of that best and most effectual refreshing, when the Lord feeds His own people with His own Body and Blood, and so gives them spirit and strength to go on their journey to their true home, and to fight with their invisible enemies. But as the preparation for this blessed feast cannot be without many bitter thoughts, deep remorse for transgressions committed, and serious fear of the effect of present imperfections, so this refreshing, prayed for in the Collect and betokened in the Gospel is mingled with our Lenten exercises, and cannot be complete without them. Now, how is this, that mortification, and self-denial, sad thoughts of past sins, and lowly bowing down of ourselves under the wrath of our offended God, should be full of refreshing and comfort? It is apt to seem all dismal and melancholy beforehand. In those days and in those countries wherein Lent was kept (outwardly at least) more in earnest than it commonly is among us, of course it was a dreary time to many, when they found Ash-Wednesday drawing on, and had to look forward to so many days, so many weeks, of unusual hardness; fasting, sackcloth, ashes, neglect of the body, lying all night upon the ground, to say nothing of what men had to bear in humbling themselves before their brethren, (for sometimes they had to kneel or prostrate themselves every day for many days at the entrance of the Church, asking pardon from God and the people). These and other like penitential doings are very startling to us now we read of them; and no doubt seemed before they were tried, very very dismal and severe to the men of those times. But they had faith to try them: they saw such things mentioned in Scripture, and those who had authority recommended

Y

them as good for their souls: they set about their penitency therefore in faith, and can you doubt how they felt, while it was going on, provided only they continued in it with patience and humility? Depend upon it, they found it very refreshing: their fasting proved Angels' food to them: and as our Lord, against what many think our natural feelings, declared, "It is more blessed to give than to receive," so we need not doubt that David and the other blessed penitents, of whom we are told in Holy Scripture and Church history, had more refreshment in their severe exercises, than ever the children of this world had in its gaieties and pleasures. Why even as we, in our poor way, endeavour earnestly to keep these holy seasons, they surely come to us full of refreshment, full of a deep and inward satisfaction which before-hand we could not understand, nor dream of. Our prayers indeed are very weak and wandering, yet surely, on the whole, when we look back calmly and thoughtfully, we must own that our prayers have been a great deal to us: we could not have done without them; they have been a true refreshment. I speak to each person, so far as he has ever felt alarm and fear because of his sins; and surely many here must have felt it before now, many must have wondered what would become of them, and in what it all must end, when they read or heard the strict sayings of the Law and the Gospel, and compared them with their own lives. Think for example, of the words which we heard in the Epistle last Sunday: "Fornication and all uncleanness let it not be once named among you, neither filthiness, nor foolish talking, nor jesting, which are not convenient.

... for this ye know that no unclean person... hath any inheritance in the Kingdom of Christ and of God." How many, alas! are there, who have gone on for their whole lives from their boyhood in utter scorn of this fearful and distinct warning: have made a mere jest of all abominable sins, which the Apostle sets his mark upon in these words. When such an one has come by God's mercy to know and feel what he has been doing, what a dreadful sentence stands against him actually pronounced in the Book of God? how could he go on at all, how could he bear himself or anything else, if he might not and could not pray? His prayers may have been, and may still continue, imperfect in the highest degree, they may seem to him little better than so many fresh sins, so very loose, wandering, and heartless is (perhaps) his whole way of saying them. Yet when time has passed on, and he looks back and considers where he is, he may find that by God's unspeakable mercy, even those prayers have proved to him a very great blessing: he may find that in some way which he can hardly trace, the chain of his sins has been broken, and although he must always go on in shame and humiliation, he is not now, blessed be God, going on in wilful sin. The time spent in such prayers is indeed a time of refreshing; and so are the times spent in holy reading, in studying the Bible, in hearing it read, in remembering and musing over what they have heard out of it. In this again it may often seem to us, it may seem to many at this very time of Lent, that their reading and hearing has been almost without profit, and void of all blessing; but depend upon it, it is far otherwise; unless indeed you have been going on wilfully in some serious sin. Depend upon it, your hours spent over the Bible with a serious mind will not return unto you void, however little comfort they seemed to bring you at the time. But I should think that many, by His mercy, have found at the time of their reading and hearing, present help and comfort, going straight to their hearts, in a way which could not be mistaken. The aweful texts which have brought them down on their knees before their offended God, come back now to them full of comfort, for now they perceive that it was Christ Himself, present with them, and speaking to them, as a grave and loving Father, for the good of their souls. The very wounds which the Word of God makes in our conscience are soothing and healing, if we rightly take them: like the sores which the skilful surgeon opens here and there in the body, to draw off the hurtful humours from within, as it is written, "Faithful are the wounds of a friend."

But if even the very threatenings of the Lord are turned into comforts for the penitent, much more will he find consolation from time to time in the regular exercise of his penitence. The Church services will come home to him continually in ways which he could not have imagined; the sayings and doings of good and kind friends or of strangers, if it should so happen; or such as he may read or hear of in books; will light upon him like arrows from a bow drawn at a venture: he will feel that they touch the very point which required to be touched, he will say to himself, this is the Hand of God: God is with me, unworthy as I am: God is dealing with my soul: I recall His gracious and wonderful dealings to my mind: therefore I have hope, for all mine evil conscience: therefore I am sure He will not fail me, if I am not wanting to His merciful invitations. In all these ways and in many more the Physician of our souls knoweth how to turn His bitterest medicines into sweetness. Thus the time of Lent, the days of mourning and penitence, are turned into times of refreshing, times of which, when they are gone, the memory will be more fragrant and precious than of many joyful and festival times. Why? because in the hours of penitence and conversion the merciful Saviour especially reveals Himself. It is His Presence which makes the difference, the times of refreshing come from the Presence of the Lord: as it was said to the children of Israel when they were humbling themselves for their sin in making the calf, so it may be said to Christian people, trying to make a good use of these penitential times: "My Presence shall go with thee, and I will give thee rest." When they most vex and punish themselves, then He shews Himself most graciously to them, and they know in their hearts that His will is to give them rest.

We may hope then even now for refreshing, and may thankfully take it when it comes: but we must remember that it is *only* refreshing. It is not entire deliverance, nor final rest: we may not expect to find it always with us: the consolations of the penitent are as breathing times, in the midst of hard, up-hill work: or like refreshing breezes in the course of a long season of hot weather: they come and go: we must make up our minds to do without them, it may be for the greatest part of our time. We must not at all fret, we must not too much disturb ourselves, when our comforts seem to be withdrawn, and we to be left to our own weariness. It were wrong to fret, though we cannot help being pained: because these are matters which our Lord keeps in His own Hands, we must leave it to Him: He only knows when and how we need to be comforted, when and how to be left desolate, and for how long. And there is another thing to be carefully borne in mind, viz., that the refreshing which God grants to such as we are, and at such times as this of Lent are after all the refreshing of penitents: not innocents fresh from their baptism, but of fallen persons under discipline. Therefore it must be more or less of the nature of punishment: it must be like, the more part of medicines, more or less unpleasant. We should have reason to fear that we were going all wrong, that we were under some strange and dangerous deceit, if we found no bitter mingled with His heavenly consolation. And what sort of penitents should we be, what kind of followers of Christ, if while He is fasting in the wilderness, and agonizing in the Garden for our sins, we had no feeling of shame and compunction, nothing but assured comfort in our hearts?

No, we must make up our minds, all along in our great work of penitence, to take the bitter with the sweet; so will it give out all its sweetness. We must welcome God's fatherly chastenings as well as His consolations, that is the way to make the most of things, now in the times of Refreshing, and to be prepared for that other more aweful time which will very soon be here, the Day of Redemption and Restitution of all things. God grant we may be found ready.

SERMON XXXIII.

PERSEVERANCE.

PASSION SUNDAY.

JUDGES xi. 35.

"*I have opened my mouth unto the Lord, and I cannot go back.*"

I HAVE taken these words from another part of the Bible history, because they answer so exactly to the mind of Moses the great Prophet, concerning whom the Church instructs us during these last Sundays of Lent. For Moses, good and faithful as he was, did most unwillingly undertake the hard duty to which God called him, of leading his people out of Egypt, and through the wilderness, and many and many a time he had sad misgivings in doing his work. But "he had opened his mouth unto the Lord:" and he felt that "he could not go back." He had put his hand to the plough, and by looking back he knew he should forfeit the blessing. He had escaped for his life; how should he look behind him? Therefore, though in fear and trembling, and with many a heart-ache, and sometimes sadly complaining to his God, still he went dutifully on, and so became a pattern to us all : and to those perhaps especially, who from time to time become amazed and affrighted when they consider how much they have to answer for.

Even in that small portion of the great Prophet's history, which is contained in the two first lessons for this Sunday, we see the beginning of his long disappointment and trouble, and what it was that carried him through it. Let us, as we may, compare it with our own case, how it has been with us, and how it now is; what God has set us to do, and how we may best hope to accomplish our task. It will be, please God, a good meditation for us, now that we are drawing again towards the end of this holy time of Lent. For surely if we have any religious thought at all, we must at this time be more or less oppressed with the consideration of the great eternal concern which is before us, and very welcome to us will be all the assurance we can obtain of God's gracious help granted to our feeble endeavours.

What then is the picture which the Holy Spirit draws this day before the eye of our Faith ? The waste barren wilderness, with the aweful rocks of Mount Sinai, and the sheep which Moses was leading scattered all around, and all of a sudden there is a flame of fire in a bush, the fire blazing, yet the bush not consumed, Moses, as is natural, turns aside to see this great sight, why the bush is not burned. He, learned as he was in all the wisdom of the Egyptians, thought, most likely, that it was some strange natural appearance, and was going to inquire into it accordingly, with no very special thought of the Presence of God. But the voice which had so often called to his forefathers, to Abraham, and the rest, now made itself heard by him; he was called by name, Moses, Moses; and so came to understand that it was no natural thing, but a wonderful miracle, in which he himself was greatly concerned. In a moment he became aware of the Lord's overpowering Presence: that there might be no mistake, the vision first bade him put off his shoes from his feet, even as we are bidden to uncover our heads when we go into a Church, because the place is holy ground: and then He declared Himself to be no created Angel, but the Lord God of his fathers, of Abraham, Isaac and Jacob. Moses trembled and durst not behold. He hid his face for he was afraid to look upon God.

Now the holy fathers teach us, that this vision of the fire in the bush is a token of the wonderful Incarnation of God the Son. It was a type, that when He should in His good time take upon Him to deliver man, He would not abhor, but would honour, even by inhabiting Himself a while, the chaste womb of the Blessed Virgin Mary. As the fire did not burn up the thorn tree, or whatever the tree was, in which it was blazing, so the Godhead of our Lord and Saviour does not in any wise consume or do away with His Manhood, but both Godhead and Manhood are joined in one Person, even in our Lord Jesus Christ for ever; He was from the moment when the holy Virgin conceived Him, perfect God and perfect Man, He is so now, He will be so to all eternity. And again, the bush burning and not consumed, is generally understood in the Church to mean that blessed

Mother's continuing a pure Virgin, even after the birth of her Divine Son. We then, Christians, wanderers, naturally, in the wilderness of this world, when we come to the mountain of the Lord, which is His Church, are so far like Moses drawing near to mount Sinai, that before all things we are called upon to turn and see this great sight, the Word made Flesh, the Incarnation of God the Son, the lower nature not swallowed up in the higher, but continuing along with it though infinitely glorified and ennobled, the taking of the Manhood into God. This I say is the first and chiefest thing which presents itself to the eye of faith, on turning aside from the ordinary matters of the world to contemplate the wonders of the Kingdom of Heaven. The Incarnation of God the Son is more than any one article besides the foundation of the Christian faith. It was the beginning of our redemption; the commencement of God's saving work by which He proposed to undo the destroying work which the devil had wrought in Paradise. And accordingly because it was the greatest thing which ever happened to mankind, we date all our time from it: we count our years by it.

Now, this Incarnate God, our Creator and our Brother, calls upon each one of us by name, as He called, Moses, Moses. He gives us a new name, and calls us by it in our Baptism. And when we grow old enough, He teaches us by His Church to believe in Him, thus made Man for us, and to fear and love Him before all things, as He began by telling Moses what reverence He expected of him: draw not nigh hither, put off thy shoes from off thy feet, for the place where thou standest is holy ground. That is the first thing : to learn reverence for the great God Who has come so unspeakably near to us. That is the beginning of all piety : even as reverence and love to our earthly parents (as Joseph's example taught us last Sunday) is the natural training and preparation for it.

In the next place Jesus Christ having shown Himself thus wonderfully to us, hath appointed for each of us *a work*. He did not call to Moses in the wilderness merely to dazzle and overawe him with His astonishing Presence, but He gave him a task, a commission, I have surely seen, He said, "the affliction of My people which are in Egypt, and have heard their cry, by reason of their taskmasters, for I know their sorrows : and I am came down to deliver them out of the hand of the Egyptians and to bring them up out of that land, into a good land and a large, unto a land flowing with milk and honey. Come now therefore and I will send thee unto Pharaoh, that thou mayest bring forth My people the children of Israel out of Egypt." This was Moses' task : and what is yours and mine? Is it not in its measure and degree, somewhat of the same kind ? Yes truly, so far as any of us have wandered back into sin, so far as we have broken the holy vows which have been laid upon us ever since our Baptism, so far we have gone back to Egypt again, i. e., to the wicked world, from which His grace had delivered us, while we were children : so far we have put ourselves anew under bondage to that evil spirit, more tyrannical than even was Pharaoh : and our work is plainly given us, our holy Lenten work, to break by His gracious aid, the chains of those sins which we have suffered to wind themselves again around us, to undo the heavy burdens under which we have wilfully stooped; if we have wronged any, to set it right; if we have been angry with any, to forgive; if we have contracted a bad habit, to break it; if we have indulged a shameful desire, to do penance for it; if we have left off holy duties, to begin them again. All such doings on our part, undertaken for Christ's sake, all that God puts in our hearts to do towards the conversion of our souls from sin, is as truly our task set us by God Incarnate, as it was Moses' task taught him out of the burning bush, to deliver the Israelites from their Egyptian bondage: although he had a great nation to deal with, and we each one of us, it may be, his own soul alone.

We own His presence, and His calling, His special calling on each one of us: else why are we here? yet as Moses was backward and unwilling to set about the work of delivering God's people, though it were never so plainly laid upon him, so which of us, my brethren, is without his misgivings and temptations, too often effectual in hindering him from working under God for the recovery of his own soul? Moses drew back from the thought of anything so dangerous and difficult as what he was called on to do: partly, no doubt, from the recollection of past disappointments: for it was now forty years, since he had of his own accord, thought much of redressing his countrymen's wrongs, and had even begun to act upon it, but they would not understand him, and he had been compelled to fly from the country. And now that he had been full half his life, leading a quiet family life, and his younger and more eager and more ambitious mind had passed away, it might well seem too hard and too strange to him to quit all his peaceful comforts, only that it was the Lord Himself who called on him to do so.

Well, my brethren, and how is it with each one of us? We too perhaps, in former years, have made some endeavours to serve God, to break off the chain of our sloth and other sins. We began and went on, for more or less time, refraining from evil indulgences, mortifying corrupt desires, attending neglected ordinances, communicating, perhaps, when we had omitted to do so. We had made a beginning: but difficulties occurred, temptations came across us, excuses were at hand, and we fell off again by little and little.

I grieve to say that this is too clearly the case with not a few, as concerning Holy Communion. Some who appeared to have made a good beginning, seem as if they had entirely forgotten it; very many are far less frequent and regular than they had engaged themselves to be. I dare say (as I have often told you,) there are some here who would be quite startled were they to hear plainly set before them, what they promised in that respect, and how long it is since they left off keeping that promise. I trust and hope that it is not all wilful backsliding. Most likely there are many misgivings not unlike those of Moses. One man may say to himself, "I was too hasty once in coming: I am now really afraid to come." Another "I am slow of speech, I am no scholar, I know not how to deal with my spiritual enemies;" and so he dares not come, any more than Moses, (until God absolutely bade him) durst come before Pharaoh, not being eloquent, nor at all feeling competent to go.

But God overruled and silenced Moses' objections by His own positive command, and by the signs and wonders which He wrought. He promised to be with him: He gave him a token, that they should serve God on that very mountain of Sinai: He made Himself known to Him by His name Jehovah, His high, aweful, everlasting Name: He gave him his brother Aaron for an helper; and when Moses first spoke to the people, God moved their hearts to believe, the people bowed the head and worshipped. So depend on it, it will be with each one of you, if you will simply hearken, as Moses did, to God's plain command, accept God's answer to your objections and difficulties, and set at once about doing what He bids you do for your souls. You will find the way smoother than you seem to think. Only take courage and begin. He offers you all help, at this time especially. How can you mistrust Him, when you think of the days that are coming on, the remembrance of Christ's Passion? He that spared not His own Son but freely gave Him up for us all, how should He deny you the grace to break your bad habits and become a worthy Communicant? In the midst of His agony He left His prayers to warn some that were asleep: fear not His being unmindful of you, if you will but try to seek Him with wakeful hearts. And having by His grace, taken up your work anew, be sure you break it not off again. Moses though greatly and continually discouraged, kept on his work when he had once undertaken it. Very soon, as we hear to-day, he began to complain, why hast Thou sent me? Thou hast not delivered Thy people at all? But he never ceased labouring, nor praying. Will not Moses' perseverance be our condemnation, if we, being called, and pretending to answer, and having made perhaps some sort of beginning, turn aside or loiter, and leave our work undone? God give us better minds: grace to gather up our broken vows and promises, and the fragments of our time which remain: God preserve us from the sin and folly of saying, "I will not, I cannot, I dare not," when we ought to be about His work.

SERMON XXXIV.

HOW SINNERS MAY DARE TO LOOK UPON THE PASSION OF THE LORD.

PASSION SUNDAY.

Exodus iii. 6.

"*Moses hid his face, for he was afraid to look upon God.*"

WE have heard in the first lesson what it was that Moses hid his face from. It was the Angel of the Lord, the God of Abraham, Isaac and Jacob, appearing to him in a flame of fire in a thorn tree. At first he turned aside to see it, as one might turn aside to see any wonderful sight. Then the Voice of the Lord came to him and warned him not to venture near in rashness. "Draw not nigh hither, put off thy shoes from thy feet, for the place whereon thou standest is holy ground." He was to put off his shoes, because that was in those eastern countries, and is now, the way to shew respect to holy places, just as we uncover our heads. He was to sanctify himself in soul and body, and the next words told him why: "I am the God of thy fathers, the God of Abraham, the God of Isaac and the God of Jacob." At the first words he trembled and durst not behold:

he knew not Who was speaking to him, or what was going to happen. At the second address of the aweful vision, coming to know Who it was, he was still more overwhelmed. He "hid his face, for he was afraid to look upon God."

In Moses, thus coming by degrees to know Who it was that spoke to him, we may see a kind of image of ourselves. Baptized in our childhood, and brought up as Christians, we have grown up, none of us so thoughtful as we ought to have been, yet none of us, I suppose, altogether without a kind of feeling, that something very wonderful and heavenly was going on in our sight, and round about us. We have not been left to wander at large, through the waste howling wilderness of this world: the Bush has been burning in our sight: Christ, the Son of God made Man, has been ever giving us signs, more or less, that He is near us in some remarkable way. In different degrees and measures we have been aware of a great and holy Presence: but *how* great, *how* holy, none of us could at first apprehend: our very childhood hindered us, to say nothing of our sinful and careless ways. By degrees however, as we grow older, or it may be suddenly, by some great overwhelming interference of the Almighty, we become aware of the aweful yet transporting truth of our condition. Moses turning aside at first to see this great sight is the figure and token of our first serious thoughts, when we feel that there is another world, another world for us, besides this which we see with our eyes, and that it is even now very near us. As when Moses turned aside to see, the Voice of the Lord declared Who He was: so those first serious thoughts

z

of ours, if we dutifully attend to them, and turn away, because of them, from worldly pleasures and profits, are rewarded with nearer and more distinct knowledge of our Saviour. We come to know, not only that there is a Kingdom of Heaven, and that it is at hand, but that we are already in it: not only that there is a God, and that He hath been made Man, but that He hath made us members of Himself. If we tremble, and dare not behold, at the first Voice of the Lord, the first indistinct sense of the great things which have been done for us; surely we had need hide our face, and fear to look on God, when a second and more distinct Voice tells us of the unspeakable things which have been done in us. O joyful yet fearful mystery, which hath been hid from ages and generations, but now is made manifest to the Saints: Christ in us, the hope of Glory: all things gathered together in Christ: the Father and the Son coming to him who by the Holy Ghost loveth Christ and keepeth His word, and making Their abode with him: sinners partaking of the Divine Nature, baptized into the Name of the Father, the Son and the Holy Ghost, and called to believe not only in God the Father, Who made us and all the world, and in God the Son, Who redeemed us and all mankind, but also in God the Holy Ghost, Who sanctifieth us and all the elect people of God! Who is sufficient for these things? What eye hath seen, or can see? Who may stand before this holy Lord God? Who would not hide his face and fear to look upon Him, so near, so gracious, so mighty, and so deeply offended by our many backslidings?

All men naturally hide their faces, when these

aweful thoughts are brought into their minds; not all however with the same purpose and meaning. Adam and Eve hid themselves from the Presence of the Lord God, when they heard His Voice walking in the garden in the cool of the day; and Cain's lot, after his great sin, was to go on shrinking and hiding himself from the face of the Lord; and Pharaoh went into his house, and would not see Moses any more; and Felix sent S. Paul away, until a more convenient season. Of all these it might be truly said, "they trembled and durst not behold:" "they hid their faces, for they were afraid to look upon God." They hid their faces as Moses did, but surely with a very different mind and heart. Elijah on the other hand, when he wrapped his face in his mantle, and stood in the entrance of his cave on this same Mount Horeb; S. Peter, when he fell down at Jesus' knees, and said, "Depart from me, for I am a sinful man, O Lord;" and the humble Centurion who would not that our Lord should come under his roof; these and others like them do, in a sort, hide their faces from Jesus Christ: they seem to do outwardly the acts and speak the words of the unbelieving ones before-mentioned: but how great the difference in their mind and heart, and in the consequence of what they did! The one sort are cursed, the other blessed: the one are patterns of Christian devotion, the other of heathen unbelief and of a reprobate mind.

Now let us mark well wherein chiefly the difference between them lay. Moses and Cain each hid his face: but the one did it, not bearing to look upon God; the other, not bearing for God to look upon him. And this makes all the difference. It must be fearful for a sinner to understand that the Eye of his offended Saviour is upon him, but the penitent sinner is content to endure this fear; he would not for the whole world have that searching Eye taken off from him; his continual prayer is, "Cast me not away from Thy Presence, and take not Thy Holy Spirit from me," although he knows that that Presence is a consuming fire to them that work iniquity. He prays for that Presence, though he feels in part how fearful it is, because he longs and labours to be delivered from working iniquity; it is not the punishment only which he fears, but the sin. But the false, self-deceiving penitent is he whose heart is still set upon the wicked indulgence, who still keeps allowing himself to wish it might be had without such severe penalties; who in his secret heart would be glad, if he had never been told how wicked it is; he is such as the Prophet describes the Children of Israel, in the worst days before the Captivity: it comes into his heart that he would fain be as the heathen, as the families of the countries who serve wood and stone. He would fain be like them, in order that he might without scruple take his fill of this world as they do. This is the false penitent, who, though he has the truth, tries and contrives to hide his face away from it, because he has no touch of love for Him Who is the Truth. God forbid it should be a true account of any of us! But indeed all persons are in danger of it, in whatever measure they permit themselves to be carried away with the things of this world. And the only security against it is the true and continual practice of that other and better way of trembling at Christ's Presence, whereof Moses in the text sets us an example. That is, that we should hide our faces *before* God, not *away from* Him: not as pretending to conceal our sins from Him, but as overwhelmed with shame and grief that we have such a burthen to bring before Him. Far from attempting to conceal anything, the very wish and prayer of the penitent heart is that the all-seeing Eye should notice all, in order that the all-healing Touch may reach every where, and cure all. What sick person, that has common sense, hides any part of his grief from the physician on whom he really depends for his cure? So neither will the heart that is truly contrite ever wish that it could hide any thing from Christ. If the thought of our sins seem in itself too dreadful, if nature herself turn away from it, yet let us remember that in true loving penitence the miserable thought of past sin is not left alone in the heart. God's merciful grace ever joins with it more or less of comfortable hope, the hope and sense of Christ's gracious Presence to receive our confession. How is it when little children who love their parents have done wrong, and their hearts are in a manner breaking with the thought of it? Is not the very coming to their parents, to confess their fault and ask pardon, a great relief? The being allowed to draw near and speak to them, is of itself a stay and comfort, over and above the hope of pardon. So it is with penitent Christians coming before God, as before a forgiving parent, to confess their sins. Two thoughts are ever present in their minds, the one serving to balance the other: the thought of their sin, and the thought of their Saviour: the first causes them to hide their eyes, afraid to look on God; the other causes them, even with their faces thus covered, to cling to the hope that He is still regarding them; and so with all the desire of their hearts they commit themselves entirely to Him.

Confession in words, secret and open, general and particular, in Church and out of Church, is the outward token and manifestation of this good mind; the body, so to call it, of this penitent soul. For see what is of course to be understood, when we come before our Lord in humble confession. On the one hand we have a heavy burthen of sin; else why do we come to make confession at all? on the other hand we have good hope in our gracious Lord's love and mercy: we are sure He is near, and we trust that He will bow down His ear and hear us: else why do we confess to Him? This may be one reason among many, why so large and gracious promises are made in Scripture to humble confession of sin, viz., that it joins in one both those tempers which best dispose a sinner to receive God's merciful Absolution. It brings people to the foot of the Cross, deeply aware indeed of their own miserable condition, but having this one inestimable hope and comfort, that Christ, Who knows it far better than they do, permits them to draw near and lay it before Him. Christ, Who died for them, has His ear yet open to their prayers, and if they go on in true penitence, will by no means allow the price of His Blood to perish.

Consider now if this be not the very disposition of mind which may best help us to think worthily of the great Mysteries of the Holy Week which is coming. Christ is going once more to be evidently set forth, crucified amongst us. On the one hand we feel ourselves quite unworthy to look on Him: we scarce dare turn these hearts and imaginations of ours, polluted, alas! too often and too lately with indulgence of sinful thoughts; we scarce dare turn them towards the most Holy Place, where the most fearful and adorable and perfect Sacrifice is going on. It seems almost profanation to fix upon the wounds and stripes of the Son of God those eyes, which not long since perhaps were lifted up unto vanity, or were otherwise obstinately wandering where they ought not. For such reasons we might well feel inclined to hide our eyes when the Cross is lifted up: we might well fear to be counted with the rude, hard-hearted multitude, who stood beholding and deriding, or at best with the ordinary people, who did but smite their breasts and return. But then on the other hand we dare not turn away from Him, so many and so earnest are His invitations to look towards Him. "[n] Is it nothing to you, all ye that pass by? Behold, and see, if there be any sorrow like unto My sorrow." And again, whereas Moses hid his face, for he was afraid to *look* upon God, the Lord's own call is, "[o] *Look* unto Me and be ye saved, all the ends of the earth, for I am God and there is none else." And the brazen serpent was lifted up in the wilderness, that whosoever was bitten by the fiery serpents might *look* up towards it and live. Looking towards Him is still the very word; we shrink from it because of our unworthiness, but His kindly compassion invites and helps us to do it.

[n] Lam. i. 12.   [o] Isa. xlv. 22.

Let us then, my brethren, with fear and trembling, yet with hopeful and earnest hearts, let us this day set ourselves to the more direct and express contemplation of the great Mysteries of our suffering God and Saviour. This Sunday is called Passion Sunday, for the very reason that the Church of old appointed it for the beginning of that course of meditation on our Lord's Sufferings which will end on Easter Day morning. Let us in heart follow where the Church would lead us; let us go on step by step in contemplation of those Sufferings for which His Incarnation did but prepare Him. Let us paint Him in our mind's eye, at supper with His disciples, breaking and blessing that which is His Body and Blood; and again in the garden, praying in an agony, prostrate, sweating blood, not refusing the bitter cup; betrayed with a kiss, shamefully entreated and spitted on. He for our sake would not shrink from all this: He hid not His face from shame and spitting: we must not then hide away our faces from Him. Behold Him tied to a pillar and scourged, crowned with thorns, dragged along, bearing His Cross, stripped, nailed to the Cross, the Cross raised up, mocked by those present, looking down on His afflicted Mother, feeling as if God had forsaken Him, in thirst, in desolation, in death; and then laid for a time in a hastily prepared grave. Of all this we are to draw a kind of picture in our minds, and think on it, study it, muse on it day by day: we are all to do so: but can we all do it safely? We may, if we chasten our thoughts all the time with the remembrance that we have trifled with His redeeming love, and are unworthy to look towards

Him at all: and that He Who thus suffers is the Most High God, and has His Eye all the while on our hearts. We may, if we make His Sufferings our own, fearing greatly lest we should regard them in a rude hard way, as people are apt to read and hear of strange and fearful calamities happening to others, or to look at sad accidents, in which, as they think, themselves have no concern. Not so will a true believer study the Passion of his Lord: he will try to make it all his own, he will pray and strive to feel more and more, that his own sins brought all this on his Saviour, and to hate and renounce them accordingly. And thus, beginning with an holy dread, how far such an one as he may venture to look on his Lord at all, he will end with a no less holy hope and confidence, that he has not forfeited his part in the Blessed Atonement; that the Blood of the Cross is truly applied to him; that he may without presumption rejoice with the Saints at Easter. Even as Moses, we read, began with hiding his face, for he was afraid to look upon God: and ended with being God's own highly favoured one, with whom He spake face to face, as a man talketh with his friend; and whose countenance, when he spake to others, shone with somewhat of God's own brightness; and as he feared to look upon God, so Aaron and the Children of Israel were afraid to look upon him. Such is the blessing of the true worshippers, men of penitent hearts and lives, continually meditating on the Passion of Christ.

SERMON XXXV.

CHRISTIAN LIBERTY.

PASSION SUNDAY.

S. John viii. 36.

"*If the Son therefore shall make you free, ye shall be free indeed.*"

THE conversation between our Saviour and the Jews, of which the Gospel appointed for to-day is part, directs our attention to a subject, always of great consequence to be rightly understood by Christians, but never perhaps more so than at this particular time, and in this particular Church and Nation of England. The subject I mean is, Christian liberty: or, as S. Paul calls it, "the liberty wherewith Christ hath made us free." It is a word which lays hold of people's hearing and imagination. Every body likes the thought of liberty, because it carries with it the thought of pleasing one's self and having one's own way. Thus it happens that even very corrupt, worldly minded, selfish, sensual people, when they hear the Gospel spoken of, as a law of liberty, feel inclined to favour it, and take up with it, expecting it to prove something very favourable to them. When they hear that Christ makes us free, they say in their hearts, "then I will be on Christ's side:" imagining that to be made free means somewhat less strict, less severe, than real holiness of life and keeping the commandments. The proud and self-sufficient, and all such as are wise in their own conceit, like to be told of their Christian liberty, because they presently think with themselves that they are free to judge and choose what they will believe, how they will understand the Scriptures, and how worship Almighty God, without submitting to the Creeds and Prayer Books of the Church. The easy and self-indulgent, love to hear of Christian liberty, flattering themselves that by it, God gives them full permission to enjoy themselves to the uttermost, in every way, which is not directly sinful: and so they play on to the very verge of ruin, within a hair's breadth of what themselves would allow to be most grievous sin. Nay, and all of us, every single person, spiritually slothful as we are, have a secret pleasure in the notion that we are left at liberty, and need not, as we think, be always anxiously striving after something better and holier than we have as yet attained to.

These are the world's notions, our own rude and carnal notions of that good thing which our Lord meant, when He spoke of being free indeed. Now let us see what notion He Himself, in that same discourse, taught us to entertain of the liberty or freedom which He won for us at so dear a rate. Certain Jews, says the Gospel, moved by the marvellous words which He spake, and by His heavenly way of speaking, while they listened, believed on Him. They could not resist the wisdom and the spirit by which He spake. So far was so good: it is better surely to be convinced in one's mind that the Gospel is true and good, than to doubt or disbelieve it: but such conviction, such belief as this is not yet true faith, and brings not after it the unspeakable gifts of the Holy Ghost. Our Lord gave those His new disciples, if they could be called disciples, a caution accordingly. " Then said Jesus to those Jews which believed on Him, If ye continue in My word, then are ye My disciples indeed: and ye shall know the truth, and the truth shall make you free." In these few words there are four points contained, four warnings most necessary to be considered, by all who seem to be turning to God: and as those Jews were greatly offended with Christ for saying those words, so we find by daily experience that nothing affronts persons more, than when we give them the like cautions and warnings, lest they should too easily conclude that they are true believers, and in a safe and good way.

The first of these four points of warning, which our Lord's words contain, is this, that they were not to depend too much on their own perseverance. "If ye continue in My words, then are ye My disciples indeed." "If ye continue." You perceive at once that the saying implies a doubt, whether they would so continue. Now this is generally very unpleasant to new converts, to first beginners in the way of faith and penitence. They are apt to be like S. Peter in the hour of his false confidence: "Though I should die with Thee, I will not deny Thee in any wise." How positively do we hear them say, as they lie in pain and weakness under God's hand, or as they are just beginning to revive, that they are quite altered men, they are sure of it, they shall never go back to their old sins: and when the messengers of Christ, knowing from much sad experience how little such feelings may be relied on, come in with a caution, the sick person, according to his temper, is sometimes more or less affronted, sometimes he scarcely seems to understand what we mean; it is well for him, but it does not often happen, when he fears for himself, and seeks strength in God's grace only. But unreal converts, like the Jews to whom Christ was speaking, are almost certain to take offence at their perseverance being doubted of, not knowing that perseverance is the special and crowning gift of Almighty grace, for which the highest Saints have need to cry earnestly to the very end of their lives: so little reason have those to feel certain of it, who are but just turning from Satan to Jesus Christ.

But if they are affronted at having their perseverance doubted of, much more if a word be spoken which seems to charge them with not being in earnest. Now the next warning words of our Saviour seem to speak in that way of the Jews. "If ye continue in My word, then are ye My disciples indeed." As if they might yet, for all their fair professions, not be His disciples indeed. This again is very trying to the humility of those who say they are penitents. If they doubt and fear their own goodness so much as not to be angry when others seem to doubt of them, it is a good sign of their judging themselves, so as not to be judged of the Lord: if on the other hand they give way to anger, and cannot bear even to be cautioned against deceiving themselves, we may well fear that they are no true disciples of our Lord, and that they are likely enough to go back and to walk no more with Him.

But thirdly, our Lord's words imply that their knowledge was very imperfect: and this again is provoking to carnal minds. Men do not like to be called or supposed ignorant. And the Jews especially prided themselves on knowing the truth, and approving the things that were more excellent, being instructed out of the law. To such of course it sounded very unpleasant, to be told, "If ye continue in My word, ye shall know the truth:" as if they did not know it already. They thought themselves perfect men, full grown, of full age; and behold He treats them as if they were babes, which have need of milk and not of strong meat.

But lastly, and this seems to have affronted them most, Christ speaks to those Jews as if they were no better than slaves. "Ye shall know the Truth, and the Truth shall make you free." If they wanted to be made free, they were as yet in bondage. But this they could not endure to have said. Slaves were, I suppose, in their judgement, as in the judgement of all persons who give way to their natural proud feelings, altogether a lower sort of beings. We know that it is so generally now, in those countries where slavery is practised. In those places it is a great trial of men's Christian humility and submission to the rules of the Church, to treat such as happen to be slaves with brotherly kindness, as one Christian should treat another. Christian freemen, except they be Christians in heart, can hardly be brought even to receive the Holy Communion at the same time with Christian slaves. We may therefore easily understand how the Jews to whom our Saviour was speaking, might have all the deep and secret pride of their hearts stirred up by such a saying as this, "The truth shall make you free." They answered angrily, "We be Abraham's seed, and were never in bondage to any man: how sayest Thou, ye shall be made free?" Being Abraham's seed, they could not, by the law of Moses, be in perpetual slavery but by their own consent; and of this they were very proud, and so much the more intolerable did Christ's words sound to them.

But He in His merciful condescension goes on to explain Himself to them, and in so doing teaches us, and all His disciples for ever, the true doctrine of Christian liberty. "Verily, verily, I say unto you, He that committeth sin is the servant of sin." Here is the sad and humbling truth: sin indulged is slavery. Every habitual sinner, how great and independent soever he may seem to himself, is a servant of servants, a bondsman of sin, death, and the devil. For what is it which we mean by a slave, as distinct from an ordinary servant? Surely this: that an ordinary servant may give warning, and withdraw from his place when he finds himself aggrieved; but a slave cannot do so. He is his master's property, like a dumb creature: he cannot release himself at will. Now the melancholy and miserable condition of habitual sinners is like this. In proportion as their sins have been long indulged and are grown into their character, to be part as it were of themselves, they are become the property of their master the devil, like horse or mule which have no understanding, to be led captive by him at his will. They cannot free themselves; they cannot of themselves give warning to their hard and cruel master, and say to him, Get thee hence, command me no more, I will not obey thee, I will seek a better master. They cannot say and do this, if left to themselves: so long they are in the sad helpless way which the Prophet describes in such aweful words: "ᵃCan the Ethiopian change his skin, or the leopard his spots? Then may ye do good who are accustomed to do evil." Too surely may each one of us know this by his own miserable practice: how helpless do we grow, in a very little time, in respect of any sin which we unhappily suffer to get the dominion over us! how hard, how next to impossible, to command our tempers, to be mild and forbearing, when we have allowed ourselves in anger; to be sparing and charitable in thought and word, when we have taken delight in evil-speaking; to govern our thoughts and eyes, when we have permitted them to range uncontrolled; to deny ourselves, when we have taken our pleasure. These things are necessary to be done, else there is no true repentance; but who of himself is sufficient for these things? not one. Habitual sinners may think they are free, they may pride themselves upon being their own masters and having their own way, (they may say, as some in the Psalms, "ᵇWith our tongues will we prevail; we are they that ought to speak; who is Lord over us?") but in truth they are base and wretched slaves.

But even as in a family of slaves, if the Master's dearly beloved Son should earnestly plead with his Father, deliverance might be obtained, and the oppressed allowed to go free: so says our Lord, "if the Son make you free, ye shall be free indeed." If God the Son come

ᵃ Jer. xiii. 23. ᵇ Ps. xii. 4.

down from Heaven to deliver you, you may yet be free from this long and sad captivity into which you have been brought by indulging your evil desires. The devil, powerful as he is, is Christ's subject and creature, and cannot keep any one in bondage, when Christ gives the word for the chains to fall off from his hands. This, says our Lord to the Jews, this, and nothing else, is true freedom. This is Christian liberty: not as the world thinks, a liberty to please one's self for the greater part of one's life, and then make all right by believing that our Saviour has made satisfaction for all: not a liberty to compare one Church and religion with another, and follow that which pleases one's own judgement and fancy: not a liberty to do without Church ordinances, provided only a man seems to himself to be exercising good thoughts at home: not a liberty to think little of God's Law, and excuse one's self from obedience to it: but Christian liberty, the being free indeed, is when the Holy Gospel, "c the Law of the Spirit of Life in Christ Jesus, hath made me free from the law of sin and death:" when bad habits of every kind are gone: when the eyes are free to turn away from base objects, the tongue free to speak only good words, the heart free to mount upward to our Maker and Saviour, all the passions and thoughts free to serve God only, sin having no more dominion over them. This, and nothing short of this, is Christian liberty: we are to measure it, not as the Jews did theirs, by outward privileges of birth and education; they thought they were free because they were Abraham's seed; and what if some of us should

c Rom. viii. 2.

A a

fancy ourselves free because we belong to a Christian country, or because we have been bred up in much light and knowledge, or because we are not so blinded in some things, as we suppose many of our brethren to be? Would not our Saviour say to us as to the Jews, "If ye were Abraham's seed, ye would do the works of Abraham?" If you value yourselves on believing as the Saints did, take care that you do the deeds of the Saints. Will He not say, So long as ye go on in your evil habits knowing them to be such, be sure ye are not of Abraham but of the devil: especially if ye go on in spite and with a murderous mind, or if you use to make any manner of lie, for "the devil was a murderer from the beginning," "he is a liar and the father of it." As sin, indulged, shews you to be children and slaves of the devil, so on the other hand the love of Christ, which is the keeping of His Commandments, is the sure and only sufficient token of our being really children of God, really in the state of freedom, to which He introduced us by Baptism. If God be our Father, we shall love Jesus Christ, "for He proceeded forth and came from God." Love and obey Jesus Christ for love, ye who desire to have the blessing of liberty: that service only is perfect freedom, either in earth, or in Heaven itself.

We see by this account of Christian liberty, how we should understand the many places in Holy Scripture which speak of Christians as being free, and of the Gospel as a Law of liberty: as when S. Paul says, "ᵈbrethren, ye have been called unto liberty:" when he says, "ᵉstand fast in the liberty wherewith Christ

ᵈ Gal. v. 13.   ᵉ Ibid. 1.

hath made you free." In all such places we are not to understand that Christians are more free to please themselves, than if they were not Christians, but quite the contrary; that their rule being far more perfect, far stricter and more exact, is yet a rule and law of liberty, because they have grace to keep it. They have yet a yoke and a burthen to bear, but the yoke is made easy and the burthen light by the Spirit of God shedding His love abroad in our hearts.

By this too, we may judge of our own condition. So far as any of the commandments, any Christian duty, is unpleasing to us, and we therefore leave it out of our practice, so far we are gone back from our Christian liberty; we are fallen from grace; we are in a sort of Jewish imperfection, knowing our duty but content without grace to do it. We are so far sinking back, by our own fault entirely, into that most wretched state which the holy Apostle describes when he says, speaking as an unregenerate man, "'The good that I would I do not, and the evil that I would not, that I do." The Jews, and still more the heathens, could not help this condition; they were providentially born in it: but what are we to think of ourselves, how, think you, do the holy Angels judge of us, when we, by committing known sin, voluntarily plunge ourselves into that mire again, out of which God had mercifully brought us?

I beseech you, be not content for a moment to go on in such a way as this, making God's grace, which hath freed you, void, and enslaving yourself again to the wretched yoke of Satan. And you know to Whom you must go in order to be delivered: even to

f Rom. vii. 19.

the same Saviour Who in Baptism would have delivered you once for all, if you would let Him. The Son must make you free from this second burthen of sin committed after Baptism, as He did make you free from the first burthen, your part in Adam's sin. And as you were then brought to Him for Baptism, so now you must go to Him in such ways as He has ordained; in the ways which He has appointed for penitents. His words are such as these; "ᵉTurn ye to Me with your whole heart, and with fasting, and with weeping, and with mourning, and rend your heart and not your garments." Especially He would have you do this in the solemn time between this and Easter. For now the days are fast coming on, in which the Bridegroom shall be taken away from us; and it is His word, that we shall fast in those days. Turn then to Christ with your whole heart, with sorrow and self chastisement often, and with amendment at all times; and prove Him, whether He will not, in His good time, make you free indeed: whoever you are, and however sadly you have sinned. The freedom, indeed, which He will restore to you, the willing heart which will make you serve Him joyfully, He will not restore it all at once, but by degrees: at least so it generally happens. The gift of Baptism is of course given in a moment, but the gift of restoration after penitence commonly takes a long time to perfect. But it is not the less certain, if we do but persevere: and if we pray and strive continually, by the gracious help of the Good Spirit, we shall persevere.

ᵉ Joel ii. 12, 13.

SERMON XXXVI.

UNBELIEF IN THE PRESENCE OF CHRIST,
NOW ALSO, DEADLY SIN.

PASSION SUNDAY.

S. JOHN viii. 24.

"*If ye believe not that I am He, ye shall die in your sins.*"

IN speaking last Sunday of the duty and necessity of making to God a distinct and particular confession, I tried to point out to you the great need of observing the differences of sins, how some are deadly, some are rather called sins of infirmity. Common sense itself would shew us that there is such a difference: and the Bible and the Prayer book plainly teach the same. "There is a sin unto death, and there is a sin not unto death." Both for ourselves and for others we have need to remember this. In many instances, the difference is very plain. No one fancies that the wilful murderer is no worse in respect of his murder than the man who indulges a fit of anger a few minutes longer than he ought: or that he who is sometimes inexcusably inattentive in prayer commits equal sin with one who never prays. But there are some cases where the difference between slighter sins and those which are deadly is by no means so plain at first sight. God has on purpose forborne to draw the line, that He might put us on our trial, whether we would serve Him with a dutiful heart or no. As if a parent should say to his child, If you go too far in that direction, you will come to a dangerous place, and not tell the child exactly how far he might go: of course the child would feel it his duty to be very cautious, and rather stop short too soon, than go on at all too far. So, inasmuch as we know for certain that there is such a thing as deadly sin, but are not in all cases quite certain whether this or that action is an instance of it, our business as dutiful children of God is plainly to refrain from that action. To do otherwise, is fearful trifling with our God and with our own souls: as it would be trifling with our bodily life, to swallow something which we thought might be poison, because we did not know for certain that it was so. It is tempting the devil to come nearer and nearer to us; it is shewing him that we are not unwilling to be deceived; like Balaam, when he sought an excuse to go along with the messengers of Balak.

Whatever our special temptation be, whether to lust, pride, or anger, or any other sin, there is always this danger of our taking dangerous liberties because we are not exactly told when the faults begin to be positively mortal and deadly. And besides, there is this great and exceeding danger, the daily ruin of multitudes untold: that if people's consciences do not point out to them any particular crime or course of sin, whereof they are undoubtedly guilty, they think all is well enough. How many go on as moral, decent people, paying their way, shewing kindness and courtesy to others, well spoken of in all the neighbourhood, and yet neither having nor seeming to have any serious sense of religion, any deep thoughts of God and Eternity at all. Now such persons as these have not the least notion that they are going on in deadly, in mortal sin: and yet they assuredly are so: their days and years are spent in the deadly sin of sloth, spiritual sloth, undutifulness to their God and Saviour.

Now I suppose that this is pretty nearly the case described by our Lord in the Text. The Jews to whom He was speaking were not, as far as appears, the worst of the nation; there is no sign of their being open scandalous sinners, they were greatly affronted at something being said which sounded as if they were a low, discreditable set. "We be not born of fornication," they said: "we have one Father, even God." As if people now a days should say, We are not outcasts nor reprobates, we do not live in open swearing, drunkenness, or adultery, we go on quietly and decently, and have the same hope as other Christians: why trouble us so much about keeping Lent and Advent, about self-examination and confession, and very particular repentance? In a word, these Jews claimed to be "respectable" spiritually, as well as outwardly "respectable;" yet see what aweful words He speaks to them, "ye shall seek Me, and shall die in your sins:" and when they did not know how to take this, He explained to them that it was not for this or that particular crime, but in general, because their minds and hearts were still in earth, they were of this world, whereas our Lord was not of this world: and therefore they could not believe; as He explains to them, "Ye are from beneath, I am from above: ye are of this world, I am not of this world, I said therefore unto you, that ye shall die in your sins: for if ye believe not that I am He, ye shall die in your sins." He does not say, For ye are adulterers, or murderers, or defrauders, or blasphemers, or in any like open sin, and so must die in your sins, but simply "If ye believe not." For all that appears, they were good moral decent men; their one sin, not believing that He was the Christ. But this was so bad, that it was enough to kill them for ever.

"If ye believe not that I am He, ye shall die in your sins." O my brethren, beware of imagining that those aweful words are nothing in particular to us: that we are surely true believers in Christ Jesus, and so far in no danger of dying in our sins. As in other sins especially of a spiritual nature, such as pride and envy, so in this way of spiritual sloth and unbelief, it is but too possible for us to be in mortal, deadly sin, without knowing it. The Jews would not believe that Christ was He, that this Jesus of Nazareth was the Person promised of old to save them from sin and make them happy: and so, for all the decency and morality of some of them, they died in their sins, they lost the grace of pardon. What if there should be here or elsewhere any one calling himself a Christian, who will not believe, will not acknowledge, that Christ is really present among us, as He has promised to be? His word was, "I am with you always, even unto the end of the world." To deny His peculiar Presence then in His Church and people now, is as truly denying and contradicting Him, as when the Jews denied that the lowly Jesus Whom they saw among them, was Christ. Would you know whether you are yourself guilty of such sad unbelief, or of something near it? Do not say at once, It is impossible: I say the Creed without misgiving, I believe all that the Church believes: but go back in your thoughts to this very morning, when you rose and began the day. How did you begin it? Did you really acknowledge Christ's Presence? Did you really and truly say one Christian prayer, as to Him, and not as to yourself? as beseeching Him, really present, to hear, and not as a mere exercise of meditation and instruction for yourself? Did you *try* to pray in this real earnest way? If you did not so this morning, did you do better yesterday? or the morning before? or any morning? Are you at all seeking after the habit of speaking to Christ really in your prayers, as to a present Saviour, Who is listening to every word? If you are not even *trying* to do this, ought you not to fear, whether all is so right in regard of your faith, as you have imagined it to be? Do you really believe that this is He, your true Saviour, your only Hope? If you do, surely you will not be contented to pray on all your days, in this absent, lukewarm way. But if you do not believe in His Presence, you know His own word; there is no help for you; you must "die in your sins."

So again, you will find, if you consider, that every evening is a trial of your faith in the matter of self-examination. If you said no really Christian prayer this morning, I should fear that you hardly tried and judged yourself in a Christian manner yesterday evening. Yet, who that really believes in the aweful Presence of the Lord Jesus, would willingly fail to open his heart, and truly confess to Him any night of his life? Who that considers, could bear to lie down to sleep with the weight of the day's trangressions upon him? especially since it is quite uncertain whether he shall ever wake again in this world. Ought it not then to make us very thoughtful, if our conscience tells us that we have almost or quite neglected this regular evening duty of self-examination? that when we have done it, we have done it lightly and after the manner of dissemblers with God? For it is too much like unbelief; too much as though we did not really account our Lord to be present; and then will not the saying hold against us, "Ye believe not that I am He: therefore ye shall die in your sins?"

And there are too many who give this other sad token of not really believing, that they come so very irregularly where our Lord has promised to be, that is, to this Holy Place. He has promised to be here: there is no doubt of His Presence. Perhaps one might truly say, that the trial of persons in such a place as this, whether they will come religiously to Church and Communion, is very nearly the same to them, as it was to the Jews of old time, whether they would believe or no that Jesus is the Christ. If so, it is to be feared that a very large proportion of us would have been unbelievers at that day, and would have brought our Lord's severe sentence upon themselves. For how very many are there, who have no standing rule how often to come to Church, who come now and then, when they happen to be so minded, but easily allow themselves to be hindered by all manner of causes. Could this be, if they had faith in the special Presence of our Lord in this place; and if they also believed Him to be their Saviour and Deliverer? No, surely: if we had but faith as a grain of mustard seed, the slightest portion of that faith which caused Daniel in wicked Babylon to pray regularly three times a day, with his windows open in his chamber towards Jerusalem; I say, the slightest grain of that faith would bring us here, not occasionally but regularly; we should make our rule about coming to Church, and we should keep it; it would not be as it is now, when many allow themselves to be so irregular that they are not themselves even aware, and would be astonished if one should tell them, how long it is since they attended here.

Of course, brethren, if men neglect Holy Communion, that is a clear sign that they do not as yet believe the full doctrine of our Lord's Gospel concerning His Presence in this place. They do not from their hearts believe, "This is My Body; This is My Blood; Do this in remembrance of Me." Else they could not be indifferent to so great a thing. They would either be actual Communicants, or seriously preparing themselves for Communion. If they doubted about it, their doubt would be a real distress to them: and for the sake of knowing what their Lord would have them do, they would not mind the trouble nor, if need were, the shame, of opening their hearts to Christ's Ministers, and receiving His instruction and comfort through them. O, if men really and considerately believed what they constantly profess in the Creed and Catechism, how very much more indeed would be going on of this kind; the people coming to the House of the Lord, not accidentally and as it were dropping in now and then, but regularly and often; as regularly as they seek their daily meals or their weekly wages; nor yet coming to the prayers and sermon only, but seeking their Lord constantly in His Holy Communion; either attending there or preparing to attend: not slurring over the difficult task of self-examination and amendment, but looking over *all* their ways, trying to confess *all* their sins, omitting *no* method of cure which the Gospel has prescribed: neither would they always think they could manage this serious work for themselves: many, and not here and there one, would be coming to the Lord's Messengers to open their grief, and to receive, if need were, the benefit of Absolution, together with ghostly counsel and advice. Our Communions would then by God's mercy be more blessed than they now are, our works of sacrifice and charity more worthy of Him Whom we profess to serve; the holy fire would spread more freely from one to another; we should be far more courageous in our Lord's service; and lastly, we may hope, our death beds would be more peaceful and more blessed.

These are not mere words; a pleasant dream, and no more. Such things have been before now, and by God's grace are yet in Christian Parishes: and there is no reason, but our sin and infirmity, why they should not be in our Parish. But will our sin and infirmity be our excuse, or rather our condemnation, before the Judgement Seat, when He Who hath given us so much shall come as He hath said, and require much from us? I beseech you, let us all once more turn our minds seriously to those most fearful words, "If ye believe not that I am He, ye shall die in your sins." If you do not earnestly set your minds to think of Christ as actually present in His Church, in prayer, in self-examination, in public worship, and especially in Communion, " you will die in your sins," very likely without knowing it; you will live and die unawares in the fatal deadly sin of spiritual sloth; and too likely, O misery of miseries, you will even pass away in this state of self-deceiving error; you will be one of those who will say by and by, "Lord, Lord, have we not done many things in Thy Name? and He will say, I never knew you." You will go to Hell, as one has fearfully said, with your faces turned all the way towards Heaven. Think what it will be to pass from this world into the dreary and dismal state of those who are kept waiting in their prisons of darkness: all one's vain hope gone in a moment, as though it had never been, and nothing for the future but a sad and certain expectation of wrath which shall never end. Think of the day which will be here before long, when all expectation shall be ended. Think of the Eternity which will come after that day. Think of these things, and fear to die in your sins: and that you may not die in them, believe that your Lord is here; believe earnestly, believe thoughtfully, the gracious Presence of Christ your Saviour, now about to be sealed anew to you by the yearly remembrance of His Death and Resurrection. Believe and consider that the Saviour and Judge Whom you read and hear of, is even now close to you, closer than you can imagine. He is every hour reaching out His gracious Hand for you to lay hold of. No decency, no goodness towards man will save you, if you are undutiful to Christ. Only believe that it is He: turn not from Him: that you may not die in your sins, but live in His Righteousness!

SERMON XXXVII.

WORK WHILE IT IS DAY.

PASSION SUNDAY.

S. John ix 4.

"*I must work the works of Him that sent Me while it is day: the night cometh, when no man can work.*"

A WONDERFUL moment it was in our Lord's wonderful life when these words were spoken. He had just been hiding Himself from the unbelieving Jews, i. e., He had made Himself invisible, when they were taking up stones to stone Him for what they pretended to account blasphemy. They took up stones to stone Him, but Jesus hid Himself, and went out of the Temple, going through the midst of them, and so passed by. And as Jesus passed by, He saw a man which was blind from his birth, sitting and begging at the entrance into the Temple. And after some conversation with His disciples, He restored sight to that poor blind man, and in no long time after, declared Himself to him plainly to be the Son of God. He had hidden Himself from the Pharisees, who were in the way of boasting of their sharp spiritual sight: from them He hides Himself, but He shews Himself to the blind beggar. And in this, He tells us, He was doing His proper work, the task which His Father had appointed, and He had undertaken. "For judgement," saith He, " I am come into this world, that they which see not might see, and they which see might be made blind." He came as a refiner's fire, to try every man's work of what sort it is. This is His work, His proper work, to save us if we will believe and obey; to leave us without excuse if we will not. It was His work, when present in the flesh, with all who came within reach of Him; it is His work no less with us all, who live within sound of His Gospel, now that He is invisibly present in His Church by His Spirit. In this work, the work of Him that sent Him, our Lord is engaged continually, all the year round: yet He seems in such Seasons as this of Lent, to take it in hand in a more especial manner. For what do we mean, when we say it is the time of Lent? Surely nothing less serious than this: that now we are aware of our Lord standing and knocking at the door of our hearts and consciences, and calling upon us to let Him in. And when we say, as we do this morning, Now the fifth Sunday is come: what is this but acknowledging, that more than half the special time appointed this year for our repentance and conversion is already gone, and we had need make much of what remains?

To this kind of reflection, at such solemn times, our Lord calls us, by that very remarkable saying, "I must work the works of Him that sent Me while it is day: the night cometh when no man can work." Only think, my brethren, Who it was Who uttered these words. It was the great Almighty God Himself, He in Whose hand are the times and seasons, and all things, Whom none ever can stay from doing what He will, when He will. Even He, having made Himself for our salvation one of us, condescends to be bounded, as we are, by the limits of time. He sets Himself times and seasons, a certain number of years, months, weeks, days, hours and minutes, within which, and not before nor after, His work on earth is to be done. And this portion of time He calls His day, and likens Himself so far to any labourer among us: in that our ordinary works also require to be done by daylight. "The sun ariseth, and man goeth forth to his work and to his labour until the evening," but if he loiter and put it off, and allow himself to be taken up with other things, "the night cometh when no man can work;" he loses that day, and he never, never can recall it. Our Lord set Himself a time, and spake thus of His work, as for other reasons, so certainly for an example and instruction to us, to stir us up to do our work also. For indeed our work, as Christians, is in a certain sense His, and His work is ours, by our marvellous Communion with Him. We are members of Him, very limbs of His body the Church, so that in a mysterious way what we do He doeth, and what He doeth we do. Our doings, as Christians, are, as His were, the works of Him that sent Him, the special tasks assigned us by the Father, even as His whole life on earth, and all He did and suffered in it, was His special task assigned Him by the same Holy Father. For what He said to the Father concerning His Apostles especially, we may understand as spoken in our measure concerning ourselves and all Christians: "As Thou hast sent Me into the world, even so also have I sent them into the world." God has set each one of us a work, and a time to do it in, as it is written, "six days shalt thou labour and do all that thou hast to do." And the life's work of all Christians is in reality one and the same; one and the same, each with the other's, and all with their gracious Lord and Saviour. We are "fellow-workers with God;" for our task is to help in accomplishing what God came to accomplish on earth, the salvation of sinners by dutiful faith in Him. To do this well, to do our part towards saving our own and others' souls, is the one thing for which we came into the world; and all inquiries, pursuits, fancies, employments, which are not made to help in this work, are merely vain, or very far worse than vain. So this answer of our Lord to His Apostles teaches. They, seeing a man whom they knew to have been blind from his birth, asked Him, "who did sin, this man or his parents, that he was born blind?" It was just the sort of question which people are apt, not perhaps to ask in words, but to wonder about in their own minds, why God orders things so and so, what sin it was in our neighbours, which brought such and such a trouble upon them. Our Saviour, correcting such vain imaginations, turns our minds towards our own work, "Neither hath this man sinned, nor his parents; but that the works of God should be made manifest in him." You are not to fancy, that, wherever you see sorrow, it is of course the punishment of especial sin: it may be for the manifestation of God's glory in some other way. What you are to think of is, how you may do your own work aright: even as I am now setting you an example. And remember, there is a set time to do it in, and if you wait till that time is over, you will find that your chance of doing it at all is gone. "The night cometh when no man can work." "Yet a little while is the light with you: walk while ye have the light, lest darkness come upon you." Remember the fearful word, "too late."

My brethren, you are all, or almost all of you, working men. You can understand our Saviour's meaning in this kind of parable very well: some of you know better than you could wish, what a serious thing it is to lose a day's work, to find when evening comes, that you have trifled the hours away, and have no wages to receive. We know such a thing cannot be, without hurting both ourselves and those to whom our work is due. Persons may say, they did not give it a thought, they only wanted to amuse or rest themselves, so the moments, minutes, hours, passed away before they were aware. They may think their fault very pardonable, but none of them thinks it at all hard that he should go without his pay for those days in which he cannot deny that he has done no work. If they were only thoughtless in so behaving, the ill effect comes upon them nevertheless; they and their children have to starve for their idleness.

Depend upon it, my brethren, so and much more will it be with us, if we allow ourselves to be careless of God's work. To each of us there is a time set, and if by the end of that time our task is not fulfilled, it never can be fulfilled. That which cometh, is a night in which no man can work: the very eleventh and twelfth hours will be past, and there will be no chance of earning the penny, which the bountiful Master and Owner of the Vineyard hath agreed with the labourers for. How foolish would you think it, if when we are mourning for any dead person, and saying one to another, how sad it is for his wife and children to lose the help he was providing for them, how senseless at such a time would you account it, were any one to say, How do you know, but he may do some work for them, he may earn something for them, where he is gone? Why? Because when he is departed, you are sure he can do no more work for his family. And are you not equally sure that he can do nothing for his soul? Yet people go on to the very edge of death, as if God had promised them another place of work and trial beyond the grave, wherein to set right what they had allowed to go wrong here.

And then, to make our case still more awful, we know that the time we shall have to do the work of Him that sent us, is fixed indeed and certain to Him, but to ourselves it is quite uncertain. None of us may say to his soul, "Soul, thou hast yet a good while before thee, are there not twelve hours in the day? and thou hast passed but one, two, or half of them: thou hast so many remaining in which to make sure thy calling." Alas! while people are calculating and planning in that way, very often the destroying angel is already at their door, and before many hours they are gone, and the time which they had vainly said in their hearts they should have to do God's work in, that time they will have to spend in astonishment and anguish, unable to do anything, only awaiting God's punishment. True it is, that according to our Lord's unsearchable mercies there are some who have stood all the day idle, yet being called at the very last, the eleventh hour, obey the call, and receive their penny at last; but there is no word which tells us that those who were called early in the morning, might safely have waited with the intention of answering the call at the sixth, ninth, or eleventh hour. There was no promise that they should be ever called again: there is no assurance for any one of us, that, if we put off God's work of which He is even now reminding us, we shall live to be reminded of it more effectually a day or an hour hence.

One thing we are sure of, it is a short time we shall have at most. The days of our life are three-score years and ten; and, O my younger brethren, I wish I could once make you understand how earnestly you will long some day for the minutes and hours which you now trifle away, trusting to have enough and to spare! How will you regret by and by the health and strength, the powers of the body and mind, which you are now wasting in mere pleasures, too much of it in absolute sin: if, by His grace, you are then minded to set about your duty in earnest, yet will you never cease deploring the sad loss of the morning of life, never, never, to be repaired. You will find too late, it is a very different thing to begin God's work at sixty years, and at sixteen or twenty; you will be wishing, many times a day, for the life and spirit, the health and energy, which God gave you to serve Him with; and what, alas! are you now doing with it?

You cannot surely for a moment persuade yourselves, that your appointed task is not large enough to fill up all your time. What is that task? It is preparing yourself for Heaven, your soul and your body, for He in His great love is preparing there a place for both. Now what a work is this! To wean the heart from its foolish, childish fancy about pleasing itself in all things; to use it to think of God and Christ, and all the great things out of sight; to break it of indulging evil thoughts, shameful, unclean imaginations, unkind suspicions, and jealousies, covetous and greedy desires! What a long hard labour, to get the mastery of the tongue, unruly member as it is, to break it thoroughly of its customary evil words, till it have become unboastful, undefiled, reverent, exactly true! What a severe, incessant task to set one's self rules for the whole of one's conduct and behaviour, alone and in company, and to be, on the whole, in the way of keeping those rules. "Who is sufficient for these things"? Not one, not the wisest and strongest of us all, were it not for the grace of God which is given us. But with that grace, the weakest and simplest may do all things, only he must not trifle with God's work: and surely it is sad trifling with it, knowing what it is, to put it off till our best days are over.

But if, as is the case with too many of us, we have already passed the turning point of our lives, without really and heartily setting about our Father's work, there is so much the more need surely to set about it this very moment; for then we have not only to learn God's lessons, but to unlearn also the lessons of the devil: the miserable and shocking past, though it cannot be undone, yet causes a fearful increase to our burthen and our work, seeing that we have the traces of it to wear out, the scars of it to heal: like children who have written their copy altogether wrong, and have to erase it before they can put another in its place: it is twice the trouble, and requires twice the time, while yet they have only the small remainder of their time to bestow upon it. And then there are the chances of darkness coming on, the overclouding and paralysing of the soul, so that it can neither see nor feel its way towards Heaven: and there is the sad helplessness of the body, when we long to be up and doing the good works which we neglected while we were able to do them; and the evil spirit tempting us to give up the fight in despair; and all the chains we have wilfully wound about us, of evil habits, bad company, thoughts of mischief coming unawares, and the like; how hard, how painful will be the task of breaking them! Certainly those chains may be broken, there is nothing too hard for the Lord; but at best, our hearts must ache all our lives long with the sense of our great sin in so putting off our Father's work. And what if the time be not allowed? What if in most just judgement for our thoughtless, unthankful ways, our sun should go down while it is yet day? What if our eyes should be closed in death, before we have at all accustomed them to look towards God and Heaven? These and other like words will then perhaps come back to you, and will not the thought be intolerable, that you treated them as words of course, such as old men and clergymen think proper to speak to younger persons, and so you turned a deaf ear to them? O, think better of it, attend to Christ's merciful warnings; lose no time. For indeed, if you are ever so young, you have no time to lose; if you are ever so old, ever so near death, earnest, entire repentance can never be too late.

SERMON XXXVIII.

THOUGHTS OF THE CROSS INTOLERABLE TO THE EARTHLY MIND.

PASSION SUNDAY.

S. Matt. xvi. 22.

"*Peter took Him, and began to rebuke Him, saying, Be it far from Thee, Lord: this shall not be unto Thee.*"

As the Holy Week of our Lord's Passion comes on, and we feel that we ought to look forward to it ourselves, more and more earnestly, it seems natural to turn to the Gospel accounts of those who were beforehand warned of it, more or less clearly: to see how they took the warning, and to learn from our Lord how they should have taken it: if haply we may find help in preparing ourselves for the sacred time.

One of the most remarkable of these warnings is that given to the Apostles in the 16th of S. Matthew. Our Lord, after a great miracle, the healing of the Canaanitish woman's daughter who was grievously vexed with a devil, had retired into the coasts of Cæsarea Philippi, a distant place, where He and His disciples might be quiet: thereby giving example and encouragement to those, who try to be, as much as they may, alone and in retirement from the world, i.e., from their own temporal pursuits, when they are called on especially to remember His Sufferings. Being thus alone with them, He asks them first what others said, then what they would say themselves, of His own Person and Nature: on which S. Peter before all the rest made that good confession, "Thou art Christ the Son of the Living God:" and our Lord in reply gave him a very great blessing and promised him the keys of His Kingdom. But lest their thoughts should dwell only on these glorious things and high hopes, He saw fit presently after to speak more openly than usual of the Sufferings through which He should enter into His Kingdom. "[a] From that time began Jesus to shew unto His disciples, that He must go unto Jerusalem, and suffer many things of the elders and chief priests and scribes, and be killed, and the third day rise again:" and He spake that saying openly (not as before in doubtful sayings, about the Son of Man being lifted up,) and Peter still more eager and forward than the rest, "took Him and began to rebuke Him," apart, as it seems, from the rest; "saying, Be it far from Thee, Lord; this shall not be unto Thee."

Now it is easy enough to understand, why S. Peter should have been thus earnest in speaking against such things as our Lord had seemed to say. The rest no doubt had much of the same feelings; but Peter spoke out, because it was his way to do so: he was zealous and fervent, and could not remain silent. And doubtless his love to our Lord was that which moved him most. It was like stabbing

[a] S. Matt. xvi. 21.

him to the heart, to tell him that his Beloved should be so ill-treated, even to the death. True, He was also to rise again, but what this meant, none of them knew: and S. Peter, in his vehement words now, did but express the same mind which caused him, when Christ was actually seized, to draw his sword and wound the high priest's servant. The words of Jesus appeared to mean something so sad, so unworthy, so shocking, that he could not believe them, could not bear them: he made up his mind they must mean something else. He therefore comes close to our Lord, and affectionately but positively ventures even to rebuke Him, Him Whom he had just before owned to be the Son of God, for prophesying such things: "Be it far from Thee, Lord: this shall not be unto Thee."

Now I suppose our ordinary feeling, at this point of the history, is, that of course it was wrong in the great Apostle to be so positive, and almost disrespectful, still of itself it would not strike us as anything so *very* wrong. Considering how it was mixed up with great and true love to our Lord, we should have expected to find it gently rebuked: perhaps that Christ would be even more pleased than displeased, as a commander might be with a soldier who seemed a little too daring. We should be little prepared, most of us, for so severe a rebuke as really proceeded from our Lord's lips on this occasion. S. Mark (or rather S. Peter himself by S. Mark) describes it very particularly. There was something wonderfully solemn, wonderfully full of deep and serious meaning, in our Lord's manner at that moment, "when He had turned and looked on His disciples, He rebuked

Peter, saying, get thee behind Me, satan: thou art an offence unto Me." What sharp, what fearful words are these! to be called satan: to be ordered out of Christ's sight: to have the very same words spoken, which had been spoken to the tempter in the wilderness; to be told, "thou art an offence unto Me:" whereas but to offend one of the least of Christ's little ones is to bring a woe upon the world, and upon one's self something worse than the most shocking death. What can be the meaning of this? Something, it would appear, which concerns the other disciples as well as S. Peter: since our Saviour turns so earnestly towards them whilst He speaks. And seeing them all, as we may well believe, astonished at His peremptory way of speaking, He at once adds the reason of it. "Thou art an offence unto Me, for thou savourest not the things which be of God, but those which be of men." That is, in other words, It is not heavenly and eternal things, the things of God, which take up thy mind, but earthly and bodily things, the things of men, the things of this present world. Or, to speak as S. Paul did long after, "thou art not spiritually minded, but carnally minded: thou mindest the things of the flesh, not the things of the Spirit." This, when we consider it, explains the severe words of our Saviour. S. Peter, and the other disciples with him, could not bear the thought of Christ's sufferings, for another reason besides their love to Him; they were still but as children, inclined to measure things by outward appearance and present feelings. They were disposed to walk by sight, not by faith. They had indeed forsaken home, friends, all that they had, to obey the calling of Jesus Christ, and follow Him: and so far, they shewed that they had in them the foundation of true faith, but as yet they did not quite rightly understand whither they were to follow Him. They might still have in them more or less of the expectations in which all Jews were brought up, that Christ, when He came, would do great earthly things for them, that they should be richer, more respected, more comfortable, here in this world. And S. Peter in particular, who knows but he might be a little lifted up by the great and special promises which had been just made to him? If he was to be in some sense the rock, on which our Lord would build His Church: if he was to be entrusted with the keys of the Kingdom of Heaven, he might think himself no unfit judge of what it behoved Christ to suffer: he might well enough be startled and disappointed to find men rejecting, insulting, crucifying his Master. This was natural, even for S. Peter, when God left him to his own judgement; although just before, speaking by the Holy Ghost, he had made that good confession, "thou art the Christ, the Son of the Living God."

Our Lord therefore calls him satan, because he was, though unknowingly, acting the tempter's part; saying words which, if he had been speaking to a frail deceivable being like himself, might have turned him aside from his duty. He commands him out of His sight, for an example to all us His disciples, how we should deal with those even, who are dearest to us after an earthly manner, when they become as tempters to us: He tells him that he is an offence, or stumbling-block, for so he was, as much as in him lay, endeavouring to make his Master stumble at the rough and severe trials which God would put in His road.

The sum of the matter is, that even this famous Apostle, along with the other disciples, being a sort of child in heavenly things until he was changed by the Holy Ghost on the day of Pentecost, could not make up his mind to the cross, either for his Master or for himself. Much less could he have done so, had he been like the greater part of men, selfish and worldly-minded, the slave of mere gain or pleasure. The Cross of Christ is hateful to such, as it is alarming to the childish and thoughtless. In one way or in the other, I suppose there is no one of us who needs not some special examination and correction of himself, lest he fail to profit by that Cross, now that it will be once more by God's mercy lifted up in his sight and for his good.

First, there can be no doubt that our natural tendency is to shrink, as do children, from every thing that gives immediate pain. Though we are told never so positively, on authority which we cannot gainsay, that such and such troubles and hardships are to be endured, before we can attain to this or that desired good, we feel as if we could not altogether receive the saying. We still keep looking wistfully round and round, if perchance we may find some easier course, some way of getting to our journey's end without hardship, pain or sorrow. Lent and Passion week, if we at all consider them beforehand, are not times which we delight in forecasting. Evermore, at the bottom of men's hearts, excepting perhaps some few, whom very great grace has brought nearer the condition of saints, we are inclined to rejoice when such times are over, we do not love to think of them coming on. We know that they are good for us, yet we would fain do without them. What little fasting and other restraint we are to practise is apt to seem irksome to us beforehand: we are tempted to wonder whether it is necessary, to contrive other methods of doing ourselves, as we think, the same good. Much more do we shrink beforehand from real pains of body and mind: sharp anguish and bitter thoughts, inflicted on ourselves, or those dear to us. "A sword shall pierce through thine own soul also." Who would willingly hear such a sentence addressed to himself by a prophet of God?

Further: suppose there be no grievous suffering, no serious illness in the case, yet the whole Christian life, and especially the life of a penitent, is full of hard work and denial of self. It is a journey, a race, a warfare: there is no time in it, properly speaking, for mere rest or mere enjoyment. Who, if he might choose, would choose such a condition, for himself or for his friend? Who that has serious thoughts at all has not been startled at one time or another of his life, on finding his task in life so very unlike what he expected? Even if no special affliction befal us, the mere effort to suit ourselves, day after day, in thought, word, and deed to what our condition requires of us, and God expects, is burthen enough and too much for most men to take up.

Thus it is with us, as long as we, like S. Peter when as yet unsanctified, savour not the things of God but the things of men. So long our life will be passed, at best, in unwilling endurance of pain, or in restless endeavours to avoid it. And, alas! we have most of us, over and above this, earthly pursuits which are too dear to us: passions to be mortified, bad habits to be corrected. Sensual desires lay hold of us; proud, covetous, angry fancies get the dominion over us; night and day they haunt us, craving to be satisfied, and besides the guilt and misery they bring in themselves, make it a great deal less easy for us to embrace the cross which our Saviour reaches out to us. Look at any young boy or girl, not a particularly unruly one, but such as the generality are, light and giddy, self-pleasing and undisciplined. You see and feel how difficult, how impossible without Divine grace, it must needs prove for that child to choose with purpose of heart the serious self-denying ways of the Gospel; such for example, as are taught in the sermon on the mount. Look at the same child again when it is now grown into a man or woman; it is much if the hard task have not become ten times harder. The stubborn child may have become a proud man; the indolent child a sensual man; the crafty child a false, hypocritical man; the selfish child a covetous man; then what chance remains of his really taking up the cross, really trying to conform himself to Jesus, the humble, the pure, the true, the merciful One? Speaking after the manner of men, the case would indeed be desperate. Our Saviour has told us so Himself. "With men it is impossible, but not with God; for with God all things are possible." As He by His Spirit entirely cured His servant Peter of that childish mind, so is He able and most willing to cure us, one and all, of our carnal and proud minds. As He changed Peter so, that from a stumbling and an offence, he became a chief strengthener of the brethren, so He may change any one of us, who may seem now to have least ground of hope. And He will do so, if we tire not of seeking Him heartily.

Only we must leave off flattering ourselves that we may knowingly keep any part of our earthly mind, and yet have the benefit of the saving Cross. We have lived on too long, many of us, in an error of that kind. We have too easily satisfied ourselves, that God's commandments cannot be in earnest kept, and that no one ever did keep them: and so we have dreamed we were taking up the cross, though we still reserved to ourselves some one darling evil passion or habit, unmortified and uncured.

Now Christ gives us another trial: now by the near return of His Passion hours, He is warning us as He warned S. Peter,—"The Son of Man must suffer many things, and be crucified:" if you will come after Me, come take up your cross and follow Me. Whatever our childishness, whatever our wilfulness may have been, now is the time to get the better of them. Cost what it may, either outwardly or in the hidden pangs of the heart, the price is worth paying: for what says Christ presently after? "What is a man profited, if he shall gain the whole world, and lose his own soul? Or what shall a man give in exchange for his soul?" Is it not worth while keeping yourself in order, and beseeching God to help you, for the sake of everlasting life? You will not doubt it in that day, when in the presence of all the Angels, we shall be asked whether we have done so; and alas for those who shall find no answer! Alas for those who by faith, and prayer and self-denial, and by humble meditation on the Cross of Christ, might have learned the love which makes the cross easy, and chose rather to be childish or wilful all their lives long!

SERMON XXXIX.

THE UNCHANGEABLE PRIESTHOOD OF CHRIST.

PASSION SUNDAY.

Heb. vii. 25.

"*He is able also to save them to the uttermost that come unto God by Him, seeing He ever liveth to make intercession for them.*"

WE are preparing to keep the yearly solemnity of our Lord's Death and Passion. The Cross is once more to be lifted up·in our sight, and Jesus Christ to be evidently set forth crucified. In spirit we are to be present where He is bound, dragged along, smitten on the face, blindfolded, buffeted, spit upon, blasphemed. They condemn Him to death, they hale Him before Pilate, in scorn and spite they cry out "away with Him, crucify Him:" they give Him over into the hands of the heathen: and we shall see Him brought very low, as a worm, and no man, by the usage of those wicked soldiers: scourged, crowned with thorns, wrapped in a ragged purple garment, "a very scorn of men and the outcast of the people;" "He hath no form nor comeliness, and when we shall see Him there is no beauty that we should desire Him."

When we see Him thus humbled, brought so very low for our sakes, it may be that some of us may not rightly remember His glory. Those who were by at the time could not know of that glory: even the better sorts among them, the women that bewailed and lamented Him, could not but be grieved and shocked to see so holy a person so cruelly and shamefully used: but they did not, they could not, know for certain how great and holy and glorious He is; the most High God Himself, the Eternal Son of the Father, come down to suffer for us in the very truth of our nature, in all things like unto us, only without sin. They could not know that He Whom they saw dying on the Cross was Very God: and we who do know it, who have been taught from our earliest days, even we, I fear, do not always rightly remember it. I once myself heard a well-meaning person say, when mention was made of our Lord's Sufferings (it was long before I knew this place) "And to think of their behaving so to so good a Christian as He was." You see, my brethren, what that good person meant; she meant nothing but what was respectful: but you see also plainly that she was not used to think of Jesus as of the most High God, equal with the Father; the God Who at that very moment was looking down into her heart. And I suppose there are many like her in this. I hear and read the Name Jesus very often used in far too familiar a way. Even serious persons, often times, make too free with that Holy Name, and so and in many other ways, they shew plainly that, whilst they are willing to take our Lord for their best friend and only Saviour, they have by no means learned to reverence Him as their God and Judge. Beware of this, dear brethren; use yourselves to bow the very knees of your heart at every remembrance of Him, Who though He so demeaned Himself for you, was, is, will be for ever, the Eternal Word of God, with God, Himself Very God, of One Substance with the Father. When you hear, verse by verse, of His sad Sufferings in the Lessons of next week, say to yourselves very often, "It was God Almighty Who endured all this; God Almighty Who sat down and ate the Passover with His disciples; God Almighty Who brake the bread and blessed it, and said, 'This is My Body;' God Almighty Who washed His disciples' feet; Who sweat blood in His agony; Who permitted Judas to kiss Him; Who was chained, dragged along, reviled, buffeted. The face in which they spat was the Face of God; the body which they tore with their scourges, was the Body of God; it was the Head of God which they crowned with thorns, the Hands and Feet of God through which they drove their cruel nails; it was God Himself, appearing among them, Whom they put to death amid their railings and blasphemies." O, never forget it, never cease to think of it, else you will never think as you ought of your own sins, or of His mercy. You will never have the right faith until you have used yourselves to think of Christ, not only as your Saviour, but as God your Saviour.

Our salvation itself, my brethren, depends upon this. If He were not our God He could not be our Saviour, such a Saviour as we need. To be such a

Saviour, He is both God and Man, and so His great Names signify; Emmanuel, i. e., God with us, God making Himself one of us and abiding with us; and Jesus, i.e., the Lord, the Most High God, our Saviour God, reigning for ever in Heaven, far above all suffering, made for a little while lower than the Angels for the suffering of death, the worst of deaths, the death of the Cross: "God of the substance of the Father, begotten before the worlds: and Man of the substance of His Mother, born in the world." And thus He was the Saviour we needed; for being Man, He could suffer; as the Apostle says, " ᵃIt behoved Him in all things to be made like unto His brethren." And as the children are partakers of flesh and blood, He also Himself likewise took part of the same. As Man, He could suffer: and as God, His Sufferings had that power and virtue in them, that they were able to redeem a lost world. As Man, He took true Blood of the Virgin Mary: and as God, His Blood was capable of washing away sins.

Because Jesus Christ is very God, He was able to reconcile us by His death: and for the same reason, we being reconciled, He is able to save us by His Life: so the Apostle tells us in the text: "He is able to save to the uttermost them that come unto God by Him."

We are not to think of our Lord's Sacrifice as of a thing past and done, in such sense that we sinners may have the blessing and benefit of it, without anything done on our part, and without any more merciful interference on His. True; He died once for all; the day of Calvary can never come again: Christ hanging on the Cross was "a full, perfect and

ᵃ Heb. ii. 17.

sufficient sacrifice, oblation and satisfaction for the sins of the whole world." But even as He created the world once, and the act of creation needs not to be again, yet still there is need of His constant preserving power to uphold the things which He hath made, and to give life and being to each of His creatures in particular, as they come into His world one after another; somewhat in the same way it is in the matter of Redemption. He died once for all mankind; but He lives again, lives for ever, to communicate the benefits of His Death to the Church which is His Body, and to each Christian in particular. While you remember His Agony and Bloody Sweat, His Cross and Passion, you must not forget His glorious Resurrection and Ascension.

"[b] I am He that liveth and was dead, and behold, I am alive for evermore." That is the Christ Whom we have to wait upon, to follow to the Cross, to lay in the grave, now in the sad and aweful week which is drawing so very near us. The Holy Church bids us think of His crucified Body and His saving Wounds, not only as His friends and mourners saw them on Good Friday, but also as the blessed Saints and Angels see them even now in Heaven. The Holy Church, I say, bids us think of Him so; in that she directs us to read at this time what the Epistle to the Hebrews teaches of Christ having come as an High Priest of good things to come, and having by His own Blood entered in once into the holy place.

The Son of Man, our High Priest and Saviour, obtained eternal Redemption for us by what He

[b] Rev. i. 18.

endured upon the Cross: but for you and me and each of us to reap finally the fruit of that Redemption, we must be partakers of that which He is now doing for us in Heaven. Let us reverently consider what Scripture tells us of this: consider, I say, and that reverently. For only think, dear brethren, what a shame, what a danger it must be, when our good Lord in Holy Scripture opens, as it were, a door in Heaven, and allows us sinners to look in and listen, and see and hear a little of what He is there doing for our good, and we choose rather to go to sleep, or amuse ourselves with looking round upon each other, or with any thing else that comes into our poor frail fancies; therefore I say again, attend to me, or rather attend to the Holy Ghost, and that reverently, and consider what the Bible tells us of our Lord's doings in Heaven, where He is now, in the way of saving our souls. How does He apply to you and me and the whole Church the blessed infallible medicine which He provided for us by His Death and Passion? How does He bring home His Salvation to each one of our souls? First, you know, He is our King in Heaven, He sitteth there at the Right hand of God. There, ever since His Ascension, all power in Heaven and earth has been exercised by the Man Christ Jesus. And all for the salvation of His elect, His own sheep, that hear His voice. Heaven and earth, Angels and men, all powers and creatures whatsoever are wonderfully ordered and overruled by Him so as to work together for good to them that love God. And most especially He, as our King, sends down His royal gift, the Holy Spirit of the Father and the Son, to dwell in our hearts to unite us to Him, to sanctify and prepare us for joy and glory.

But that is not all, there is another high and wonderful office which "He that liveth and was dead and is alive for evermore" vouchsafes to exercise for us in Heaven at His Father's Right Hand. He is not only our King but our Priest. This is what S. Paul speaks of, "He ever liveth to make Intercession for us." To make Intercession, i.e., to intercede. You know what "intercede" means; it is when a person wants a favour of another, and gets a friend or favourite of the other to ask the favour for him. So our Lord, not exactly as one praying, at least Holy Scripture does not say so, but as a Priest offering a sacrifice and pleading for another, appears before God for us. If He appears as a Priest, He must have some sacrifice to present, as S. Paul himself argues, "c every High Priest is ordained to offer gifts and sacrifices: wherefore it is of necessity that this man have somewhat also to offer."

What is the Sacrifice which our Lord offers in Heaven? The very same which He once for all offered on earth: the Body which was broken, and the Blood which was shed on the Cross. That Body and Blood which He took of the Virgin Mary, which He offered once for all with pain, suffering and death, on Good Friday, but which on Easter Day He united again, and on Ascension Day carried both Body and Soul into Heaven, there to appear night and day in the Presence of the Father for us: not without Blood, His own Blood whereby He continually pleads for His Church and each one of

c Heb. viii. 3.

His servants on earth, and is our Advocate with the Father, through that same love which caused Him to make Himself here a bloody Sacrifice, a Propitiation, i. e., a reconciling gift, for our sins. Thus He pleads and intercedes in Heaven, standing before the Father as a Lamb that had been slain. He does not forget us for one moment. As often as we say an earnest prayer in His Name, as often as any poor distressed sinner begs mercy and grace of the Father, as our Prayer book teaches, "through Jesus Christ our Lord," so often, depend on it, our merciful High Priest in some unspeakable way makes His heavenly memorial of what He endured on mount Calvary. And the Lord smells a sweet savour, and accepts our prayers, as incense in His Tabernacle, for the sake of Him who unites them to His own Sacrifice. And as if this was not love enough, behold what He has done besides for us; according to the delight which He has in being with the sons of men and doing them good. Though He has taken up His Blessed Body and Blood in its outward and visible form unto Heaven, there to remain until His second coming, He has nevertheless in a Sacramental manner left us that same Blessed Body and Blood on earth, to be set before His Father, in the way you know of, by the appointed use of Bread and Wine, and so to be pleaded on our own altars for a memorial of His precious Death. And observe, this memorial on earth, as well as the memorial in Heaven, is made by Christ Himself. Outwardly to the eye indeed, it looks as if we earthly priests offered the sacrifice, and made the memorial. But the truth is, we earthly priests are as nothing in that great work, it is not we that consecrate but our Lord Himself, though we say over the words. And since He has said, "I am with you always, even unto the end of the world," we cannot doubt that He is present, then especially when we sanctify and offer the Precious Blood and Body of our Saviour. He is there; He pleads for us on earth by that bread and wine which is His Body and Blood, as surely as He pleads in Heaven by His natural Body, with its visible wounds, in the very form which He has shewn to a few of His saints. The priest, be he who he may, is but an instrument in the Lord's hand, as the rod in the hand of Moses. Christ, the Living and Eternal Word of God, is the true Priest, the true Consecrator; just as in the other Sacrament it is He who really baptizes: the clergyman whom you see sprinkles the water, but it is Christ and Christ alone who baptizeth with the Holy Ghost.

So you see, my brethren, the offering in the Holy Communion is the same remembrance of our Lord's Sacrifice on the Cross which He offers to the Father continually in Heaven: and it is the same Christ Who pleads and offers it: here in an image and under a veil, there openly in His own human form, in the sight of the Angels. And for whom does our gracious Lord thus continually plead and offer Himself? For those, no doubt, whom He prayed for on earth: for those whom He mentioned in that wonderful prayer immediately after that first Holy Communion. You may read it in the seventeenth chapter of S. John: for His chosen Apostles, and in them for the whole Church; and not for them only, but for all who should believe on Him through their word, i.e., for all Christians, for us, my brethren, for us, sinful and unworthy as we are, unless we unthankfully reject His Intercession. For us He then prayed on earth; for us He now intercedes in Heaven: and what is the blessing, the special end of His prayer and Intercession? Is it earthly joy and comfort, health in our bodies, peace in our homes, success in our undertakings? and the like.

No, my brethren, none of these did our High Priest ask for us in that prayer at His First Communion, but what He did ask was, "That we all might be one, as the Father in Him and He in the Father." Christ in us and the Father in Christ; that we may be with Him where He is, and may behold His glory which the Father hath given Him. This is what He asked for us on earth, and for this He pleads on our behalf where He now is, in Heaven. In respect of all other things, He orders them, and pleads for them, in such manner and measure as He knows will work together for good to them that love Him and keep His Commandments.

Thus you see what a High Priest we have, "holy, harmless, undefiled, separate from sinners and made higher than the Heavens, and able to save us to the uttermost." For what more could we ask or think of, were we the purest and highest Angels in Heaven than being one with Him and He with us? Much more, being as we are sinful souls and bodies, worthy of nothing but hell. He is able and He is willing to save us one and all, to the uttermost. But one thing is needful. We must come unto God; we must not refuse or hang back, when His loving voice calls; when His loving hand draws us on, we must come unto God, and we must come by Him. What is coming by Him? Not only praying in His Name, but really doing and suffering for His sake; not only saying at the end of collects, "through Jesus Christ our Lord," but joining in His Sacrifice by worthy Communion. Mind, I say, worthy Communion. That word "worthy" gathers up all into a point. If that be right, all is right: without it, there is no promise of life.

SERMON XL.

SUFFERING THE MEASURE OF LOVE.

THE FEAST OF THE ANNUNCIATION FALLING ON PASSION SUNDAY.

S. Luke ii. 35.

"*Yea a sword shall pierce through thine own soul also.*"

WONDERFUL are the ways of the Most High, and unsearchable His counsels! we might have thought, that as God by His Very Nature is Blessed, and incapable of all suffering, so the creatures which He hath made, in proportion as it might please Him to lift them up nearer to Himself, would be incapable of suffering also. We might have expected, that if there were any one of the children of men whom it should please the Almighty and Blessed One to raise up nearer to Himself than the rest, that person would surely be raised far above all pain, affliction and disappointment, all trouble both of body and mind. In this sense, cruelly and profanely as the word was uttered, it was still but the natural thought and expectation of men's hearts, when those who stood by our Saviour's Cross cried out, "let Him deliver Him, if He delighteth in Him." This is what we might have expected. But here is one taken out of the world to be blessed above all who were ever naturally born of Adam, and she is appointed at the same time to most grievous affliction and anguish; part of her very calling and commission is, "yea, a sword shall pierce through thine own soul." By the voice of the Holy Spirit Mary the Mother of Jesus Christ was three times declared to be blessed: first, when the Angel came to her, saying, "Hail thou that art highly favoured, the Lord is with thee, blessed art thou among women." Next, when her cousin Elizabeth being filled with the Holy Ghost spake out with a loud voice and said, "Blessed art thou among women, and blessed is the Fruit of thy womb," and once again, when she herself, by the same Spirit accepting Elizabeth's salutation, made answer and said, "behold, from henceforth all generations shall call me blessed." And no doubt by the same Divine teaching, the Church has all along been fulfilling this prophecy, putting the word "blessed" before the name of the Virgin Mary, and will do so to the end. Yet a sword was to pierce through her soul. As she was to be the most blessed of mothers, so was she to be the most sorrowful and distressed. The nearer God drew her to Himself, the more heavy was her burden to be.

And why? Holy Scripture appears to tell us in one word, where it teaches, that God is Love. "[d] God is love, and he that dwelleth or abideth in love, dwelleth in God, and God in him." The more we love, the more like we are to God, the nearer to

[d] 1 S. John iv. 16.

Him, and so the more blessed and happy. But fallen and sinful as we and all our race are, it is also true that the more we love, the more we suffer. The more truly we love God, the more keenly and bitterly we feel our own unworthiness and sad separation from Him; the more truly we love our neighbour, so much the more do we feel his miseries and mourn for his sins. The more we love both God and our neighbour, the more earnestly shall we embrace that Cross, which is the only means of truly approaching to our God, and doing our neighbour real good. And thus it cometh to pass, that suffering is in us, sinful children of Adam, the true test or standard or measure of love: and if of love, then of blessedness also, for to love God is to be blessed and happy. And the Mother of our Lord and our God, Jesus Christ, as she was nearer to the Most High, more highly favoured than any other merely human being, so it stands to reason that her sufferings should be sharper and deeper than those of any besides; always of course excepting her Son, Who was no mere human being, but true God made true Man as on this great Day, that He might endure her burden and the burden of us all, a load inconceivable of torment and agony, beyond that of all mankind put together.

And if this seem a hard saying, as indeed to flesh and blood it may well seem hard and incredible, that the more a person suffers, (if he suffer as a Christian) the nearer he is to God, and therefore the more blessed and happy, let us consider for a moment how it is, even in worldly matters, which we all more or less understand. What is there to make a person tolerably happy, even in this imperfect world, but true love and affection? and where and how, generally speaking, is that to be had, without more or less of suffering? A mother's love: what is there more tender and exquisite, more naturally full of joy and gladness? But we know that by God's appointment it has had its beginning in very sharp sorrow and pain and dauger, ever since the word was spoken to Eve, "in sorrow shalt thou bring forth children." A mother's love begins in travail and anguish, and it goes on in watching, anxiety, and fear; and in a thousand cares and distresses such as none but mothers can know, both during infancy, and when the sons and daughters are grown up. "Can a woman forget her sucking child that she should not have compassion on the son of her womb?" but if she has compassion, she must feel for her child's sufferings, for any trouble he may fall into, and more especially (when he is old enough) for any sin; any danger that may assault and hurt the soul. The truer the love, the greater the distress, and the greater the happiness also: is it not so? If you did not love your children so as to feel their falls and calamities more grievous than death, you would not be capable of tasting the joy, better than life itself, which a true loving mother experiences in seeing her offspring good and happy. Thus you see how naturally suffering accompanies a mother's love; and it is much the same in respect of the other affections which make up the joy and comfort of this world. Even the ordinary books, which people read for mere amusement, may teach us so much as this, that the course of true love, as one said who knew well, seldom or never runs quite smooth. That love which is the best human beginning of happiness in the Holy estate of Matrimony, how many disappointments, fears, doubts, anxieties, delays, are commonly, in God's Providence, sent to try it! and of course, the truer, and purer the love is, the greater the joy when God blesses it, and the sharper every one of its trials. But the mind of one who is in earnest in such a case will be like that of Jacob, who served for Rachel seven years, and they seemed to him but a few days, for the love that he bare her. The greater the love, the greater the blessing; but the greater also the suffering and self-denial. You see how this holds true in respect of earthly love; can you not understand how it may be the same in respect of heavenly love also?

Or think of children's feelings towards their parents. Joseph loved his father Jacob with a most earnest and dutiful love; it was a great part of his life's comfort; he could not have been happy without so loving him; but how much had he to endure in consequence, separated from Jacob and full of anxiety about him, for all those long years after he was sold into Egypt. Or think of friends. David and Jonathan, we know, loved each the other as his own soul; their love was a part of them, they felt as if they could not live without it; they would not have given it up for any consideration; but it brought very sore trials upon them: Jonathan felt himself persecuted in every thing that his father did against David: David, when he lost Jonathan, was distressed for him, as for a brother. Thus, all through life it is plain, that so far as men find their happiness in loving, i. e., so far as they have feelings and thoughts higher than those of the brutes that perish, so far they must make up their minds to suffer for that love's sake. The suffering is God's way of trying the reality of the love.

But as all these earthly affections are but as the faintest types and shadows of God's holy and heavenly love in Christ Jesus towards us sinners, and of the dutiful love of His faithful people towards Him and towards one another, so the sufferings and self-denials which the various forms of earthly love bring with them, are sure tokens of His will that there must be affliction, and that, willingly borne, to try His true lovers, and prepare them for spiritual blessings. It is a kind of law of His kingdom, If we suffer, we shall also reign with Him: not else. And those who love Him with true child-like love, come by degrees not even to wish it otherwise. To find pain in overcoming temptation, to part with things we would gladly keep, to lie awake all night, and spend wearisome days, weeks, months, in bodily torment, and feverish restlessness; to be bereaved of dear friends and relations; to fail in the dearest wishes of one's heart; to be scorned, mistrusted, slandered, forsaken; all these and all other temporal calamities, bitter as they must be to the natural man, are in the mouth of the believer as honey for sweetness, if he can but regard them as signs of his Lord's love, and also as means graciously allowed him, whereby to prove the sincerity of his own love. And if this is so in regard of the common troubles of life, in such visitations as we all of us know, much more when it comes to actual and express suffering for the truth's sake. When ye endure this, and are nothing terrified, it is as S. Paul tells the Philippians, a manifest token to you of salvation, and that from God Himself, when He grants unto you on Christ's behalf, not only to believe in Him, but also to suffer for His sake. The suffering also, patiently and thankfully endured, is a token to us from His own self that we really love :—the very point on which we are doubting, and to be assured of which from Himself is worth all the world to us. This in a more eminent degree was the spirit of the holy and faithful martyrs. Their torments were often such as that, even now when we read or hear of them at a distance, many thousand miles off, many hundred years ago, it is too trying for us; we shut the book, we stop our ears, we turn away our eyes as from a fearful picture, which is sure to haunt us with disagreeable remembrance; and yet the persons themselves who had to bear those agonies, entirely longed for them and rejoiced in them, and had such perfect faith in the blessing which accompanied them, that they took it as a joy and a glory when they heard of their near kindred, parents or children, wives or sisters, having to go through the same. Why? because they knew that loving martyrdom was the very crown of all love, and what could they wish greater or more blessed to their dearest on earth, than to love God as well as ever they might, as well as ever any had loved Him, with a love stronger than death.

And no wonder that in us, sinners by nature, God should always keep this order and law of His kingdom, that those who will be happy must love, and those who love must suffer; since His own Divine Son, Who knew no sin, and could not in His own Nature suffer, did in His inconceivable love become one of us, that He might suffer for us, and so, having purchased us to be His own, might unite us to Himself, enabling us in our poor measure to love Him in acknowledgement of His love, and to suffer gladly in communion with His sufferings. He was made perfect through sufferings; He entered not into His glory before He was crucified. And as it was with the Head, so it must be and has ever been with each of the living and abiding members: first humiliation and suffering for love's sake; then blessedness and glory, still all of love: only in Christ our Head, these were all perfectly and infinitely; in each one of us His members, according to our measure of holiness and grace from Him.

Of course that holy and highly favoured one, whom we especially remember to-day, the Blessed Virgin Mother of our Lord and our God, by how much she was nearer to Him than any other of the Saints, surpassed them all, we may well believe, in the sorrow she had to endure. First, in the very miracle itself, that unspeakable gift to her alone, that she should be the true and real Mother of Him, Who is the most High God; even in that glory and joy there was a bitterness, "How shall this be, seeing I know not a man?" And many and sad, it would seem, must have been the thoughts and searchings of heart, during the time which the Evangelist speaks of, when he says, "[b]she was found with child of the Holy Ghost, and Joseph her husband being

[b] S. Matt. i. 18, 19.

a just man, and not willing to make her a public example, was minded to put her away privily." By and by came the second trouble. Simeon with the Holy Child in his arms had uttered the mysterious prophecy, which could not be quite understood until the lifting up of the Cross. "This Child is set for a sign which shall be spoken against; yea, a sword shall pierce through thine own soul also." This the Blessed Mother kept, and pondered in her heart, a grave and sorrowful warning to be remembered among the consolations of her holy home all through those thirty years, until the time came for her Blessed Son to go out, and be separated from her. And we may be sure that was another time of sadness for her, when she found that His hour of glory for which she longed was not yet come, and she had to listen to the evil reports which His enemies were spreading abroad concerning Him, and to know how He was wandering abroad, not having where to lay His Head, and how much He was going through in so many ways. Well might she say with that afflicted mother of Tobias, "ᶜ Now I care for nothing, since I have lost thee my son, the light of mine eyes." But all this, and whatever else her love for the Holy Jesus caused her to suffer in His life-time, could be nothing, just nothing at all, to compare with what she must have suffered at His death; when, as a true mourning mother, she stood by the Cross of Jesus, seeming in a certain way to gather in one, and to bear in her own single person the grief of all bereaved mothers, from Eve weeping over Abel, down to the last who shall lose her child.

ᶜ Tobit x. 5.

It was like parting with all in one, to part, and that by so cruel a death, with Him from Whom all mothers and all children derive their love for one another. O that was indeed a sword, a most unpitying sword, piercing through her tender soul, when without the least power of helping Him, she had to look up and behold the Son of her love hanging upon His cruel wounds, to hear His sad cry as He felt forsaken of His Father, and the cruel reproaches of His enemies on every side; to be witness of His dying thirst, and not be able so much as to offer Him a drop of water; to be present, but not to close His eyes, when at that last unspeakable moment, He bowed His Head, and gave up the ghost. Who is sufficient to imagine the thousandth part of what this blessed Mother then endured? No man: because no man can tell the thousandth part of the blessedness of conversing with Him as His own Mother, with Him, Who is the Life and the Light, with Whom is fulness of joy; of Whom it is written, He is love. The misery of so parting with Him could only be measured by the bliss of abiding with Him.

May we not in some way discern, my brethren, in this most mysterious and gracious example, how the love of Christ, as it is the only blessing which can fill and perfectly gladden the heart, so on the other hand, it may be expected to draw after it the very sharpest of trials and sufferings? Nor is this so very strange, when we come to consider: for where such love is deep in the heart, there must needs be great tenderness of spirit and of conscience. True love is keenly alive to every thing that would hurt or trouble the beloved. Aware that He is always present, it is disquieted at every thing that falls out amiss or contrary to His holy Will. How then can it have one moment's perfect quiet, so long as it remains in such a world as this? Truly it is as if one, with a perfect and exquisite ear for music, were every moment compelled to listen to the most harsh and jarring and untuneable sounds. And then think of our Lord's love of souls, how much stronger it was than death, and how sincerely and how deeply all who love Him must care for those whom He hath bought with His own Blood. And look around, and see which way the greater part appear to be too evidently going. Alas, what is it but our sad imperfection in the love of Him, which makes even the best of us, by comparison, so faintly touched with the daily corruption and ruin of those for whom Christ died? We can be very anxious for the bodily comfort and health of our brethren, and it is well to be so, if we are patient withal; but which of us cares, as he ought to do, for the immortal souls perishing on every side of us, at our own doors, perhaps in our own houses? There was once one who did so care; who could cry out concerning himself, "[d] Who is weak and I am not weak: who is offended and I burn not?" It came upon him daily, the care of all the Churches; and this also was as a sword piercing through his soul, part of the sorrow which his nearness to Christ brought upon him. The world of wilful sinners is continually crucifying our Lord afresh, and His Saints have to

[d] 2 Cor. xi. 29.

bear this Cross especially after Him, whatever may be their lot in respect of the things that are without. And then there is the sorrowful sense of our own continual failures, our longings to be better than we are, felt by us as vain and fruitless.

What then, my brethren, is the special blessedness of His true and loving children, which makes their lot, even in this world, such, that nothing would induce them to change it? What is that joy which depends on their suffering, and grows out of it, outgrows it, so that they would not, if they might, give up any portion of the healthful pangs which their Father sees good to lay upon them? It is just this, their believing hope in Him. Their Lord's own word was, "*Therefore doth My Father love Me, because I lay down My life . . . No man taketh it from Me, but I lay it down of Myself." And what He says of Himself, He says of all His members. The Father loveth them so much the more as they willingly suffer more for His sake. This trust in Almighty love is so great and divine a blessing, that it far overpays all the troubles, inward and outward, of this our time of trial.

What was it to the Mother of our Lord that the sword pierced through her soul for a season, in comparison with the joy of knowing that she was the Mother of our Lord? What is it to any of us, to bear trouble inward and outward, as much as ever it may please Him to lay upon us, if we may but have a reasonable hope that we are doing the will of God? For to all such His promise is clear

* S. John x. 17, 18.

and certain: "ᶠ Whosoever shall do the will of My Father which is in Heaven, the same is My brother and sister and mother." Observe, this promise is not to a few favoured ones, but to all who will do His will, quietly, each one in his own place. There is not one here, nor in any other Christian congregation, to whom this hope is not held out, that he may be accounted the brother or sister, or mother of Christ. Blessed hope! God grant that we may none of us wilfully throw it away.

ᶠ S. Matt. xii. 50.

SERMON XLI.[a]

OUR LORD'S OWN ACCOUNT OF CHRISTIAN FASTING.

S. Luke v. 35.

"The days will come, when the Bridegroom shall be taken away from them; and then shall they fast, in those days."

"By Thy Baptism, Fasting, and Temptation, Good Lord deliver us." How, we may reverently ask, by His Fasting? even as by His Baptism and Temptation. It was part (if one may so speak) of the process whereby He made Himself entirely one with us; going before us, doing what He would have us do, and suffering what we justly deserved to suffer. And this, not merely as our example, but as our Head and Surety. He was baptized with water and the Holy Ghost, not that He needed the mystical washing away of sin, or that He was not from His Incarnation "anointed with the oil of gladness above His fellows," but that the washing and anointing might overflow, as "from Aaron's head to the skirts of his clothing," might overflow and be communicated to each one of us, His members. He was tempted of Satan, not that such probation and exercise was His

[a] Preached at Penzance on Ash-wednesday, 1863.

appointed way, as it is ours, to moral perfection, but that He might mysteriously sympathize with and succour us when we are tempted.

In like manner, our Divine Lord fasted, not that His Flesh required, as ours, so to be subdued to the spirit; God forbid! but as the Head and Leader of His people, to sanctify and bless their fasts; to shew them how to fast; to expiate, as it were, by His sacred hunger all the sins of our eating and drinking, our intemperance when we have enough, and our impatience when we are in want. Such, we may humbly believe, were some of the purposes of our Incarnate God's mysterious and miraculous Fasting in the wilderness, besides any other influences, secret to us, which so wonderful a transaction may have had on the worlds visible and invisible.

Now in this, as in other manifestations of His Sacred Humanity, the Spouse from the beginning was taught by the Holy Ghost to enter into the mind of the Bridegroom. Few, if any, pages of the Prayer-book come to us with greater authority of God's Word, than that which we turn over to-day · nor is any season in the Christian calendar more distinctly sanctioned in the Bible than Lent. The Law and the Prophets forecast it by unmistakeable types in the persons of Moses and Elijah; Moses, by his twice-told forty days, teaching the double use of religious abstinence; to prepare the flesh and spirit for holy communications, and to do penance, and obtain grace in aid of the penitent; Elijah, by his retirement for the like space of time, instructing the Church how to chasten herself, and cry mightily unto God in time of decay and rebuke and blasphemy.

To God's ancient Israel, fallen as it was, the lesson was repeated in the time of Joel, and it is taught us year by year, as on this day. And lest men should imagine that all this is legal and outward, and not in harmony with the spiritual service of the Gospel, our Master and Lord has spoken so plainly that we cannot choose but hear, in that Sermon which He preached to us all to be the alphabet of our Christian duty. "When ye give alms, when ye pray, when ye fast, do so and so." Whatever difference the customs of men may have made, no one surely can be so shameless as to doubt or deny that our Lord here takes it for granted that His faithful people will, in some way, fast; that it will be a matter of course with them, as much so as that they will pray and give alms. Is this, think you, duly considered by the majority of even well-meaning Christians in our land? Is there not some danger, that, in our great care not to appear to men to fast, we may be found, in the end, to have gone without fasting at all? And if He is to be taken at His own word, will not that be the same kind of loss as if a man should live and die without almsgiving or without prayer?

Over and above all this, the Church from very ancient times has found special warrant for keeping her Lents, in those remarkable words of our Lord which, literally taken, seem to fix a particular time when His disciples should fast. "Days will come, when the Bridegroom shall be taken away from them, and then shall they fast." If you consider for a moment the circumstances under which He was speaking, you will find, I think, that the saying has three distinct bearings: that it is at once a prophecy, a ritual precept, and a principle of Christian morality. To explain its force as a prophecy; observe that it arose from a discussion between certain Pharisees on the one hand, and on the other certain disciples of S. John Baptist, "about purifying." S. John being now in prison, the transition from his ministry to our Lord's was becoming more and more evident; his disciples were more and more attracted to Christ, according to the tenor of the parable which John himself had addressed to them, by way of farewell, as it would seem, shortly before he was cast into prison. "[b] He must increase, but I must decrease, He that hath the Bride is the Bridegroom: but the friend of the Bridegroom, which standeth and heareth him, rejoiceth greatly because of the Bridegroom's voice: this my joy therefore is fulfilled." When, in obedience to John, they had regularly resorted to our Lord, still questions would naturally arise, as before, "about purifying;" i. e., I suppose, how a sinner can be made clean before God. Such a dispute occurred about fasting. The Pharisees and S. John's disciples were at a certain time solemnizing a fast. It must of course have been a voluntary fast, not one of those ordained by the law of Moses, or kept by any sufficient authority of the Jewish Church; otherwise our Lord's own disciples would have joined in it, for they were taught by Him to "walk orderly and keep the law." But in this case, they did not join in the fast. This seems to have occurred more than once, and so John's disciples, being rather disturbed, naturally put the question to our Lord, Why

[b] S. John iii. 29, 30.

are Thy disciples often eating and drinking, going on with their ordinary meals, while we and the Pharisees are fasting and making solemn prayers? Our Lord in His answer refers them to His forerunner's parable of the Bridegroom, which they had so lately heard; as if He should say, "You have learned out of the Psalms and the Song of Solomon and the prophecies of Isaiah, and John has lately reminded you, that the coming of My Kingdom will be like a wedding; Myself the Bridegroom; My Church or people the Bride; John Baptist the 'best man,' or friend of the Bridegroom. You will readily understand then that My disciples are as children of the bridechamber, bridesmen and bridesmaids, waiting on the nuptial Feast." But His words imply, as the truth is, that the wedding would not be completed, nor the Bride taken home, until after some time. "As yet it is only a betrothal, at which they are assisting; I am still with them, and they can hear My voice, and rejoice greatly because of it." It is a time of joy: they cannot now mourn, nor fast: it were unnatural to do so, because the Bridegroom is with them, and sorrow and sighing are out of season at present. But by and by the Bridegroom will be taken from them. By a special dispensation of Providence, before the time of Betrothal is fully over, and the time of the wedding Festival and of the Bride's reception to her final home has arrived, the Bridegroom will have to depart out of sight, and, as long as He is away, there will be mourning and fasting.

You see plainly, my brethren, the drift of this prophecy, which must have sounded very strange to those who heard it; being, as I apprehend it will be found, the first warning which He publicly gave of His own Sufferings, and of the seeming failure of His great work for a time. It was the first time of His sounding the note, which regulated afterwards the general strain of His prophecies, and thereby of all the prophecies of the New Testament. It seems as if it were one of His purposes to correct His hearers' natural expectation of nothing but good days to come. I need only just remind you, that the tendency of all minds in Israel, believers as well as unbelievers in Him, was to look for a kind of golden age, "halcyon days" as the heathen might have called them, perfect peace in their time, a people all righteous, Paradise literally restored on earth. Well may we understand their having such thoughts, but our Lord now begins to warn them that it would be far otherwise. The betrothal would still go on; but before the marriage supper, before the wedding was completed, the Bridegroom would be taken away. Thus He would prepare them, first for His Passion; then for the long and sore and wearying trial, which would come even after His Resurrection, when He would be out of sight, and His Church to a great extent, be rejected, decay, and apostatize. The very sound of His words may call to remembrance a later prophecy in S. Luke. "[c] Days will come, when ye shall desire to see one of the days of the Son of Man, and ye shall not see it." The Son of Man delaying to come, and faith seeming almost to vanish from the earth; iniquity, the anti-Christian lawlessness, abounding, and the love of the greater part waxing cold: these are the

[c] S. Luke xvii. 22.

mournful, but undeniable anticipations which He Who is the Truth, instructs us to form of what shall be in the last days of all, immediately before His Coming. Were it not that He is love also, well might all men cry out with the prophet, "[d] Alas! who shall live when God doeth this?"

So much for the predictive meaning of the text. In such measure as any generation of Christians may perceive it in course of accomplishment; faith vanishing; Church authority despised; discipline laid by; and God's best worldly gifts, knowledge, peace, liberty, national wealth, used not to His glory and in subordination to His kingdom, but to build up daily a great Babylon, which man hath made for his own self, until it not only rule, but fill the whole earth;—in such measure, I say, as Christians in any time or country shall behold any thing approaching to this, how can they choose but mourn and fast, and make much of their Lents when they come, remembering what fasting and prayer have been able by God's mercy to do in times past? If we of the Church of England, even now at this very season, will set ourselves to seek our Lord as earnestly as Daniel, or Esther, or the Ninevites did, indeed humbling our souls greatly, who knoweth but He will return and repent, as He did in Daniel's and in Esther's time, and spare us the shame and misery, which we have now some reason to fear, that this people may lose their faith in the holy Word of God, as they have already, alas! too generally lost their faith in His Church and Sacraments.

We have this encouragement, that in such use of

[d] Num. xxiv. 23.

Lent, we shall not only be acting in the spirit of our Lord's saying, but in all likelihood obeying the letter of it. For it is certain that, besides the *prophetic* force of the text, the words of it were taken in very early times, as a *ritual* intimation, or hint, from our Holy Redeemer, that He would have the days and hours in which He made perfect our Redemption by His Death, kept as days of humiliation and mourning. The Church, therefore, probably from the very beginning, kept Good Friday and Easter Eve strictly, as times of fasting and abstinence. Afterwards, in consideration of His mysterious Fast, whereby He had vouchsafed to prepare Himself for His Passion, the forty hours were extended into forty days; and thus the holy time stands before us, every year, like a solemn avenue, along which we are to walk steadily with Christ, towards His Cross and Grave, which we see at the end of it. For a like reason, Friday has His mark set on it, to be, as it were, a Lent in every week. In truth, that institution, one need not scruple to say, has at least as much countenance in the New Testament, as our resting on Sundays, instead of Saturdays. This should be more thought of than it is, for the sake of Christ's truth, as well as for our own perfection. I mean that if the days of humiliation had been as duly kept as those of thanksgiving, the balance of Christian doctrine might possibly have been more exactly preserved among us; there might have been less danger of our people's dwelling only on what gives comfort, and refusing to contemplate the aweful side of our Lord's Atonement, and the terrible voice of most just judgement. Perhaps as years roll on, and this material world becomes more comfortable to live in, as there is more of commerce, liberty, education, refinement, and whatever is bound up in the reigning idea, civilization; as all sorts of appliances for ease and enjoyment abound, and especially as people live more and more in sight of each other, Christian self-denial may become in one sense more difficult: i. e., the temptation to neglect it will be stronger. But in another sense, if you mark it well, it will be easier; for with the comforts of life the opportunities of self-denial multiply; if a person cannot punish himself in respect of food, yet every pleasure within his reach, literary, artistic, conversational, social, may supply, if you will, an occasion of virtual fasting. And true loyal lovers of Christ will be on the watch for such occasions, and will use them discreetly and quietly as best they may.

Here we are come to the *moral* meaning of our Lord's rule in the text, the great Gospel principle implied in it. Both our fasting, and our festival joy, in whatever form, and for whatever special purpose, must be animated by the love of Christ. The two things are equally impossible for the friends of the Bridegroom, to mourn while the Bridegroom is with them, or to refrain from mourning while He is taken away from them. By the waters of Babylon the spouse must sit down and weep, while she remembers thee, O Zion. The eyes of Hezekiah must fail with looking upward; the great Apostle must be in a strait betwixt two, having a desire to depart and be with Christ, which is far better.

By such measures, Christian brethren, by the sayings and doings of the true and approved friends of the Bridegroom, let us try and prove both our Lents and our Easters: our times of rejoicing, and our times of mourning. And at this time especially let us see to it, as well as we can, that what we do in the way of self-denial be really done for Christ. Something of course we must do. He plainly expects it from us. And it is best done, where circumstances allow, by rule. The very endeavour to keep the rule is a sort of self-denial in itself. Strict, more or less, and ascetic (for I will not shrink from the word) ascetic more or less it must be; but it must not be either ostentatious or morose: it cannot, if it be kept penitently, and for love, with a heart set upon His Lenten promise, "* Ye now therefore have sorrow; but I will see you again, and your heart shall rejoice, and your joy no man taketh from you."

* S. John xvi. 22.

SERMON XLII.

THE PRODIGAL SON.
Part I.

S. Luke xv. 11, 12, 13.

" A certain man had two sons; and the younger of them said to his father, Father, give me the portion of goods which falleth to me. And he divided unto them his living. And not many days after, the younger son gathered all together, and took his journey into a far country, and there wasted his substance with riotous living."

As years roll away, and we come nearer our latter end, I suppose we all feel more and more, among other serious lessons which God's good Providence is continually teaching us, how much we ought to value these holy seasons and times, in which He calls us nearer to Him, and further away from the world, to humble ourselves in His more immediate Presence. I say, my brethren, as we live longer in the world, we may well feel more and more aware of the preciousness of such times as this, and alas! more and more ashamed of the way in which too commonly we have hitherto trifled them away. This sort of penitent feeling, I am sure must be good both for you and for me. We should encourage it, if we have it: if we have it not, we should pray God of His great mercy to put it in our hearts. We should seek and try, in every way, to make this Lent, which is fast passing away, a blessed time, a time of penitence and prayer. It has come into my mind that we may find help in this necessary work by considering together, as carefully and reverently as we can, some portion of Holy Scripture, when we assemble here on the Friday evenings of Lent. And the portion which I have thought of is the parable of the prodigal son, in the fifteenth chapter of S. Luke: which parable contains in short a whole Gospel for the penitent sinner; good tidings of great joy for us all: the very salvation of our souls, if we will lay it to heart. But, as I said, we must consider it together. Both I who read or speak, and you who come to hear, must be minding what is said, and inwardly in our hearts endeavouring to be the better for it: else we shall both lose our blessing.

Let us then consider together what Christ would teach us by this most merciful parable : and in doing so it will be convenient to divide the parable into so many portions, and take one portion for each of the Fridays in Lent: that so, if it pleases our heavenly Teacher, we may be the fitter and readier to kneel down under His Cross on that best and greatest Friday.

I suppose that we many of us know in general the substance of the parable of the prodigal son. But I will read it over to you out of S. Luke's Gospel. And as many as can, I advise them to turn to it in their own Testaments, and look it over as I read. It will much help their attention and understanding, both now and on other evenings. " A certain man had two sons; and the younger of them said to his father, Father, give me the portion of goods that falleth to me. And he divided unto them his living. And not many days after, the younger son gathered all together, and took his journey into a far country and there wasted his substance with riotous living. And when he had spent all, there arose a mighty famine in that land; and he began to be in want. And he went and joined himself to a citizen of that country; and he sent him into his fields to feed swine. And he would fain have filled his belly with the husks that the swine did eat: and no man gave unto him. And when he came to himself, he said, how many hired servants of my father's have bread enough and to spare, and I perish with hunger! I will arise and go to my father, and will say unto him, Father, I have sinned against heaven and before thee, and am no more worthy to be called thy son: make me as one of thy hired servants. And he arose, and came to his father. But when he was yet a great way off, his father saw him, and had compassion, and ran, and fell on his neck, and kissed him. And the son said unto him, Father, I have sinned against heaven, and in thy sight, and am no more worthy to be called thy son. But the father said to his servants, bring forth the best robe, and put it on him; and put a ring on his hand, and shoes on his feet: and bring hither the fatted calf, and kill it; and let us eat, and be merry: for this my son was dead, and is alive again; he was lost, and is found. And they began to be merry. Now his elder son was in the field: and as he came and drew nigh to the house, he heard musick and dancing. And he called one of the servants, and asked what these things meant. And he said unto him, thy brother is come; and thy father hath killed the fatted calf, because he hath received him safe and sound. And he was angry, and would not go in : therefore came his father out, and intreated him. And he answering said to his father, Lo, these many years do I serve thee, neither transgressed I at any time thy commandment : and yet thou never gavest me a kid, that I might make merry with my friends : but as soon as this thy son was come, which hath devoured thy living with harlots, thou hast killed for him the fatted calf. And he said unto him, Son, thou art ever with me, and all that I have is thine. It was meet that we should make merry, and be glad : for this thy brother was dead, and is alive again : and was lost and is found."

An attentive person will readily perceive that the history here related by our Lord divides itself into five parts. The first, tells us how the son became prodigal : the second, how miserable he made himself; the third, how he returned to his father; the fourth, how his father received him; the fifth, how his brother complained, and how he was answered. These five parts seem to contain in them the whole blessed doctrine and discipline of Christian repentance.

The first part, which tells us how the son became a prodigal, begins at the eleventh verse, and goes on to the end of the thirteenth. " A certain man had two sons; and the younger of them said to his father, Father, give me the portion of goods that falleth to me. And he divided unto them his living. And not many days after, the younger son gathered all together, and took his journey into a far country, and there wasted his substance with riotous living."

By the Father, of course, is meant Almighty God, "of Whom the whole family in Heaven and earth is named," Who with impartial love and kindness vouchsafed in the beginning to be the Father both of Jews and Gentiles: of His own people and of strangers; and again, Who made Himself by Holy Baptism the Father both of those who should abide with Him, and of those who should fall away from Him: just as this father in the parable was the father alike both of the one son and of the other; of him who turned out wild, and of him who stayed quietly at home. Earthly parents cannot of course know how their children will turn out: no wonder if they look with equal fondness on the one and on the other: on him who shall afterwards prove reprobate, as on him who will be the comfort of their old age. But Almighty God our heavenly Father, He knows beforehand, He knows from the beginning, all the sins, negligences and ignorances by which so many of His children would grieve Him and dishonour His name, and yet He did not the less adopt them for His children. He knew, before we were born, how many things we should do to affront Him, how we should set at nought His plain commandments, and scorn His gracious ordinances; how we should dislike His House and grow weary of His Presence, what perverse pleasure we should too often take in following after His enemy, and spoiling His work. Yet for all this He loved us and chose us in Christ Jesus, before the foundation of the world, that we should not be heathens, but Christians: not strangers, but inmates in His family. Before we could do any thing for ourselves, He did all for us: He saved us, and called us with a holy calling: He made us members of His Son, His own children, inheritors of His kingdom. It was His will to have us such, though He knew from the beginning how ill we should behave. There is an unfathomable mystery in this love of His, both in respect of those who shall be the better for it at last, and in respect of those who shall perish.

As S. Paul writes concerning it: "it is in God a sweet savour of Christ both in them which are saved and in them that perish." In the beginnings of both, there is the sweet savour of love. He was, from the beginning, content, if I may say so, to have two sorts of sons in His family, the elder and the younger: those who should serve Him constantly, and those who, He knew, would fall away. Remember this, and be humbled with the thought, how ill a return you have made for this great, this unspeakable love. Remember it, you especially who are cast down under the burthen of your sins, and take the comfort which He surely intended you from it. If He loved you so from the beginning, and became your Father in spite of the wickedness which He foresaw you would commit, doubt not but He is ready to forgive you all that wickedness, when He sees that you have truly turned away from it.

What follows in the parable may help you to recollect and mourn over the manner of your falling away. "The younger of the two sons said unto his father, Father, give me the portion of goods that falleth to me." He would not be content to wait his father's time, but wanted his share of the property at once. Here we see how it was with many of us in our own eager youth, when the world with its pomps and pleasures was opening before us, and we thought, surely it is a bright and beautiful world, and we were eager to begin taking our part in it: to be away from those who kept us in order: to be choosing for ourselves, and taking our own way. And so in respect of the great Father of all: when persons have been received into His family, and are quietly enjoying, if they will, the holy and happy gifts which He offers in His Church, the Evil one comes, and whispers to their hearts, by nature leavened with sin and discontent; There are fairer and brighter things abroad than any which you can find here: look and see how others are enjoying themselves: why should not you have your liberty as well as they? Thus the Evil one whispers to us, and we have generally some bad companions to say the same: and so one Christian after another becomes uneasy in his safe and happy home: instead of thankfully receiving God's gifts as a child from a father, he wants to become independent, to manage and provide for himself, to have things for his own.

The father, we read, listened to the restless son's prayer; "he divided unto them his living." So is it, that by the Providence of Almighty God we are all of us after a time left more or less masters of ourselves. He tries us, as the householder in another parable tried his servants, by entrusting us with the proper number of talents, and so withdrawing Himself out of our sight. So the younger son, of whom we are discoursing, was trusted. He had what he asked for, his share of his father's property. He is left to his own will. Is he happy then? Alas! no; he goes on from bad to worse. Hitherto he had wished indeed to be allowed his own way, but it does not appear that he had begun quite to hate his home and his father's presence. But now that he has so much more at his command, new mischiefs begin to work in him: desires and fancies, more and more violent hurry him away from the places which ought to be dearest to him. "Not many days after he gathered all together, and took his journey into a far country." Thus when Christians grow older, and God gives them means and opportunity, how seldom do their hearts and minds stay contentedly in their quiet home, the Church, and under the immediate eye of their great and good Father! How do they make haste to gather all together, all the treasures which God has given them, the affections of their hearts, their powers of mind and body, their skill and strength, their money and their credit, their cheerfulness and their cleverness, those who love them, and those who look up to them; how do they gather all these together, and go with them at once, not a little way, but into a very far country; into the country of sin, the kingdom of the devil, which is very far indeed from the blessed home of Christ and His saints, to which they before belonged. And O, how eagerly do men act thus, as the Scripture says, with all the desire of their heart: sinning, as they ought to love God, with all their heart, soul, mind, and strength! How do they spend and throw themselves away, themselves and all the good gifts which their God had enriched them with! and so fulfil what is said next in this parable, "he wasted his substance with riotous living." Alas, my brethren, how sad to think that something too like this has been the case with many of us, with some openly, with others secretly. God had given us the treasures of His grace, a living indeed, the means of everlasting life: and we made haste to get away, as well as we could, out of sight of Him: we made haste to forget Him, that we might the more enjoy our own ways; and so we have miserably wasted more or less of His unspeakable gift, Baptismal grace, if not openly in riotous living, in fornication and uncleanness, in gluttony and drunkenness, yet secretly and not less fatally in spiritual, unseen sins, sloth and envyings, anger and covetousness, pride, and low and worldly imaginations.

And what have we gained by it all? What is the sum of this sad account? Grace wasted, God provoked, the world, if seemingly enjoyed for a moment, now fast fading away out of our sight; the happy home of our baptismal innocence far, far away from us: what can we do? is there any hope? Yes, by His unutterable mercy, my brethren, there is a sure and certain hope, as the rest of this parable will shew. Though our shipwreck were ever so sad, a plank is thrown within our reach on which we may lay hold, and save ourselves in the mighty waters. That plank is true repentance. God give us grace, without waiting longer, to lay fast hold on it, and to keep that hold all the rest of our lives; and to help us in so doing, may He guide us to the right understanding, both here and elsewhere, of the words of His Son.

SERMON XLIII.

THE PRODIGAL SON.
II.

S. LUKE xv. 14, 15, 16.

"*And when he had spent all, there arose a mighty famine in that land; and he began to be in want. And he went and joined himself to a citizen of that country, and he sent him into the fields to feed swine. And he would fain have filled his belly with the husks that the swine did eat: and no man gave unto him.*"

THE second part of the history of the prodigal son sets him before us as he was in the far country, when his few brief hours of wild enjoyment were past, and he had wasted all his substance in riotous living. During that short time he, poor miserable man, was lifted up perhaps with a keen sense of pleasure; he pitied those who stayed quietly at home serving God and their parents, and praised and congratulated himself that he knew better. But this could not last long. Even if he felt no pang of conscience, no misgiving at the very time, yet after a very little while the heat of his eager passions abated, and another state of things began to shew itself. "When he had spent all, there arose a mighty famine in that land, and he began to be in want. And he "went and joined himself to a citizen of that country, and he sent him into his fields to feed swine. And he would fain have filled his belly with the husks that the swine did eat, and no man gave unto him." Here are several points, describing between them the sad condition of the sinner yet impenitent. First, it says "When he had spent all." His father had trusted him with a full, a bounteous portion; he had it all with him when he set out from home; but now it is all gone. See in this the wastefulness of sin. We set out from our Father's house, from the baptismal font, abundantly laden with the rich treasures of His grace, to help us on our journey through the world. Too soon and too easily, if we listen to sin, will all those treasures be consumed. God gives us time: we waste it in idleness or folly, or, still worse, in abusing and hurting His good creatures. God gives us money, that, offering it back to Him, we may lay up for ourselves treasures in Heaven; we throw it eagerly away on that, which corrupts others and ourselves: the money goes first, then the fancied pleasure and enjoyment which was to be had for it, and we have nothing left but the wretched thought that it is gone for ever, except so far as it will appear against us in God's book at the Last Day. God gives us health and strength of body; we waste it in idleness or wicked pleasures. God gives us a hopeful mind, and cheerful spirits; it is one of His best gifts, as far as this world is concerned; it is given us to make us hearty in our duty, and help us through difficulties; what a pity it should be thrown away, as we too often have thrown it away, in mere diversion and nothing more; or, what is worse, in making a mock of sin, and putting goodness out of countenance. God gives us deep and warm affections; by the very nature of which we are partakers, He puts it into our hearts to love our companions, and delight in being with them; how dreadful when He shall call us to account, and we have to confess, that we have spent our warmth and eagerness of heart upon things altogether vain and sinful, perhaps (for so it too often happens) upon things not fit to be named among Christians, "working all uncleanness with greediness." Lastly and infinitely worst of all, God in Baptism and Confirmation has given us His Holy Spirit: and every deadly sin, every course and habit of known sin, is so much of the grace of that good Spirit, as a spark of holy fire, trodden out or smothered, until at length, by repeated incorrigible sin, the whole seems gone and quenched for ever. Alas! many of us know too well the process of this miserable change: how when Christians, falling away, have given themselves up to work any sin with greediness, the Holy Spirit, at first resisting the evil, begins after no long time to withdraw Himself and permit them to sin in silence: and if so it go on with them, they are lost for ever.

But Almighty God in His great mercy did not so leave this unhappy prodigal to himself. Trouble came upon him, and brought him to a better mind. When he had spent all, "there arose a mighty famine in that land, and he began to be in want." What is this famine, but the feeling, sure to come on after a course of sin, how dreary and desolate all things are, how utterly insufficient to make a soul happy:

the hopeless hunger and thirst of immortal beings, left to provide for themselves in a perishing world? What is it, but the same which the wise king complained of, so sadly and earnestly, after his shameful fall? "ᵃ Whatsoever mine eyes desired, I kept not from them, I withheld not my heart from any joy. Then I looked on all the works that my hands had wrought, and on the labour that I had laboured to do; and behold all was vanity and vexation of spirit, and there was no profit under the sun." Such is the end of all worldly, sinful delight. In a very short time it will be all spent, and he who is now well pleased with himself will awake as from a dream, and know that he is "wretched and miserable and poor and blind and naked." This is the famine which arose in the land, to which the unhappy prodigal had wandered: all who dwell there, all who have wandered away from their true home, feel that famine sooner or later: and by and by it came to that prodigal's turn. He began to be in want. Often and often he had been warned beforehand, over and over had his father foretold him, before he had left him, what would come of such ways: but he had turned a deaf ear to all: but now it is come home to him: now at last, in spite of himself, he is forced to own that what they said was true, as it is written in the book of Proverbs: he mourns at the last, now his flesh and his body are consumed, and says, "ᵇ How have I hated instruction, and my heart despised reproof, and have not obeyed the voice of my teachers, nor inclined mine ear to them that instructed me."

[a] Eccles. ii. 10, 11. [b] Prov. v. 11, 12.

He begins to be in want. He feels and owns his misery, but as yet he knows nothing of the remedy. In a reckless kind of despair, he does but plunge himself deeper into misery. He went and joined himself to a citizen of that country. Not knowing where to get bread to eat, he hires himself to a person there living: and seems to make the chance less and less of his ever being delivered. So when the sinner has spent all his spiritual treasures, and the sharp and bitter famine of the soul is come upon him, the Evil one, if he can, will persuade him that all is lost: he will try to bind him over, as he did Judas, to a kind of perpetual slavery under some deadly sin or other, some citizen of his own country: for all deadly sins are natives and citizens of hell. For example, the devil says to one man, There is nothing to be done: you can but endeavour to drown your present cares and fears in strong drink, and let alone thinking of what is to come. To another he says, To be sure, you are miserable enough: but it is just the condition of the world, there is no help for it: you can but overpower the sense of it by much business; you can but hurry faster, and pant more eagerly, after riches and pleasures and such like. Thus he leads them more and more captive at his will, and as they become more subject to him, he puts upon them more shameful and degrading work. "He sent him," says the parable, "into his fields to feed swine." When a man in reckless despair gives himself up to deadly sin, there is no saying how low he may sink, what horrible, shameful things he may do and submit to, what swine, what foul, unclean passions, he may give himself up to feed and cherish.

"And he would fain have filled his belly with the husks that the swine did eat." This represents the vile and shocking ways, most degrading as well as most miserable, towards which we move when we enter on wilful sin: such as S. Paul describes, when he says of the heathens of old, "ᶜthey, being past feeling, gave themselves over to lasciviousness, to work all uncleanness with greediness." *"Past feeling:"* when men come to that surely they are come to the worst. If God leave them so, if they are permitted to have their will, their low and wretched will, without stint or misgiving, what remains but that they perish utterly? This prodigal was not left. His sad craving continued: he could not have enough, even of the husks which he longed for: no man, we read, gave unto him. This was God's mercy: disappointing his low desires, and causing him still to feel hungry, that he might not reject, but welcome, the thought of returning to his father, when it should strike him. And is it not still more God's mercy, when He causes the fallen Christian to meet disappointment at every turn, denying him the husks which the swine eat, the base pleasures of this world, until He has even forced him, by His loving Providence, to turn his face homewards again? O let us learn with all our hearts to thank Him for His severe yet gracious doings. When in earthly matters we encounter disappointment and anguish, let us acknowledge the Presence of the Good Shepherd, turning us back from tempting paths, in which

ᶜ Eph. iv. 19.

He knows we should otherwise be lost, and urging us toward the only right way. Let us never despair: for behold this wanderer was reduced to the food of swine, and not enough of that, and yet returned, recovered, and was pardoned. Yet let us walk in great fear and trembling: for after all, as I shall shew you another day, his was a very narrow escape: and though told us for our comfort, is full likewise of aweful warnings.

SERMON XLIV.

THE PRODIGAL SON.
III.

S. Luke xv. 17, 18, 19.

" And when he came to himself he said, How many hired servants of my father's have bread enough, and to spare, and I perish with hunger ! I will arise and go to my father, and will say unto him, Father, I have sinned against heaven, and before thee, and am no more worthy to be called thy son : make me as one of thy hired servants."

WE have considered the wanderings and the distress of the young man in our Lord's parable : his wanderings and extravagance being the type of our sins; his distress and famine, the type of our misery and helplessness, the natural effect of our sins, and the just judgement of God upon them. The next part of the parable sets before us his repentance; the type of ours. "When he came to himself, he said, How many hired servants of my father's have bread enough and to spare, and I perish with hunger." "He came to himself." This gives us to understand that his condition before was that of one beside himself. His whole soul was weakened, confused, bewildered, by the extremity of his misery. The famine had made his very appetite unnatural, like the cravings of a brute beast. "He would fain have filled his belly with the husks which the swine did eat." So it is with the habitual, deadly sinner when he finds that the world and the flesh fail him, but as yet has no heart to turn to God in earnest. He plunges lower and lower in base pleasures. He would fain fill himself with the very husks. He goes on till you would think him beside himself: and so indeed in one sense he is: his mind and senses out of order, his appetites all false and distempered, nothing appearing to him as it really is. This is the condition we bring ourselves to, by giving entire way, though it be but to one mortal sin. Yet all the while, if we would but believe it, our remedy is within our reach. That prodigal, had he chosen it, might have turned his thoughts at any time towards his first and true home. So the fallen Christian, as long as it pleases God to continue him within reach of His Gospel and Sacraments, may turn his thoughts, if he will, towards his Saviour. Well for him, if he do so before he come to that extreme point of misery: but even then, if he repent in earnest, it is not too late. This is what our Saviour so graciously teaches in the next part of the parable. The prodigal "came to himself:" he recovered his senses: he had a chance given him of not going on, like a castaway, with the swine for ever, and what is the first token of his better mind? He thinks of his father's house. The happy remembrances of his innocent childhood come strong upon him, and take place of the diseased and miserable dreamings which had possessed him of late. He thinks of it as his home; he loses for a moment the sense of his distance from it, and of the frightful and wretched things which are now around him; he says to himself, what if I were there once again? He thinks of the order which is there: father and children, master and servants, every one knowing his place: whereas in the wild and famished country, to which he had wandered, all was confusion and irregularity. He thinks of the peace and quiet of that sober household; so different from the brawling and disturbance, so sure to prevail where riotous living is. He thinks of the plenty in which he had been brought up: "the meanest of the hired servants there has bread enough and to spare, and I perish with hunger." So when a backsliding Christian turns his mind by God's grace to the merciful voice ever sounding in his ears, and begins to repent in earnest; how moving are the thoughts and remembrances of his earlier and better days! how he was taught and led, week by week and season by season, to serve God in His Church: how he was used, night and morning, to say his prayers on his knees: how quietly and contentedly the time passed with him, what peace he enjoyed, both towards other men and with his own heart, before he gave way to his restless and shameful passions: what a joy to him, then, to think of God and His Angels, and of Saints and good men in Heaven and in earth, watching him with kind and approving eyes. He thinks of the plenty of graces and blessings which in those days God offered him one after another in their due season, Baptism, Confirmation, all the holy services of the Church: and more especially of the Holy Communion, " bread enough and to spare," to which he might then draw near continually. And as in the parable that unfortunate son, on coming to himself, thought of no one so much as of his father, it was his father's bread that he longed for, his father's house, his father's servants, his father's forgiving countenance: so the one thought which fills the penitent's heart is the thought of God Almighty as being still his Father: he yearns after his place in the Church, and all the comforts and joys of his innocent young days, because there his Father, his Heavenly Father was: His gracious Presence was the root of all the blessings: if they are ever to return, it can only be by His owning us as children again. This indeed is the difference between true repentance, and the mere selfish dread of the impenitent: the one is the feeling of children to an offended father, whom they still love, and own as their father: the other is the feeling of slaves, trembling before a master whom they do not love. One mark of the better sort of penitence is, that he does not even dream of a good place for himself, although he had been a dearly beloved son; he dares not now hope for anything beyond a hired servant's allowance.

This is the beginning of repentance in such sad cases, when men have wasted the grace of God. He mercifully puts it in their hearts by His Spirit to remember with longing regret their first good and gracious beginnings, to think of Him as a Father, however grievously offended, and to desire earnestly the very lowest place, so it be but in His house: to desire it, because they cannot do without it, yet to shrink from it, as knowing it far too good for them. This is the beginning of penitence, or rather the preparation for it: but the next step is the great thing:

it is actually setting about the work. And what is the next step? It is forming good resolutions, making up his mind, resolving what to do. The prodigal son does not only dwell, as in a kind of dream, on the comforts of his father's house and presence, but he settles it in his heart, that he will really seek them again, and that, without loss of time. "I will arise and go to my father, and will say unto him, Father, I have sinned against Heaven and before thee, and am no more worthy to be called thy son." "I will arise," he says; not, "I wish I could arise, but my evil nature prevents me; not so, but I make a resolution. I declare before God that I really do mean to arise, I will do my part to be forgiven: I hope it may not be in vain, but at least I will try." Take notice of this, my brethren: for indeed there is a very great difference between wishing to do right, and really resolving to do it: and we are all of us too apt to be contented with mere wishing: which is much the same as if we were pleased with ourselves for dreaming about some good action, which in our waking hours we had no heart to perform. He must not do so, who would find mercy with the prodigal: he must not lose time in fancying how happy it would be to repent and be forgiven: he must steadily make up his mind to walk henceforth by the rule of true penitents: and having resolved, he must begin so to walk.

For the next thing we read of this young man, is, "He arose and came to his father." He did not only say to himself, "I will arise," but he actually arose and went. He got over the bad habits, the false shame, the foolish fondnesses, which might still have bound him captive in that far country and set out at once for his former home. He went as to his father, not in mere dread and shame: his bowels yearned after that pardoning love, which he knew by sad experience to be so much better than any thing he could find elsewhere. He did not despair: he had so much trust in the love which had encompassed him in his childhood, as that he could still pray, could still say, "Father, I have sinned." His heart was thoroughly humbled within him: he made up his mind to confess all, both his sin and his unworthiness: to leave out nothing which he had done amiss either against God or his father. "I have sinned," he says, "against Heaven and before thee." He chooses beforehand the very lowest place, as the only one fit for him. "I am not worthy to be called thy son; make me as one of thy hired servants." In these resolutions he exercises himself during the whole of his long and dreary journey. I call it long, because we know that he had wandered into "a far country;" and dreary, because he was all the while in doubt, how his father might receive him: but he did not therefore sink down or draw back. He went on humbly and penitently, thinking with himself, "where else shall I go, or what else shall I do? My Father alone hath the words of pardon and blessing."

Mark him, follow him, take up his word, ye who have wandered from your God, ye who have wasted your heavenly portion. Arise, leave your base and low pleasures, your fretting cares of this life, and go to your Father, with humility in your heart and the words of confession on your lips: and see if He will not come out to meet you with pardon and grace beyond what you could ask or think.

SERMON XLV.

THE PRODIGAL SON.
IV.

S. Luke xv. 20—24.

"*And he arose, and came to his father. But when he was yet a great way off, his father saw him, and had compassion, and ran, and fell on his neck, and kissed him. And the son said unto him, Father, I have sinned against heaven, and in thy sight, and am no more worthy to be called thy son. But the father said to his servants, Bring forth the best robe, and put it on him; and put a ring on his hand, and shoes on his feet: And bring hither the fatted calf, and kill it; and let us eat, and be merry: For this my son was dead, and is alive again; he was lost, and is found. And they began to be merry.*"

WE are now to consider the unhappy wanderer on the long and dismal journey which he has undertaken towards his ancient home, the house of his father. Mile after mile he goes on alone, well nigh naked and barefoot, and nothing left even of the miserable wages which he had earned in the far country, much less of the beautiful portion which his father at first had bestowed upon him. Mile after mile he goes heavily and sadly along, with no other companions but his own thoughts, and those full of bitterness and alarm: not so much for his increasing weariness, raggedness, and other bodily discomfort, as because every mile brings him so much nearer the dreaded moment when he will know whether he have any hope or no; whether or no there is yet any chance for his being forgiven and received into favour. Mile after mile he goes on with this sad and restless anxiety deepening and deepening on his heart. At last, while he is yet a great way off from his home, a great part of his dreary journey still to be performed, he looks up and sees one coming out to meet him. He does not, we may imagine, recollect the person at first, but it may well make his heart beat more earnestly, but to think, Here is some one in sight, who has but just come from that very home and neighbourhood, where I so long and desire to be. The person draws nearer, he quickens his pace, he is evidently hastening towards him; at last he sees who it is: his own Father!

For so it is, that while the broken hearted young man is on his sorrowful way, his loving father, who had never forgotten him, who has all along looked anxiously along the road to the far country, if haply he might see any sign of his return; his father, I say, has seen him afar off. We may lose sight of God, but He never loses sight of us. We may turn our backs upon God, but He hath not yet turned His back upon us. "ᵃ From the habitation of His dwelling He considereth all them that dwell on the earth," more especially the members of His Son. His Eye pursues them in all their wanderings: much more

ᵃ Ps. xxxiii. 14.

does He delight to watch them as they return to a better way, be it never so slowly and sadly. He sees them yet a great way off: the very faintest dawnings of repentance are noted by Him, set down in His book, encouraged by His gracious visitations, improved, if we do not hinder it, by His strengthening Spirit. As an anxious, loving parent might watch by the bedside of a young child seriously sick, and might discern and treasure up the dim and doubtful beginnings of amendment, far too dim and doubtful for strangers even to be aware of: so none of the penitent sinner's misgivings and regrets are blotted out from before the Lord. If he do but turn his face towards his home, there are eager friends leaning from Heaven to welcome even that small beginning, and assist it with their prayers.

But the father does not only see the returning son a great way off; he also runs out to meet him. Whilst he is wearily stumbling on, full of the mournful sense of his loneliness, and doubting perhaps if he have not so sinned as that no more hope can remain of his ever seeing the offended father again, behold the father has left his place and is far on his way towards him with a great blessing. What a lesson of perseverance is here, for a heart that is just beginning to have better thoughts. Who knows? perhaps the very next step on your road may bring you within reach of the light. Whatever you do, persevere: do not give it up, do not cease to make the most of what little strength you have left. Preventing grace; the father, running out to meet you, is mighty, and can and will do wonders for you, if you will dutifully give yourselves up to it.

Observe what happens next; the father and son have met. How does the offended father behave? Does he stop at some considerable distance, and say, as some I fear do say in effect, when any such thing takes place, Stand off yet a while: come not near, I am holier than thou? Is there any grudging, any unwillingness, in his way of receiving the penitent? Oh no: far otherwise. The father's heart overflows at once; he falls on his son's neck, he embraces him tenderly; he deals with him as in the days of his childhood, when his soul and body were yet tender and innocent. He falls on his son's neck, and weeps for joy, as Joseph and his brother Benjamin wept on each other's neck, when they had been so unexpectedly brought together again by God's wonderful Providence. Imagine the son's feeling at that moment! Think how the gracious touch of his parent must have brought back the lively remembrance of his blameless, happy infancy: so the hope and sense of pardon, with which our merciful Saviour vouchsafes to visit men in the early times of their penitence, recalls, without their well understanding it, the lost memory of their first days, their long passed days of baptismal purity. Nothing so melts the heart as that reviving hope of pardon, after a long and dreary banishment in sin.

But the father is not content to fall on his son's neck; he also kisses him, loses no time in giving him some token for good, whereby he may understand that his caresses are real, that it is not all a mere dream or fancy. When the penitent has been sufficiently tried, when the penance which God sees necessary is over, then the Judge admits him to peace. For that kiss is the sign of peace, and is mentioned as such by S. Paul more than once. In this place it seems to mean especially God's mercy in confirming the first feelings of hope by words of comfort out of the divine Scriptures, or by the wise reasonings and instructions of friends and pastors: whereby the soul being greatly comforted, ventures to address God yet as a Father: as a loving and forgiving Father, however deeply alas! offended.

This is the next point: the prodigal's manner of speaking. He is so far encouraged by his father's gracious demeanour as to venture on the prayer which he had long ago provided himself with; which prayer, no doubt, had dwelt on his thoughts, and haunted his memory, all the journey through. Such at least we know is apt to be the case, when people are setting out on an anxious journey, to meet some one on whom much depends. They are apt to settle beforehand with much care the very words they mean to use: they go on all the way, conning and saying them over to themselves, and wondering whether some other words would not be better. At last, they speak them in fear and trembling; and it is the greatest relief to them, when they find they are not rejected.

It is very much to be observed that this prodigal uses the very same humble words which he had thought of so long before, even now that he has met his father, and can have no more doubt of his gracious purpose towards him. He is not in the least lifted up: there is no touch of boldness or presumption, on finding how dear he still is to his parent, how much he is thought of at home. He simply makes his confession, as he had resolved to do: makes it fully, in both parts of it, "I have sinned against Heaven and before thee." His heart is still broken, to think of his grievous offences, how unworthily he had used both his earthly and his heavenly Father. He cannot get over the thought of it: the frank, free, undeserved compassion of his father seems for the time to make it keener, notwithstanding the comfort it gives him. So it is with true, affectionate penitents; such for example as S. Peter. It is the Lord turning and looking upon them His loving and forgiving Eye, which quite overcomes them. The very sense of pardon deepens the sense of unworthiness: they weep bitterly in that most joyful moment. With all their hearts they crave to be humbled; they feel as if their place could not be too low, provided only they may have some place in God's house. "I am not worthy to be called thy son, make me as one of thy hired servants."

But the truest penitent cannot take half so much delight in humbling himself, as God, the Father of penitents, takes in receiving and exalting him. Consider the picture in the parable. The father makes no direct reply, but turns to the servants, and bids them produce all the best treasures of his household, which he had prepared, knowing before what his son would need. "Bring forth the best robe, and put it on him: and put a ring on his hand, and shoes on his feet: and bring hither the fatted calf and kill it: and let us eat and be merry." The poor wanderer is ragged, from his misery and long journey; therefore he orders clothing out for him:

and not ordinary clothing but the best robe. What is this but a token of the true heavenly righteousness, the righteousness of God and of our Lord Jesus Christ, given us freely in our Baptism, and worn for a while in our young days, ere we had wandered from our home; then alas! too long despised and forfeited by our many wilful sins, but sure to be restored, on our true and earnest repentance? What is it but the wedding garment of holiness, put on us again by His miraculous mercy, that we may not be unfit to enter into His courts, and sit down at His marriage supper? The father has his servants, our Saviour has His priests, waiting ready with these best robes, to put on those who truly repent and come to Him to be forgiven; they are in a manner put on, when the word of Absolution or remission of sins is pronounced. Priests at that moment are very like the servants in the parable going out with the father to meet the returning son: and the saying, "bring forth the best robe and put it on him," is but the same in other words as, "Whosesoever sins ye forgive, they are forgiven."

Further; "Put a ring," it is said, "on his hand." "The ring," says an ancient Bishop, "is a pledge of the Holy Spirit." Such as He gave Himself in Baptism and Confirmation, such He returns, to sanctify anew the souls and bodies of those who sincerely repent. As if a wife who had broken her marriage vows, and had actually, by wilful neglect, thrown away her ring, were to receive it again from her husband on coming to a better mind.

Again, it is said, "put shoes on his feet," weary and footsore as he was with his long journey, what could be more welcome than this? But neither is the spiritual meaning hard to find. When penitents come home, neither God intends, nor do they desire, to pass the rest of their time in indolence. They must set out again, as soon as they are refreshed, but on a far different journey: to do God's work, not to follow their own pleasures. But in this path they will meet with many stumbling blocks, much that is sharp and rough lying in their way, which will be too likely to cause them to fall. He provides them accordingly with shoes: as S. Paul writes: the Christian soldier must have "^chis feet shod with the preparation of the Gospel of peace:" that is, they must keep their members watchful and prepared against temptation, fenced from all unnecessary touch of earthly things.

Being thus forgiven the past, and prepared for the future, the wanderer is in a condition to partake of the family meal: and as a final token of forgiveness, the very best that was in the house is made ready to strengthen and refresh him. "Bring hither the fatted calf and kill it: and let us eat and be merry." Thoughtful hearers will know at once, without being told, the meaning of this, as another saint of old tells us, "the calf is our Lord Jesus Christ, so called because of the sacrifice of a body without spot; and fatted i. e., rich and costly, sufficient as it is for the salvation of the whole world. And men's feeding on it, is the Christian family partaking of our Lord's Body and Blood in the Sacrament of the Holy Communion. God Himself in His infinite condescension represents Himself as a partaker in this feast." "Let us eat

^c Eph. vi. 15.

and be merry," He says. He vouchsafes Himself to rejoice with the servants, i. e., with His Angels and His Priests at the revival of the dead soul, the finding of the lost sinner.

Although then the true penitent will feel himself utterly unworthy, yet for love's sake he will not venture to stay away from this Feast: he will not disobey the gracious invitation, he will not refuse to his loving Father the joy of seeing him among the guests, in his best robe:—sanctified and prepared, by earnest and humble contrition, to do his Father, for the time to come, the very best service that he can.

SERMON XLVI.

THE PRODIGAL SON.
V.

S. Luke xv. 31, 32.

"Son, thou art ever with me, and all that I have is thine. It was meet that we should make merry and be glad: for this thy brother was dead, and is alive again; and was lost, and is found."

THERE may perhaps be some among us, who think that they have no particular part in our Lord's parable of the prodigal son: that it does not exactly apply to such as they are. They do not seem to themselves to have ever wandered far away from the fold of the Good Shepherd. Conscience does not accuse them of any deadly sin, whereby they have cast away the grace of Baptism. Therefore the history of that unhappy wanderer does not fall upon their ear as any thing in which they are very deeply concerned. They, as they believe, are still at home, never having strayed into a far country. They still have in hand their portion of baptismal grace, not spent nor wasted by riotous or unholy living. The story of the prodigal son is to them a beautiful and affecting history, but it is not to their thinking, their own history. They do not see themselves in it. If they were to meet with a picture of our Lord with the lost sheep, it would not come into their minds to point to the sheep and say, as I have heard of a penitent person saying, "that is I: that means me."

Happy, thrice happy are those Christians, who may have such a feeling as this without deceiving themselves: happy and blessed above all worldly blessings, they who have kept their first baptismal purity; so as to need not any doubtful and anxious repentance, like what this prodigal had to go through. Happy, who are such indeed! But surely there is no small danger of deceiving ourselves in that matter; and we may be quite sure that those who are very ready to believe that all is so well with them do somehow deceive themselves. Our Lord seems to speak to all such, towards the end of the parable, where He tells how the elder son received the news of his brother's return. When the joy was now at its height, for the unexpected recovery of him who had been so long lost, the elder, who had never strayed, returned from the field: and " as he drew nigh unto the house, he heard music and dancing. And he called unto him one of the servants and asked what these things meant. And he said unto him, thy brother is come, and thy father hath killed the fatted calf, because he hath received him safe and sound." Now if any person think himself not such as to be represented by the younger son, then, by his own account, he is such as to be represented by this elder son. Our Lord seems to say to such, You do not think yourself a great sinner: you never wandered, that you know of, wilfully away from your heavenly Father's house: you never wasted your heavenly treasure, the grace I freely gave you, with disorderly living. See then in the history of this elder brother, what is your special danger and temptation. It is, to be proud and scornful: to value yourself and think meanly of others. Watch, pray, strive against this: strive and pray with all your might to be not only pure, but lowly and loving in heart; then will you please God indeed, and your reward will be great in Heaven: then and not till then, will you be a meet companion for the Angels, who are not only unsinning themselves, but rejoice also with the tenderest charity over every sinner that repents.

This is in sum an account of the meaning of this last portion of the history we are considering. Now let us see how this meaning is brought out by the several particulars which our Lord has mentioned.

During the whole time of the prodigal's joyful reception, the elder son was absent in the field. He was about his regular day's work; his time and thoughts were taken up with ordinary farming employment, with the cares of the cornfield, the pasture, or the vineyard. Now so it is, that when we, any of us, are earnestly taken up with our usual employment, going on in our accustomed course much as we have done, it may be, all our lives long, we are apt to be rather impatient at any thing which calls for deep feeling of another kind. We are not in any degree ready and prepared for it: it puts us out of our way. We are conscious, perhaps, at the bottom of our hearts, that we ought to feel more than we do: and this very thing makes us more uneasy and irritable. Whether it be joy or sorrow, which we are called on to feel, makes very little difference; our tendency is to look another way, taking no notice of either. Thus, if the elder brother had come home a little sooner, or had met the younger on the road, while yet in his rags and misery, it is most likely that he would have dealt harshly with him, simply from not liking to be interrupted in his own ordinary course. If he did not pass him by, as the Priest and Levite, intent on their journey, passed by the wounded man, yet he might very likely mix a little sharpness with his relief of him. Take this then for a first warning, you who seem to yourselves to be going on in a good way with tolerable steadiness and regularity; try and keep your heart open to others, to all others, however seemingly unworthy: watch and pray, that the evil spirit of hardness and scornfulness get no dominion over you; that you look grudgingly on no man, neither on those who are better than yourselves, nor on those who seem to be worse. Keep your hearts open, that you may be able to feel for every man, to do all charitable deeds which God puts in your way, without being peevish or fretful, though you be taken a little out of your ordinary round of duties.

But let us accompany this elder son. Steady and industrious, but somewhat the harder and prouder for his entire devotion to his outward calling; let us accompany him to his father's door, and see how he takes the good tidings which meet him there. "He is angry and will not go in:" therefore comes his father out and intreats him. The father, all overflowing with love, watching to do good to all his household, impartially kind, to one as well as another, comes mildly to him, (though he might well be offended,) and intreats him: remonstrates with all longsuffering. He answers in the very tone of grudging and sullenness, "lo! these many years do I serve thee, neither transgressed I at any time thy commandment: and yet thou never gavest me a kid, that I might make merry with my friends: but as soon as this thy son was come, which hath devoured thy living with harlots, thou hast killed for him the fatted calf." Every one, as he reads or hears, feels how unamiable all this is: yet I suppose there is something not unlike it, in a corner at least, of almost every one's heart. Christians of what may be called average goodness, neither better seemingly than the common sort, nor worse, have generally something in them which makes them rebel against special mercy shewn to great sinners repenting. It was the feeling of the Jews, generally, towards the Gentiles: it offended them, made them stumble at the Gospel, when they found that the heathens and idolaters, those who had wandered farthest from God, were to sit down with their fathers in the kingdom of Heaven. It was the feeling of the Pharisees towards the Publicans: "This man receiveth sinners and eateth with them." It is the feeling, I fear, of almost every one of us, in respect of those sins, in which we suppose ourselves not guilty. The man who is strictly honest thinks it hard that the thief should be forgiven: some who are strictly chaste, may be apt to grudge pardon and Church communion to such as have sinned in uncleanness, even after a great measure of penitence. Nay, there were in old times a sect of persons who refused penitence to all who had unhappily fallen into deadly sin after Baptism. Few men now hold any such doctrine : on the contrary, the more part among us seem to think far too slightly both of the guilt of sin, and of the labour of repentance. Yet we are all too much inclined to value ourselves in our secret hearts, as often as we find any sin in others, which we account ourselves innocent of, and to look on the sinner, even though he may have repented, with somewhat of dislike and contempt.

Hear now the loving Father of us all, what He says, once for all, to rebuke these our ungodly, unloving thoughts. "Son, thou art ever with me, and all that I have is thine." If you are such as you think, all that He hath is yours. If you have really preserved your first Christian grace, free from habitual or other deadly sin, then you are still a member of Christ, a child of God, and an inheritor of the kingdom of Heaven: and what can you want more? You are ever with Christ: one with Him, and He with you; raised with Him to an exceeding height of glory: partaker of the Divine Nature. How can you be disturbed at your poor brother's receiving a portion of that pardon and mercy, to which you yourself owe so much?

Especially considering what is said next, He is your brother. "It was meet that we should make merry and be glad, for this *thy brother* was dead and is alive again." It is our brother: let him have sinned as he may, nature herself teaches us to rejoice in his recovery. Again, think of the manner of his recovery: how much he has himself suffered, how infinitely more your Saviour has suffered for him. Think of the horror and anguish he had to endure, when, his eyes being opened by divine grace, he found himself on the very edge of hell, and feared it might be too late to repent. Think of the famine, the husks, the hard and cruel bondage, the long, dreary, anxious journey. And then, as the father in the parable ran out to meet his son, so we are to think of the Most High God, the Second Person in the Everlasting Trinity, hastening down from His eternal glory, taking our nature upon Him, suffering all that torture in soul and body, which we remember at this time especially, that He might lay hold of the fallen wanderer, raise him up, and bring him home. Let us not be against Christ: let us not grudge Him the joy, with which He looks down from Heaven on every sinner that repenteth.

Nor need we fear that, by forgiving and rejoicing in God's forgiveness, we are too encouraging towards offences, leading people to think lightly of sin, if we be but careful to bear in mind that final warning of the Father and God of penitents: "It was meet that we should make merry and be glad, for this thy brother was dead and is alive again." "Dead and alive again!" the greatest of miracles: this is what the repentance of a wilful deadly sinner is likened to. Who would not fear to bring himself into such a condition, that his deliverance from it would be like raising a man from the dead? The love of our Almighty Saviour may indeed and will work such miracles: but woe to him who wilfully casts himself down, daring Christ, as it were, to raise him up. That be far from us, my brethren: let us rather resolve, now that we are finishing His merciful parable and beginning our more earnest yearly meditation on His Passion: let us resolve, I say, to give glory to Him, in our several ways, according as we stand before Him. Those who have seriously sinned, let them now give glory to the Cross by true and entire repentance, and the rest by rejoicing with them: till we all come to our prepared Home, a holy and happy family for ever and ever.

O Saviour of the world,
Who by Thy Cross and Precious Blood
hast redeemed us;
Save us and help us,
We humbly beseech Thee,
O Lord.

WORKS by the late REV. JOHN KEBLE.

THE CHRISTIAN YEAR: THOUGHTS IN VERSE FOR THE SUNDAYS AND HOLYDAYS THROUGHOUT THE YEAR.
Small 4to. Edition. Printed on toned paper, with red bordered-lines and initial letters,—Cloth, 10s. 6d. Foolscap Octavo Edition,—Cloth, 3s. 6d. 24mo. Edition,—Cloth, 2s. 32mo. Edition, Limp cloth, 1s; cloth, gilt edges, 1s. 6d. Cheap Edition—Limp cloth, 6d.

LYRA INNOCENTIUM: THOUGHTS IN VERSE ON CHRISTIAN CHILDREN, THEIR WAYS AND THEIR PRIVILEGES. Thirteenth Edition. Fcap. 8vo., cloth, 5s. Cheap Edition, 48mo., limp cloth, 6d.

MISCELLANEOUS POEMS. [With Preface by G. M]. Third Edition. Fcap. 8vo., cloth, 6s.

THE PSALTER, OR PSALMS OF DAVID: in English Verse. Fourth Edition. Fcap. 8vo., cloth, 6s.; 18mo., cloth 1s.

₊ The above Four Volumes are printed uniform in size and binding with the Fcap. edition of "The Christian Year." Together they form "The Complete Poetical Works of the late Rev. John Keble.'

LETTERS OF SPIRITUAL COUNSEL AND GUIDANCE. Third Edition. Post 8vo., cloth, 6s.

ON EUCHARISTICAL ADORATION, WITH CONSIDERATIONS SUGGESTED BY A LATE PASTORAL LETTER (1858) ON THE DOCTRINE OF THE MOST HOLY EUCHARIST. 8vo., cloth, 6s.—Cheap Edition, 24mo., sewed, 2s.

WORKS by the late REV. J. KEBLE (*Continued.*)

SERMONS, OCCASIONAL AND PAROCHIAL. 8vo., cloth, 12s.

VILLAGE SERMONS ON THE BAPTISMAL SERVICE. 8vo., cloth, 5s.

THE WORKS OF S. IRENÆUS, Translated by the late Rev. JOHN KEBLE (forming vol. 42 of the Series of the Library of the Fathers). 8vo. cloth; 10s. 6d.

THE LIFE OF THE RIGHT REVEREND FATHER IN GOD, THOMAS WILSON, D.D., Lord Bishop of Sodor and Man. Compiled, chiefly from Original Documents, by the late Rev. JOHN KEBLE. In Two parts. 8vo., cloth, 21s.

AN ARGUMENT AGAINST REPEALING THE LAWS WHICH TREAT THE NUPTIAL BOND AS INDISSOLUBLE. *Second Edition.* 8vo., 1s.

SEQUEL OF THE ARGUMENT AGAINST IMMEDIATELY REPEALING THE LAWS WHICH TREAT THE NUPTIAL BOND AS INDISSOLUBLE. 1857. 8vo., 4s. 6d.

A LITANY OF OUR LORD'S WARNINGS. WITH SUGGESTIONS FOR THE USE OF IT. 1864. 16mo., 6d.

SUNDAY LESSONS. THE PRINCIPLE OF SELECTION. Being No. XIII. of "Tracts for the Times." 8vo., 6d.

ON THE MYSTICISM ATTRIBUTED TO THE EARLY FATHERS OF THE CHURCH. Being No. LXXXIX. of "Tracts for the Times." 8vo., sewed, 3s 6d.

PRINTED BY THE SOCIETY OF THE HOLY TRINITY,
HOLY ROOD, OXFORD.

www.ingramcontent.com/pod-product-compliance
Lightning Source LLC
Chambersburg PA
CBHW051843300426
44117CB00006B/255